LIVING WITH UNCERTAINTY

New directions in pastoral development in Africa

IAN SCOONES

INTERMEDIATE TECHNOLOGY PUBLICATIONS 1994

Intermediate Technology Publications Ltd,
103–105 Southampton Row, London WC1B 4HH, UK

© International Institute for Environment and Development 1995

ISBN 1 85339 235 9

Typeset by J&L Composition Ltd, Filey, North Yorkshire
Printed by SRP, Exeter

Contents

Contributors

WOLFGANG BAYER is a consultant in tropical livestock husbandry and forage management and part-time lecturer in pasture science at the University of Göttingen, Germany. After studying agricultural biology at the University of Hohenheim and tropical animal science at the Technical University of Berlin, he was a post-doctoral fellow with the CSIRO Tropical Crops and Pasture Division in northern Australia. ANN WATERS-BAYER is a consultant in rural sociology with the ETC Foundation and works with its Information Centre for Low-External-Input and Sustainable Agriculture (ILEIA) in Leusden, Netherlands. After studying agricultural economics at the University of New England, Australia, she gained a doctorate in rural sociology in Hohenheim. From 1981 to 1985 both were involved in livestock systems research with the sub-humid zone programme of the International Livestock Centre for Africa in Nigeria. Present address: Rohnsweg J6, D-3400, Göttingen, Germany.

JIM ELLIS is the Director of the Center for Environment and Sustainable Agriculture at Winrock International. He is a systems ecologist with experience working in Africa for the South Turkana Ecosystem Project. Present address: Winrock International, Route 3, Petit Jean Mountain, Morrilton, Arkansas 72110, USA.

JOHN HOLTZMAN and NICK KULIBABA are senior analysts in the Agriculture and Natural Resources Area of Abt Associates Inc. Holtzman is an agricultural economist and Kulibaba an economic anthropologist. They have both worked extensively on the Agricultural Marketing and Improvement Strategies Project between 1990 and 1993. Prior to this they have conducted applied research on livestock economics in a number of African countries including Cameroon, Togo, Burkina Faso, Senegal, Zaire and Somalia. Present address: Abt Associates, 4800 Montgomery Lane, Suite 600, Bethesda, Maryland 20814, USA.

CHARLES LANE has experience of agriculture and livestock production in the UK, Australia and Africa. Ten years of field-work in Africa includes five years as Oxfam Field Director in Tanzania. He is currently Senior Research Associate at the International Institute for Environment and Development, co-ordinating a collaborative research and advocacy programme on pastoral land tenure in Africa. Present address: IIED, 3 Endsleigh Street, London WC1H ODD, UK.

RICHARD MOOREHEAD is a socio-economist who has been working on issues of natural resource management in East and West Africa for the last 15 years as a researcher on field projects and for bilateral and multilateral donors. His particular interest is in natural resource management institutions at the community, district and national levels and in natural resource tenure systems. He is currently a Research Associate at the International Institute for Environment and Development. Present address: IIED, 3 Endsleigh Street, London WC1H ODD, UK.

GREGORY PERRIER is the International Programmes Co-ordinator at the College of Natural Resources, Utah State University. He has eight years of experience working in West Africa and is interested in pastoral indigenous knowledge systems for natural resource management and pastoral development. Present address: College of Natural Resources, Utah State University, Logan, Utah 84322–5200, USA.

STEPHEN SANDFORD is currently a project co-ordinator with the British NGO, FARM–Africa, working in south-west Ethiopia on participatory research with peasant farmers. In the past he has prepared pastoral projects for World Bank financing, established and organized the pastoral network of the Overseas Development Institute and headed the Livestock Economics Division of the International Livestock Centre for Africa. Present address: FARM-Africa, PO Box 5746, Addis Ababa, Ethiopia.

IAN SCOONES is a Research Associate in the Drylands Programme at the International Institute for Environment and Development. His interest in rangeland management and livestock development emerged from work carried out in the communal areas of Zimbabwe. He is an agricultural ecologist by training, and is particularly interested in the challenges of dryland farming in Africa. He has been active in co-ordinating the programme of research on African range management and policy at IIED. Present address: IIED, 3 Endsleigh Street, London WC1H ODD, UK.

JEREMY SWIFT is a Fellow at the Institute for Development Studies at the University of Sussex, specializing in the economics and development of dryland and mountain land-use systems, especially pastoralism. He has a particular interest in land tenure, local organizations and food security issues. He has done extensive fieldwork in Africa, the Middle East and Central Asia. He is currently working on the economics of transformation of Mongolian pastoralism. Present address: IDS, University of Sussex, Falmer, Brighton, BN1 9RE UK.

DJEIDI SYLLA has worked with ACORD in Mali and Uganda. He now works as a Sustainable Development Advisor for UNDP in Mali. A sociologist by training, he has been particularly concerned with issues of capacity building among pastoral communities and support to indigenous NGOs in Africa. Present address: PNUD/UNDP, BP 120, Bamako, Mali.

CAMILLA TOULMIN is the director of the Drylands Programme at the International Institute for Environment and Development, London. This programme includes research in collaboration with African researchers, such as pastoral land tenure and traditional soil and water conservation; training in participatory planning and natural resource management in the Sahel; and information and networking. An economist by training, she has worked mainly in the francophone Sahel on agropastoral systems and natural resource management issues. She is currently involved in negotiations to prepare and implement a global convention to combat desertification. Present address: IIED, 3 Endsleigh Street, London WC1H ODD, UK.

Preface

IAN SCOONES

Many of the core assumptions that provided the basis for range management and pastoral development in dryland Africa have been challenged in recent years. Such terms as 'vegetation succession', 'carrying capacity' and 'land degradation' have come under critical scrutiny. It is now accepted that many dryland ecosystems do not follow equilibrium dynamics. Instead, such systems are characterized by high levels of temporal and spatial variability in biomass production. In these non-equilibrium systems, pastoralists must avoid risks by moving herds and flocks to make best use of the heterogenous landscape; they must destock and restock in response to droughts; they must seek economic diversification to support their livelihoods; and they must defend complex rights of access to grazing and water resources.

In the past, pastoralists have been blamed for the assumed environmental destruction of the drylands. But new ecological thinking highlights how this is most unlikely. The risks of environmental degradation in non-equilibrium environments are limited, as livestock populations rarely reach levels likely to cause irreversible damage. Rather it is large shifts in rainfall that are seen to be the major factor determining the availability of grass in the rangelands. Most traditional pastoral management can now be seen to be environmentally benign, and indeed customary institutions for land management are potential models for the future.

But this does not mean all is well in the drylands of Africa. Recurrent drought, civil war and economic decline characterize too many pastoral areas. The appalling record of previous attempts to support pastoral development has convinced governments and donors alike that development investment in the pastoral drylands offers little hope. The contributions to this book argue that this is misplaced pessimism. Not only are there major costs to ignoring areas which support significant human and livestock populations, but also there appears to be a growing consensus on the basic ingredients of a new approach.

The new thinking in range ecology sheds light on many of the long-running debates about development policy and practice in pastoral areas. It highlights how and why many earlier interventions failed and points to new ways forward. A concern with variability, uncertainty and flexible responses focuses attention on the ways in which government policies and development interventions can encourage the efficient tracking of the environment through opportunistic management.

Living with Uncertainty builds on the foundations provided by a recent rethinking of range ecology. It represents the second phase of a research project that started with a review of ecological research now published in the book, *Range Ecology at Disequilibrium* (Behnke, Scoones and Kerven (eds.) 1993). This book, drawing on ecological work carried out in Africa over recent years, provides firm support for the contention that many dryland pastoral areas are characterized by non-equilibrium dynamics and that many pastoral livestock and land management strategies can be interpreted as being a direct response to this. The question then follows: so what? What are the practical, policy and development implications of the new ecological thinking? These questions are the subject of the chapters in *Living with Uncertainty*.

The book arose out of a workshop held in June 1993 when a group of researchers and development practitioners concerned with pastoral development issues came together to elaborate new directions for pastoral development suggested by recent rethinking of range ecology. The chapters in this book are edited versions of the theme papers commissioned for this workshop. They are complemented by several other overview and commentary chapters which attempt to draw some of the issues together into a more coherent whole.

The book starts with an overview paper by Ian Scoones which introduces many of the themes discussed in the following chapters. This is followed by a chapter by Jim Ellis which provides a brief historical introduction to the ecological debate that underpins all of the contributions to the book. The next chapter by Gregory Perrier examines issues of planning and development in pastoral areas. He argues for the need for flexible and responsive planning processes that are in tune with pastoralists' needs.

The following three chapters deal with ways of encouraging an effective tracking strategy. Wolfgang Bayer and Ann Waters-Bayer discuss the various means of ensuring alternative feed supplies for rangeland animals. Livestock–crop farming linkages, supplementary feeding and range improvement strategies are considered. John Holtzman and Nicolas Kulibaba tackle the question of livestock marketing. They argue that increasing the efficiency and competitiveness of the marketing system is the surest way of offsetting price and supply instability. Together with Camilla Toulmin, they also note that social welfare interventions to prevent destitution are also necessary in highly variable environments. Toulmin's paper looks at destocking and restocking through the drought cycle. She examines the importance of indigenous systems of tracking, as well as the potentials for external intervention, with an assessment of recent non-government organization experience in this area.

Charles Lane and Richard Moorehead examine the issue of resource tenure in pastoral areas. They show how most conventional theories, particularly the 'tragedy of the commons' model, are inadequate explanations for actual practice. They provide a strong argument for supporting customary tenure arrangements, with the promotion of conflict resolution mechanisms.

The institutional dimensions are taken up by Djeidi Sylla. With an examination of project experience in pastoral institution building from across Africa, Sylla offers a thorough critique of past approaches. He points to the need for a diversity of pastoral organizations, recognizing that different groups may be appropriate for different tasks. For instance, permanent organizations may be formed around regular, common tasks while *ad hoc* bodies may tackle episodic events or issues of concern to more specific interest groups. Such local groups may federate into wider associations, offering opportunities for policy lobbying and advocacy work.

In the next chapter, Jeremy Swift examines the appropriate roles for state intervention and locally led development. He argues that in highly dynamic ecosystems it is important to decentralize power and responsibility to the lowest level consistent with the provision of services and maintaining accountability. The state's important residual role is therefore focused on providing the legislative framework for conflict resolution, as well as the provision of basic infrastructure and services.

The final chapter is a commentary by Stephen Sandford who offers his reflections on the potential importance of the new directions for pastoral development elaborated in the rest of the book. He concludes that the new directions offer an important way forward, but there remain significant challenges.

These challenges must be met through practical experience in the field, as well as encouraging the dissemination of new thinking through educational establishments. Without the re-equipping of a new generation of range managers and development professionals working in pastoral areas, the mistakes of the past will undoubtedly be repeated. This book will, we hope, go some way towards providing a new framework for practical action.

Acknowledgements

Living with Uncertainty is the culmination of a research project which started in 1990 with a workshop held in Woburn, England to explore the ecological dimensions of African range management. This workshop resulted in the publication of the book *Range Ecology at Disequilibrium* (Behnke, Scoones and Kerven (eds.) 1993). The arguments contained in this book have provoked much debate amongst range scientists and development practitioners working in Africa's drylands.

This prompted the second phase of the work which was aimed at exploring the practical development and policy implications of this rethinking of range ecology. Theme papers were commissioned with support from the British Overseas Development Administration (ODA) and the German Agency for Technical Cooperation (GTZ). These explored how the basic components of pastoral development in dryland Africa—planning, fodder management, marketing, drought coping, resource tenure, institutions and administration—would change if the new thinking in range ecology was to be taken seriously.

With support from the World Bank and the Commonwealth Secretariat, a workshop was held in June 1993 to discuss these theme papers. The workshop was seen as the socio-economic and policy counterpart of the earlier workshop which focused on ecological issues. While they are not responsible for the content of this book, all 36 of the participants at the second Woburn workshop have contributed significantly to the ideas contained in this book. I am particularly grateful to the following for their comments on earlier drafts of the overview chapter: Wolfgang Bayer, Roy Behnke, Andrea Cornwall, Ben Cousins, Adrian Cullis, Cees de Haan, John English, Brian Kerr, Robin Mearns, Richard Moorehead, Gregory Perrier, Brigitte Thébaud, Camilla Toulmin and Ann Waters-Bayer.

The work since 1990 has been a collaborative venture involving the Food Production and Rural Development Division of the Commonwealth Secretariat, the Pastoral Development Network at the Overseas Development Institute (ODI) and the Drylands Programme of the International Institute for Environment and Development (IIED). The research project has been co-ordinated by Brian Kerr of the Commonwealth Secretariat. Throughout, the project has benefited from his immense administrative skills and continual good humour. I am also particularly grateful to Roy Behnke at ODI who has been a central figure in forming and shaping the ideas that have become the 'New Directions' discussed in this book.

Finally, I would like to thank my colleagues at IIED, notably Camilla Toulmin, who directs the Drylands Programme, and Nicole Kenton, who has ably provided vital administrative support to the whole research programme. A special mention should also go to Fiona Hinchcliffe who has struggled patiently with some of the editing work.

IAN SCOONES
Drylands Programme
International Institute for Environment and Development
London

1. New directions in pastoral development in Africa

IAN SCOONES

Rethinking range ecology: some implications

The last few years have seen a major rethinking of some of the hallowed assumptions of range ecology and range management practice. What were once the hallmarks of the discipline are now being questioned. The utility of terms and concepts such as 'vegetation succession', 'carrying capacity' and 'degradation' are being reassessed, particularly for the dry rangelands where system dynamics are dominated by highly variable rainfall and episodic, chance events such as drought (Ellis and Swift 1988; Westoby et al. 1989; Behnke and Scoones 1993; Ellis this book).

This 'new' thinking[1] highlights in particular the differences between so-called equilibrium and non-equilibrium environments. Equilibrium environments are those that show the classic feedback mechanisms normally assumed in mainstream range management. In such settings vegetation change is gradual, following classical successional models (Clements 1916; Stoddart et al. 1975). Livestock populations are in turn limited by available forage in a density-dependent manner, so that excessive animal numbers, above a 'carrying capacity' level, result in negative effects on the vegetation. In the longer term this is assumed to cause more or less permanent damage—degradation or desertification. Such environments are typically found in wetter areas with more predictable patterns of rainfall.

By contrast, in non-equilibrium environments range degradation is not such an issue. Production potentials of both grassland and livestock are so dominated by rainfall (or other external variables) that the livestock populations are kept low through the impact of drought or other episodic events. Livestock, under such conditions, do not have a long-term negative

---

[1] As with most 'new' thinking there are some long-term precedents. Indeed ideas about non-equilibrium dynamics in ecosystems can be traced back to the early 1970s (for example, Holling 1973; May 1973, 1977). Parallel shifts have occurred in other areas of the natural sciences where interest in non-linear dynamics and chaos has provoked much debate (Gleick 1987; Ruelle 1991).

effect on rangeland resources.[2] Such non-equilibrium environments have highly dynamic ecosystems and are typified by the arid or semi-arid zones where rainfall variability is high.

In practice, the distinction between these contrasting environments is often blurred. There is clearly a gradation between these two separate ideal types. In some sites more stable, predictable equilibrium dynamics may occur in a run of wetter years, with non-equilibrium, uncertain, event-driven patterns emerging when a dry period strikes. Equally in any one area there may be certain areas which commonly show a more equilibrial pattern (e.g. relatively wetter bottomland sites where primary production varies little between years) within a wider landscape of dry rangeland which shows non-equilibrium dynamic patterns with high levels of inter-annual variability (Scoones 1993).

Pastoral populations in Africa largely live in dry environments with dynamic, non-equilibrium ecologies. Indeed 59 per cent of all ruminant livestock in Africa are reported to be found in arid and semi-arid areas. This represents a significant proportion of Africa's agricultural production. The total value of livestock products is estimated to be 25 per cent of the total agricultural output, equivalent to ' US$12 billion in 1988 (USDA 1990). If livestock benefits of manure and draught power are also included, this figure may increase to 35 per cent of total agricultural GDP (Winrock 1992). In other words, in considering the importance of arid and semi-arid production systems and the significance of dynamic, non-equilibrium ecologies we are talking of significant areas of land, supporting large numbers of pastoral livelihoods and contributing a large amount to national economies.

Recent ecological thinking suggests a number of propositions that potentially have far-reaching implications for the way we must conceive the theory and practice of range management and pastoral development in Africa and indeed other dryland areas of the world with significant pastoral populations. Three propositions summarize the recent rethinking of range ecology (Behnke 1992; Behnke *et al.* 1993; Sandford this book):

o Many arid and semi-arid grazing ecosystems are not at equilibrium and external factors (e.g. drought) determine livestock numbers and vegetation status. Grazing therefore has a limited effect on long-term grass productivity. In such situations opportunistic or tracking strategies are environmentally benign and waste less feed.

o The productivity of African rangelands is heterogeneous in space and variable over time, therefore, flexible movement is critical.

o African pastoral production systems are influenced by a range of differentiated livelihood objectives. Therefore blueprint interventions aimed at boosting single outputs (e.g. meat) using simplistic management tools

---

[2] However, impacts on tree resources are more complex, as heavy browsing or extensive lopping may affect long-term productivity due to slow regeneration rates (Bayer and Waters-Bayer this book).

(e.g. fixed carrying capacity) as part of standardized models (e.g. ranches) are unlikely to work.

The new ecological thinking suggests a number of key principles for management and policy in the drylands of Africa. The high level of variability seen in dynamic ecosystems requires an emphasis on flexible responses to uncertain events, and mobility to allow the optimal use of a heterogeneous environment. Contingent responses are critical to successful survival in a hostile and uncertain environment. Because of unpredictability, prescriptive planning and imposed solutions will not work and locally derived responses are the key to success.

Recommending that development should take note of the need for flexibility, mobility and local level solutions is hardly new. Indeed much of the social science critique of development in pastoral areas has focused on just these issues (cf. Monod 1975; Horowitz 1979; Galaty *et al.* 1981; Swift 1982; Sandford 1983). Ethnographers of pastoral societies equally have documented in great detail the way pastoral livestock keeping is adapted to environmental variability (e.g. Gulliver 1955; Dupire 1962; Dyson-Hudson 1966; Spencer 1973; Dahl 1979). What we are now seeing is a convergence of concepts, of interpretations and of analyses between the natural and social sciences. This convergence of course parallels what pastoralists have known and acted upon all along. The sad irony is that it is only now that the non-pastoralists, who dominate the professions which advise on and plan for pastoral areas, are catching up.

The last 30 years have seen the unremitting failure of livestock development projects across Africa. Millions of dollars have been spent with few obvious returns and not a little damage. Most commentators agree that the experience has been a disaster, so much so that many donors and other international agencies have effectively abandoned the dry zone in their development efforts. For instance, USAID, once a major donor in dry Africa and the supporter of many ill-fated livestock development projects, has dramatically reduced its support in this sector. Similarly the International Livestock Centre for Africa (ILCA) redirected its research focus away from dry areas and now concentrates on milk and meat production in the 'high–potential' zones (ILCA 1987–92). So should development agencies (international donors, national governments, NGOs) abandon the drylands as a 'no hope' area? Or should we reconsider, and analyze in detail why the failure has been so consistent and what lessons can be learned from the convergence of recent ecological thinking, social science critiques and pastoralists' own practices?

This book takes a positive view for three reasons. First, the costs of abandoning pastoral areas are potentially enormous. Second, many of the reasons for development failure are clear. Third, recent ecological thinking offers new perspectives and new insights that just might offer a way forward.

Conflict and civil strife dominate many pastoral areas today at great social cost, in parts of Somalia, Kenya, Ethiopia, Uganda, Mali and other areas. Such costs are borne most heavily by the residents of the pastoral

3

areas, but also by national governments and the international community who, in a variety of ways, bear the costs of insecurity and famine. Without a recognition of the problems of pastoral areas and support for development needs, problems of in security are likely to increase (Hjort and Salih 1989; Markakis 1993).

The reasons for the failure of many of the development projects imposed on pastoral areas from the 1960s are increasingly clear. In some quarters the lessons are being learned and a new era of more appropriate and apparently successful projects are emerging (Oxby 1989; Grell 1992; Vedeld 1993). The new thinking in range ecology puts much of this debate in sharper focus. In essence, the history of livestock development in Africa has been one of equilibrium solutions being imposed on non-equilibrium environments. The ranch model (and its many variants) has long dominated the curricula of professional training in range and livestock management. As a consequence the ranch model has been highly influential in development practice. But ranches with fenced paddocks, water points and reseeded rangeland are classic components of equilibrium systems. Management is focused on keeping things as stable as possible through the regulation of animal numbers and balancing grass species composition ('increasers' and 'decreasers'). Such management is ill-suited to highly dynamic ecosystems. Of course, ranchers and pastoralists making a living in dry areas recognize this. They have to, because textbook solutions do not work. They either adapt or abandon the ranch model recommendations and evolve alternative solutions that are viable. This has occurred in the US, where the ranch model originated, as well as in Africa (Gilles 1993).

The problem is that the learning experiences of pastoralists or ranchers and the intricate knowledge that is embedded in practical action is so often overlooked or ignored by development agencies. At the same time, year after year graduates of universities and training colleges in Africa and elsewhere emerge into the world of practical development as planners, policy makers, extension workers, NGO staff, expatriate advisers and so on with a blueprint model for livestock development that is basically unworkable in many settings. The institutional learning process in many donor agencies and government departments is often so slow and so poor that field experiences are rarely fed back into revising strategies and approaches. Senior professionals, who have learned much through bitter experience on the ground, are quickly promoted up and away from practical implementation activities. Livestock keepers themselves, those with the most direct experience of practical management of all, are rarely consulted let alone fully involved in programme design and implementation (Perrier this book). The consequence is that failures are repeated and repeated, apparently *ad infinitum* (Roe 1991a,b, 1993).

However, there are some encouraging signs which are beginning to gain wider currency among the development community. For instance, the World Bank has provided support for pastoral associations in the Sahel (Shanmugaratnam *et al.* 1992; Sylla this book). This followed a critical analysis of pastoral investment approaches which firmly rejected the ranch model (de Haan 1991). Similarly, the German development agency (GTZ) is emerging as a leader in exploring new ideas in field settings with pilot projects in the Sahel.

A discussion of new directions for pastoral development prompts a convergence of many strands of thinking, a weaving together of ideas and concepts that have diverse origins yet similar implications. This book concentrates on one strand, exploring the applied implications of recent ecological thinking for practical policy and management issues. There is little point in proclaiming the emergence of a new paradigm of thinking in range ecology without exploring the implications. This book attempts to ask the basic question: how will recent ecological thinking change policy and practice in pastoral development in Africa? This is a major challenge in a complex area and this book is clearly only a preliminary attempt. A significant hurdle lies in the effective translation of languages between disciplines. Ecological issues provide a starting point for the debate (see Behnke *et al.* 1993), but the policy and management implications of recent thinking are mediated by political, economic, social and cultural considerations. Finding a way of bridging between issues and interpretations will be key in finding practical ways forward. This overview chapter thus attempts to pick through a variety of interlocking and overlapping debates and suggests a number of key policy and management themes that will guide new directions in pastoral development in Africa.

This overview chapter draws on the themes developed more fully in subsequent parts of the book. The chapter starts with a discussion of planning alternatives followed by an examination of livestock–crop interactions and fodder supplementation. The discussion then turns to tracking strategies with a look at movement, destocking and restocking, as well as marketing options. Issues of resource tenure, institutional development and administration are considered next. The chapter concludes with a discussion of the investment and policy implications of these new directions in pastoral development.

Unpredictable change: alternatives to conventional planning and intervention

Pastoral areas are typified by high levels of unpredictable variability. From one season to the next you cannot know what will happen. Contingent responses to uncertain events characterize pastoral strategies. This involves seizing opportunities and avoiding hazards (Westoby *et al.* 1989). The more uncertainty there is at the local level, the more planners try to impose order through generalized development solutions. Millions of dollars have been spent trying to make unpredictable environments more predictable (e.g. through expensive early warning systems or irrigation schemes). Rather than addressing the issues of variability and uncertainty head-on, the development debate becomes dominated by unworkable, generalized solutions derived from simplistic analyses of complex problems (Roe 1991a). So, for instance, range privatization follows from the tragedy of the commons or ranch development follows from technology transfer and modernization approaches.

Under conditions of environmental uncertainty, planned intervention of any sort becomes problematic. Conventional planning and mainstream development intervention are premised on assumptions that the future can be predicted, inferred from patterns that have occurred in the past. Blueprint plans are designed and development investments approved on this basis. But is this mistaken under such conditions of variability and uncertainty?

Blueprint or adaptive planning?
There are two basic alternatives for planning in an uncertain world. The first aims to reduce uncertainties to probabilistic descriptions of variability by the collection of more and more data on more and more variables. The assumption is that more information will allow the prediction of outcomes at least in a probabilistic way. The result will be, it is hoped, a better defined problem (appropriately differentiated and accounting for recognized complexity) allowing for more effective plans. These are still blueprint plans, but better informed ones.

The alternative is to accept that uncertainty and indeterminacy are fundamental and central (Wynne 1992). No matter how much information is collected in a sensitive and differentiated manner, there is no way that all possible outcomes can be predicted and planned for. Rather than aim for 'complete' information (elaborate, multi-variate surveys) prior to intervention, it is better to act incrementally and initiate a learning process that monitors experience and feeds back lessons (Korten 1980; Schön 1983). This is adaptive management. Adaptive management relies on principles and guide lines rather than blueprints and prescriptions; it relies on a continuous learning process, rather than time-separated planning, implementation and monitoring/evaluation (Holling 1978; Walker *et al.* 1978; Walters and Hilborn 1978; Walters 1986).

These two options are obviously not mutually exclusive. For instance, adaptive management approaches may rely on pre-defined contingency planning: a suite of blueprints that allow response to a variety of circumstances. In other words, formal planning and policy-making may provide a framework within which adaptive management can operate. Despite the potentials for overlap between these two approaches to planning, the differences between them are fundamental and have important implications. If the variability that characterizes pastoral systems is unpredictable and uncertainty prevails, then we are forced to explore approaches to planning and intervention that involve adaptive and incremental change, based on local conditions and local circumstances.

These must be based on an in-built learning process, assuming that knowledge is never complete but action is always necessary (Korten 1980). Norman Uphoff comments on the adaptive learning process approach that evolved during the rehabilitation of a failed irrigation system in Sri Lanka:

6

With a learning process approach we did not expect to impose a linear logic on a non-linear world. Blueprints would not succeed because the situation was inherently uncertain and relations of cause and effect were probabilistic and contingent (Uphoff 1992b:397).

The learning process in uncertain environments is episodic. Particular events, such as droughts or disease outbreaks, provide important learning occasions. Establishing the facility to learn during and respond to episodic events requires new forms of institutional and organizational arrangement. Such set-ups must be both flexible and locally based, they must be able to change in response to both successes and failures, and they must be open to the risks and possibilities of failure.

Rethinking planned intervention in pastoral areas
There is a need to rethink planned intervention in pastoral areas (cf. Long and van der Ploeg 1989). Global solutions (e.g. the ranch model) imposed on local problems do not work. The assumption that Western science and technology can provide planned solutions to particular problems under conditions of high unpredictability and immense variability is clearly unfounded. Yet the domination of Western science has engulfed so much of the development process (Marglin and Marglin 1990), putting forward technical solutions to political problems such as poverty. Blueprint solutions so often ignore the important contextual issues of politics, history and culture that necessarily impinge on technical development.

Such imposed, blueprint plans are almost inevitably rejected, either openly or by more subtle means (Scott 1985, 1990). For instance, in Lesotho, Ferguson (1990) shows how local resistance to imposed plans involved both active sabotage and simple non-compliance. He argues that blueprint plans are not simply the result of poor or inadequate information. Instead, plans reflect political ambitions, whereby livestock development in Lesotho has acted as a smoke-screen for other agendas being played out in the development arena, ones involving the expansion of state control or the assertion of authority by local elites. Blueprint, technicist, imposed plans thus suit the wider political objectives of these actors. It is this political dimension to conventional planning approaches that helps to explain the tenacity of the blueprint planning approach.

A learning or process approach to development accepts that there are multiple sources of knowledge to draw on, both locally and externally derived; there are a diversity of perceptions and interpretations of a particular situation; there are always a variety of interests in a range of alternative options; and the process of development and change is inevitably one of negotiation, sometimes conflictual, sometimes consensual (Long and Long 1992; Scoones and Thompson 1993, 1994). In other words, development planning must recognize the variety of actors involved and accept that planning is ultimately a political process of consensus building between often divergent interests. Hybrid plans or evolving adaptations will be the most likely outcome rather than pre-specified blueprints. Such

7

process planning, if facilitated skilfully, may offer unexpected and potentially successful solutions for the challenges faced in pastoral areas.

New methods, skills and professionalism

Process planning and adaptive management require new methods, new skills and, above all, a new professionalism (Chambers 1992, 1993). Conventional livestock development has been dominated by such technical disciplines as animal breeding, veterinary science or improved forage agronomy. The applied discipline of range management has had some influence, although, as we have seen, its contribution has been almost exclusively geared towards equilibrium settings. Social science inputs have been fairly limited, with economics perhaps contributing most when questions of livestock marketing and trade are considered. Insights from institutional sociology, organizational management, social anthropology or law have been marginal. There is now a need to rethink the disciplinary balance of research expertise in livestock development. This is not to say that technical research is not required. It certainly is; there are many issues ranging from veterinary epidemiology to fodder improvement that require sustained, well-supported basic research (Winrock 1992). However, for this research to be well focused, providing the right answers to the right questions, it must be complemented with other inputs. But perhaps more importantly, there are a number of key issues that require particular social science attention. The uncertainty that dominates dryland environments means that local solutions are key, demanding flexible responses in diverse institutional settings and negotiation of interest groups with arbitration of disputes.

But perhaps even more important than reviewing the disciplinary mix of researchers is a re-examination of the context for research. Conventional, blueprint approaches to planning assume a stable world within which technical solutions can be implanted. The technology transfer model assumes that there is a more or less linear flow of information and ideas from basic researcher to applied researcher to extension worker to pastoral producer (Chambers 1983; Chambers *et al.* 1989). This transfer mode is reinforced by the structural separation of basic and applied research activities. The linear mode is also reinforced by the separation of research and extension activities, with extension expected to take 'off-the-shelf' messages or packages and deliver them to producers (e.g. through the Training-and-Visit system) (Moris 1991; Pretty and Chambers 1993). Aspects of this system may be appropriate to equilibrium environments (such as the rainfed lands of the so-called Green Revolution areas of Asia), but the transfer of technology approach is wholly inappropriate for the highly variable, unpredictable and complex environments found in pastoral areas. The context for research and extension must be changed for such settings.

Tracking a variable environment: how to support opportunistic management strategies?

In uncertain environments fodder availability fluctuates widely over time and space. Grass production may range from zero to several tonnes per

8

hectare, depending on rainfall. Such variation is spatially differentiated, with some areas showing more stable patterns of primary production while others are highly unstable. Making use of such a variable fodder resource requires tracking. Tracking involves the matching of available feed supply with animal numbers at a particular site. This is opportunistic management. Opportunistic management involves seizing opportunities when and where they exist and is thus highly flexible and responsive. Effective tracking may be achieved in four ways:

o Increasing locally available fodder by importing feed from elsewhere or by enhancing fodder production, especially drought feed, through investment in key resource sites.
o Moving animals to areas where fodder is available.
o Reducing animal feed intake during drought through shifts in watering regimes, reducing parasite loads or breeding for animals with low basal metabolic rates.
o Destocking animals through sales during drought and restocking when fodder is available after the drought.

These four strategies are discussed in turn in the following sections.

Existing livestock management strategies in dryland Africa combine all four of these options to varying extents (Box 1). Drought feeding strategies involve extensive lopping of browse species or the collection of tree pods. In some parts of Africa, particularly in North Africa where feed grain is heavily subsidized, livestock keepers maintain animals through the importation of supplementary feed. Indigenous zebu cattle are physiologically adapted to low feed intake with metabolic shifts allowing reduced need for survival feeding. The same applies to camels and small stock. Movement is central to the survival strategies of transhumant pastoral systems. Equally, local level movement is important in agropastoral systems. Drought sales of livestock are also important, although often a last resort.

Tracking is not easy and in most cases not very efficient (Sandford this book). Tracking strategies also run counter to elements of the conventional wisdom of many range managers and livestock development specialists. The mainstream view argues that a safe conservative strategy is desirable because it reduces the risk of large-scale fluctuations in numbers and output; it buffers the potentially environmentally damaging effects of temporary overstocking; and fits within the ranch model of development where particular interventions ('improved' breeds, fences, paddocks, rotations) can be implemented most effectively.

Unfortunately, a conservative stocking strategy is also inefficient and can impose heavy costs. Over time, extended periods will occur where fodder is left unused. Low stocking rates may result in additional burdens with reduced grass palatability due to undergrazing and increased fire risks. On occasions when grass production collapses completely, the conservative stocking level will itself be too high to be sustained in a limited area. Such occasions may be devastating for a rancher who, hemmed in by fences, has little option for flexible movement and is unpractised at responding to such rare events. In addition, conservatively stocked ranches

9

Box 1. Pastoral tracking strategies

During drought

○ Long-distance transport of animals to feed-surplus areas (trekking, truck transport, etc.)

○ Feed supplementation (lopping, hay-making, concentrate purchases, etc.)

○ Cereal stores to prevent needless distress sales of livestock

○ Animal health care (e.g. dosing with anti-helminthics), recognizing that animals die more of disease than starvation in drought

○ Diversification or switching of species composition within the family herd

○ Herd and family splitting

○ Supplementing or diversifying income from other livelihood sources besides animals

After drought

○ Investment/re-investment of surpluses from other activities in livestock (especially small stock with high reproductive rates)

○ Transfers of animals within social networks (whether with kinship basis, or with stock associates, etc.) on which individuals have legitimate claims

invariably have lower financial returns than opportunistically managed 'traditional' systems on a per area basis (Table 1).

The primary trade-off, however, may not be between opportunistic, tracking strategies and conservative, ranch management strategies. Conventional ranching systems represent less than five per cent of the total livestock population in Africa (Winrock 1992). In most cases they follow conservative regimes for very good reasons. Despite the rhetoric of some protagonists, ranching is not an alternative for most African livestock systems. While this has been recognized by some of the major donor agencies (cf. de Haan 1990), the ranch model, in various guises, continues to be promoted by both national governments and donor agencies.

The most important trade-off is between efficient and inefficient opportunism or tracking. The development challenge is thus not the transformation of pastoral systems into ranching systems, but increasing the efficiency of tracking (Sandford this book). How can this be done? There are a number of development options suggested by this analysis that can be grouped under the four tracking strategies outlined above. Again such options are not mutually exclusive, but each derives from an acceptance that, in order to improve the livelihoods of livestock keepers living in a highly variable, often uncertain environment, enhancing tracking opportunities and reducing the chances of livelihood loss through drought (or other episodic events) are key principles for designing practical options.

Feed alternatives to rangeland during drought

Most fodder research has concentrated on the enhancement of range productivity in 'normal' years. Reseeding with legumes or planting of fodder trees appear to provide some promise of boosting productivity in more humid agro-ecosystems, but such technologies have rarely proved viable in drier situations, especially when repeated droughts or intense grazing wipe out vulnerable grass and legume species or kill trees (Bayer and Waters-Bayer this book). The attempts by fodder agronomists or agroforesters to provide equilibrium solutions for non-equilibrium settings has thus proved very disappointing.

Understanding how most pastoral herds use the fodder landscape in dry areas, however, suggests an alternative strategy for such interventions. In dry seasons or in dry years, animals depend on relatively small patches within a wider dryland landscape. These are the 'key resources' that sustain animals in times of fodder shortage (Scoones 1994). Traditional tracking strategies usually involve strategic movement to such sites. It is these areas, rather than the open range, that should be the focus for fodder improvement. Enhancing (or even creating) key resource areas through investment in fodder management, reseeding and environmental rehabilitation appears to offer chances for productivity enhancement in good years and survival feeding in poor years (Barton 1993). For it is in such key resource areas, characterized as they are by a more equilibrium environment (often run-on sites with highly available soil water and nutrients), where legume seeding and tree planting (of existing species using existing management techniques) may have some chance of success.

Depending on the livestock species, browse may also act as an important key resource. The availability of coppiced trees and shrubs in dryland areas is often critical to the nutrition of livestock in times of drought (Le Houérou 1980; Barrow 1991). Tree pods in particular may be an important protein supplement that increase appetite and ensure maintenance of animals during periods of stress (Coppock and Reed 1992; Oba 1993). To many mainstream range managers trees within rangeland areas represent 'bush encroachment'. Great effort has been invested in cutting down such trees, removing in many cases the very browse resources that can allow animals to cope with drought. In dynamic ecosystems, the trade-offs between productivity under good rainfall conditions (where bush decreases grass growth through competition under conventional equilibrium dynamics) must be balanced against productivity under drought conditions, where non-equilibrium conditions apply and the browse component of the fodder landscape is critical. Thus for pastoralists attempting to track a highly variable environment it is important to sustain a scrub woodland where browse fodder is accessible to animals within range areas.

Pastoral–agricultural linkages

Some commentators argue that closer links between pastoral and agricultural systems and the evolution of integrated, mixed farming systems is both inevitable and highly desirable on the grounds of efficiency (McCown *et al.* 1979; McIntire *et al.* 1992). But does close crop–livestock interaction

Table 1. Comparisons between ranching and pastoral production systems in Africa

Country	Comments	Sources
Zimbabwe	All studies show that the value of communal area (CA) cattle production far exceeds returns from ranching. If actual stocking rates are used, CA returns are 10 times higher per hectare.	Danckwerts (1974) Jackson (1989) Barrett (1992) Scoones (1992a)
Botswana	Communal area production (in cash, energy and protein terms) per hectare exceeds by at least three times per hectare returns from ranches, even though technical production parameters are lower. The difference in soil erosion levels between the two production systems is negligible, despite differences in stocking rate.	Rennie et al. (1977) Carl Bro (1982) Hubbard (1982) De Ridder and Wagenaar (1984) Abel (1993)
Mozambique	Traditional systems have higher overall returns per hectare because of the multiple benefits of draught, transport, manure, milk and meat compared to the single beef output from ranches.	Rocha et al. (1991)
South Africa	Cattle production systems in the Transkei show higher returns per hectare, but lower productivity indicators, compared to ranches in the commercial white farming sector.	Tapson (1991, 1993) Richardson (1992)
Kenya	Gross output levels in individual ranches and undeveloped group ranches are comparable. Maasai multi-product outputs are higher than ranches on a per hectare basis.	De Leeuw et al. (1984) Bekure et al. (1991) Western (1982)
Tanzania	The productivity of pastoral herds in the Ngorongoro Conservation Area were found to be comparable to commercial herds. The patterns of productivity were similar to those found in Kenyan Maasai herds. Similarly high levels of productivity were found among livestock in Sukumaland.	Birley (1982) Homewood and Rodgers (1991) Homewood (1992)
Uganda	Recalculations of figures to include the full range of costs and benefits show that dollar returns per hectare under pastoralism are two times higher than for ranching. Dollar returns per animal are a third higher.	Ruthenberg (1980) Behnke (1985a)
Ethiopia	The pastoral Borana system has higher returns of both energy and protein per hectare compared to industrialized ranching systems in Australia. Australian Northern Territory ranches only realize 16% of the energy and 30% of the protein per hectare compared to the Borana system.	Cossins (1985) Upton (1989) Cossins and Upton (1988)

Table 1. Continued

Country	Comments	Sources
Mali	Transhumant pastoral systems yield on average at least two times the amount of protein per hectare per year compared to both sedentary agropastoralists and ranchers in the US and Australia.	Breman and de Wit (1983) Wilson *et al.* (1983)

imply the potential for improved tracking? Various arguments are put forward to justify crop–livestock integration. Below I will examine three of these.

Mixed farming systems are more efficient. This claim is based on a number of related arguments. The first relates to the 'inevitability' of intensification due to population pressure. As increases in population occur the premium on land grows as does the availability of labour. The result is an 'evolutionary' process of intensification (Boserup 1965, 1981; Pingali *et al.* 1987; Tiffen and Mortimore 1992), resulting in a move from extensive pastoralism to intensive mixed farming. As intensity of production increases, so the argument goes, the costs of production decrease, especially those that relate to transportation of inputs. In addition, in an integrated agropastoral system the transaction costs of negotiating contract herding or manure–crop residue exchanges disappear (Toulmin 1992b; Bayer and Waters-Bayer this book).

Despite the appealing logic of arguments in favour of livestock–crop integration on-farm, there are a number of pitfalls (Gass and Sumberg 1993). Although certain efficiencies may increase at the level of the farm unit, there are a range of inefficiencies at the broader geographical scale that arise through integration, particularly in the semi-arid zone. The production efficiency of individual animals may decrease in settled farming areas as compared to transhumant pastoral settings. For instance, Wilson and Clarke (1976) report the higher production indexes of migratory livestock in western Sudan. Other research, however, is more equivocal. Wilson (1982) found no significant differences between transhumant and agropastoral livestock in Mali, while van Raay and de Leeuw (1974) found settled livestock to be more productive in northern Nigeria because of their preferential access to prime grazing. However, generalizations are difficult to make, as there are highly efficient mixed farming systems found in the dry areas of southern Africa (Scoones 1992a; Abel 1993), where there has been a long tradition of integration.

In some settings, such as in the West African Sahel, the comparative advantages of the agricultural and pastoral areas may be lost through integration. If pastoral livestock are increasingly incorporated into agropastoral areas, and transhumant movement tracking the production vagaries of the dry rangelands is abandoned in favour of more 'efficient' settled production systems in more equilibrium environments, then the opportunity for exploiting large areas of dry range will be lost. Under conditions of

13

land pressure, to encourage the abandonment of the dry rangelands may be an inefficient solution. On top of this, the loss of pastoral livelihoods will result in additional costs as people migrate to the towns in search of casual employment or are driven to destitution. In terms of wider social welfare, in any country with a pastoral population, this can hardly be regarded as an efficient solution.

Mixed farming increases feed diversity and decreases variability in feed production. Mixed farming systems usually increase the diversity of feed available to animals compared with access to range resources alone. Crop residues, feed concentrates, agro-industrial by-products, as well as graze and browse in rangelands and between fields, offer a wide diversity of alternative feed. The variability of primary production in dry rangelands is high primarily due to rainfall variability.[3] Coefficients of variations of crop residue production in comparable areas are lower (although coefficients of variations of grain production are higher). This implies that in most semi-arid areas it is easier to track a variable environment with access to crop residues, as crop residues act to dampen some of the variability of production seen in the rangelands (Sandford 1988; Bayer and Waters-Bayer this book).

Some argue that the feed diversity and reduced variability of fodder production found in mixed agropastoral systems offer greater fodder security, making tracking variable environments more efficient in mixed agropastoral systems. However, while mixed farming systems offer a diversity of feed sources, this is also true for many pastoral systems. Flexible movement over extensive rangelands means that a great variety of grass and tree associations can be exploited, making good use of the varied phenology, production dynamics and forage quality of the different sources. In addition, pastoralists almost invariably have some access to crop residues and other agricultural by-products. Catch cropping by pastoralists often results in more fodder than grain. In addition, grazing arrangements between pastoralists and agriculturalists have long been a route for pastoralists to gain access to farm resources (Powell and Waters-Bayer 1985; Toulmin 1992b; Powell and Williams 1993). Pastoralists also purchase feed concentrates and other supplements to complement range resources and facilitate tracking.

Account must also be taken of scale. Production variations may be very high between seasons or years if a restricted single farm area is considered. However, if the scale is increased production variability decreases sub-

---

[3] Data from the southern rangelands of Ethiopia shows the coefficients of variation of grass biomass production to range between 19 and 59 per cent (short rains) and 25–47 per cent (long rains)(Bille 1982; Cossins and Upton 1988; Coppock, 1994). In Zimbabwe the primary production coefficients of variation depended on soil type and degree of bush cover; they were 59 per cent in Tuli where rainfall CV was 47 per cent and 27 per cent at Matopos where rainfall CV was 38 per cent. The highest variability of grass production over 17 years was found in thornveld, clay soil areas which had been cleared (Dye and Spear 1982; Noy-Meir and Walker 1986). In Mali, coefficients of variation ranged from 86 per cent in the northern part of the Gourma to 64 per cent in the south over the period 1984–1990 (de Leeuw *et al.* 1993).

stantially, especially if the biomass variability of different parts of the larger area is uncorrelated. This is what happens in an extensive range setting, where animals can be moved between different sites with different levels of production at any given time. This flexibility is often not feasible for a mixed farmer and the high local level variability must be coped with on a reduced scale. Landscape form will also affect the ability of livestock to respond to spatial and temporal variability. In highly dissected landscapes, such as in southern Zimbabwe, where habitat heterogeneity is high and key resource patches are plentiful, livestock may be herded in relatively restricted areas and within an agropastoral setting, except in extreme droughts when long distance movement may be required (Scoones 1992b, 1994). By contrast, in more uniform landscapes, such as the Kalahari sands areas of Botswana, more extensive pastoral production systems are required, involving frequent movement between agricultural areas and cattle posts (White 1992).

Mixed farming offers opportunities for stratification of production systems. Advocates of production system stratification argue that in order to exploit the comparative advantages of different ecological zones, it makes sense to stratify the production system, with different components of the livestock production process occurring in different areas. For instance, the dry areas of the Sahel have a comparative advantage for breeding animals. The low disease incidence, the high quality feed and the skills of pastoral producers suggest that an efficient breeding operation can be sustained in such areas. However, the dynamic ecological conditions are not conducive for efficient fattening operations. Such operations, it is argued, are more efficiently carried out in more equilibrium environments, where fodder and water supplies are guaranteed. Such areas are found in the mixed farming areas of the sub-humid savannas, with greater access to input supplies (feed concentrates, agro-industrial by-products, etc.) and output markets, which in the case of West Africa are further south on the coast (Staatz 1979; Jahnke 1982; Holtzman and Kulibaba, this book).

Again, the simple logic of the argument is highly appealing. But, as before, there are complications made more pertinent by our consideration of tracking strategies. Stratification is a poor mechanism for tracking. The logic assumes that the comparative advantage is static over time. Clearly this is not the case. Rainfall variations in the 'breeding zone' will mean a highly variable supply of young animals. In periods of drought, such animals may be in poor condition and receive low prices, thus increasing the incentives for pastoralists to hold on to them for sale at a higher price. Equally, during periods of good rainfall the 'breeding zone' may be quite a good 'fattening zone' too. In such periods where plentiful fodder exists, pastoralists will be unlikely to pass on animals that have a real potential for locally added value. Thus because of the dynamic variability of the pastoral areas, static notions of stratification are largely unworkable. However, local forms of stratification do exist. For instance, in the Sahel some farmers are diversifying into livestock rearing (e.g. *mouton de case)* as a risk minimization strategy.

15

Tracking ecosystem variability is potentially an efficient solution for dry areas. The complementarities with agricultural areas are obviously a necessary component of the future of pastoral areas. However, arguments for mixed farming must be tempered by considerations of what efficiency means in a dynamic ecological context.

Livestock movement

Movement of animals in response to spatial and temporal variation in resource availability is perhaps the most classic of all the tracking strategies (Swallow 1994). Movement allows herders to track fodder across the landscape, making use of patchy grass production caused by uneven rainfall or variations in landscape topography. Rather than manipulating herd numbers in response to climatic variability, as would a rancher operating in an enclosed area, pastoralists move and so shift their resource endowments (Behnke 1994). Efficient tracking requires movement over different scales depending on the temporal and spatial pattern of primary production variability. For illustration, let us contrast two different areas. The first is in a highly dynamic ecological setting where primary production varies enormously between years, where a dramatic fall in fodder availability is common and where similar conditions apply over wide areas. The second case is in a more equilibrium setting where primary production variability is lower, extreme droughts are rarer and the diversity of fodder sources within a relatively small area is higher. In the first case, it is clear that access to large grazing territories are required. But as production variability decreases, the scale of grazing territory required to sustain an effective tracking strategy also decreases. However, even in the second case, the occasional extremely dry year occurs and large scale movement may be necessary.[4]

In addition to the scale of movement, the regularity of movement will differ between the two cases. Under uncertain environmental conditions, movement over long distances must be a regular occurrence, as for transhumant pastoralism (Breman and de Wit 1983). In the second case, more typical of agropastoral settings, movement is more irregular. Exploitation of local level variability (local key resources, browse, crop residues) is sufficient in most years, and only occasional movements over longer distances are needed under conditions of extreme drought (Scoones 1992b).

Flexible and responsive movement requires institutional arrangements that ensure occasional access and that can resolve disputes and develop contingency plans for movement (Swift; Sylla this book). In cases where large scale movement is highly irregular, organizational and administrative arrangements are not geared up to facilitate movement. Very often large costs are imposed on livestock-owning people by regulations that restrict movement. Most administrative arrangements (movement permits, veterinary regulations, etc.) assume a stable environment where move-

---

[4] A similar contrast can be made between the mono-modal rainfall setting of the Sahel, typified by north–south movements, and the bi-modal rainfall situation of east Africa, where relatively localized and more erratic movements are common.

ment is discouraged. However, under more dynamic ecological conditions, movement becomes increasingly central and such administrative structures impose a major cost on the production system (Scoones 1992b).[5] When movement to particular sites occurs on a regular basis, negotiation of trekking routes and access to seasonal grazing must occur more frequently. Under such conditions institutional and administrative arrangements evolve that explicitly deal with ensuring movement and resolving conflicts.

Increasingly, arrangements that facilitate transhumance are no longer viable as key grazing land has been removed from pastoral use and put under the plough, or expropriated for conservation purposes. For instance, the Kenyan Maasai have lost over 1000 square miles of grazing over the past century as the Laikipia plateau, the Ngong hills, the Mara plains, the Amboseli swamp and the Mau forest area were removed from their control by other interests (agriculturalists, settler farmers, national parks) (Little 1987). This pattern continues today in Maasailand (Kituyi 1990), as well as many other pastoral areas (Galaty and Johnson 1990). Conflicts between agriculturalists and pastoralists have increased, particularly over 'key resource' sites, areas which are important for both agriculture and livestock production. Under such conditions, tracking through movement becomes increasingly difficult.

Physiological tracking by low-input animals
Adaptations of animal physiology may offset expected mortality levels during drought and increase recovery rates afterwards. Indigenous zebu cattle have energy sparing mechanisms that act as an adaptation to undernutrition and water deprivation (Finch and King 1979; King 1983; Nicholson 1987). Trials show that increasing the walking distance and decreasing the watering frequency, as might happen in a period of drought, did not result in any significant loss of weight in African zebu (Finch and King 1979). Fasting metabolic rate decreased by around 30 per cent, especially in the first 30 days of undernutrition and this led to decreased water requirements (Western and Finch 1986).

Adjustments to low feed intake are also observed among calves. Studies of Borana cattle in Ethiopia show that reduction in milk supply to the calf (through human consumption or reduced cow production due to poor nutrition in drought) does not affect the longer term target weight of calves, despite reducing calf growth rates in the short term (Coppock 1992). Recovery following drought is equally rapid. When food is available again there is a rapid response in metabolic rate levels and, with an increased plane of nutrition, conception rates greatly increase amongst mature female zebus.

Shifts in metabolic rate have two important implications. First, there are

---

[5] Clearly, there will be occasions when movement restrictions to limit the spread of contagious diseases and the imposition of quarantine regulations are warranted. However, in the design of veterinary regulations and associated administrative arrangements, the trade-off between veterinary control and mobility must be taken into account.

apparently no extra weight losses imposed by longer foraging treks and reduced water availability during periods of undernutrition in drought. Therefore indigenous animals are physiologically adapted to mobility and flexible responses to uncertain fodder and water availability. Second, due to reductions in fasting metabolism, more animals can be sustained on a given amount of available fodder during periods of drought than would be possible if there was no physiological tracking of the environment. In other words, forage needs in drought may be reduced by as much as 30 per cent through shifts in metabolic rate. This will likely result in significant reductions in drought-induced mortality among zebu cattle (Western and Finch 1986).

Healthy animals are best able to track environmental fluctuations. Animals with high parasite loads, for instance, are less resilient to stress. For this reason, veterinary interventions during drought periods (e.g. anti-helminth drug campaigns) may increase tracking ability of pastoral herds and flocks. Such interventions could usefully be complemented by support for indigenous systems of veterinary care, such as the feeding of browse fodder with anti-helminthic properties.

Pastoralists' own breeding strategies emphasize breeding for survival. Breeding occurs under conditions of stress, with selection pressures which encourage certain traits. This is unlike most conventional animal breeding where selection for milk or meat occurs under high-input conditions (Bayer 1989). It is not surprising that the introduction of so-called 'improved' breeds into areas with highly variable and sometimes very low feed availability have been disastrous. Breeding for physiological tracking and low-input conditions remains a challenge to be taken up by animal scientists.

Marketing
Livestock sales levels in pastoral areas are often correlated with rainfall. In periods of drought, pastoralists tend to sell more and in wetter periods, pastoralists tend to accumulate their herd capital. For instance in Swaziland, 25 per cent of the variation in annual cattle herd offtake rates was attributable to rainfall variation, 40 per cent to price changes and 35 per cent remained unexplained in an analysis of sales patterns from small-scale herds between 1950 and 1976 (Doran *et al.* 1979). Similar correlations between sales rates and rainfall levels are found in Zimbabwe between the 1920s and mid-1980s (Scoones 1990). The supply of livestock also depends on the structure of herds. In many pastoral areas, commercialization of livestock production is constrained by herd size (Behnke 1987) and herd composition (Dyson-Hudson and McCabe 1983). Livestock marketing in uncertain environments therefore must be responsive to highly variable levels of supply, both between years and between seasons.

High variability in throughput is experienced by parastatal marketing authorities and private traders alike. For instance in Kenya, the Livestock Marketing Division experienced an interannual coefficient of variation of purchases of 51 per cent between 1960 and 1978. Private traders equally

18

had high variability in purchase levels (CV = 36 per cent) over the same period (White and Meadows 1980).

The uncertainty of animal supply from pastoral areas is compounded by the high transaction costs involved in the marketing process. Because of the long distances between production areas and urban markets, transport costs are high. Equally, because of poor market infrastructure (holding grounds, storage facilities, etc.), the costs of marketing for the producer may be high.

Efficient tracking responses require getting animals to markets rapidly before prices collapse during drought. The availability of private traders' truck transport may increase flexibility and speed of response, but costs may be high if there is limited competition in the transport business. Most studies show that trekking is a more efficient option for large stock, especially where trek route facilities already exist (Staatz 1979; Sandford 1983; Holtzman and Kulibaba this book). Private or public investment may assist in offsetting some of these costs. For instance, government road schemes in pastoral areas may increase marketing opportunities. Private investment in transport (such as trucks), butcheries or small-scale meat and milk processing may increase the variety of marketing options in pastoral areas.

Most public investment in meat marketing in pastoral areas has failed. Large abattoirs or freezing plants often lie idle. The high overhead costs of maintaining large facilities working at low capacity for long periods means that most parastatal meat marketing systems have collapsed (Sandford 1983; Bekure and McDonald 1985; Holtzman and Kulibaba this book). But in some areas, parastatal marketing authorities have persisted. Political pressures have meant that parastatals such as the Botswana Meat Commission or the Zimbabwe Cold Storage Commission have been allowed to continue operating at a loss, on the assumption that they are fulfilling a useful rural development role and should not be considered only on commercial criteria. In drought periods such parastatals operate buying schemes in order to provide a last resort selling option for herd owners (Hubbard and Morrison 1985; Rodriguez 1986).

The mix of public and private investment in marketing systems needed to encourage tracking responses by pastoralists will vary from place to place. In general, governments bear high overhead costs and are constrained by bureaucratic procedures, while private operators are more flexible. This suggests that public investments are best directed to broader infrastructural support (roads, trekking facilities, etc.), while private investment is likely to be most responsive to particular local market conditions.

Constraints to efficient tracking

The previous sections have outlined different ways pastoralists can track a highly variable environment. It is clear that a combination of these strategies can allow a highly efficient pastoral land use strategy making optimal use of variable fodder supplies for maximum return over time. However, there are clearly constraints to efficient tracking strategies. These include the following.

Labour and skills. Tracking often involves high levels of skilled labour input. For instance, flexible and responsive movement (especially complex herd splitting and phased movement of different animal types) requires skilled herding labour. Similarly, fine-tuned fodder management through drought periods also requires knowledge about animal physiology, experience of different responses to different feed combinations and labour for fodder collection and selective feeding. Again such labour and skills may be difficult to find in some pastoral areas, due to the out-migration of male pastoralists in search of alternative employment opportunities. Very often available labour is unskilled and with limited experience. This reduces the efficacy of many of the tracking strategies discussed above.

Ownership and commitments. Today, an increasing proportion of pastoral herds are owned by absentee herd owners (Little 1985a,b, 1987; Thébaud 1993). They may be government officials, rich agriculturalists or urban businessmen with little knowledge of the complexities of pastoral production in dry, dynamic ecosystems. Hired herd managers do not own the animals themselves, and so have less incentive to invest in fine-tuned tracking management. The consequence is often a different set of objectives and a lower level of productivity in absentee owners' herds compared to those of resident pastoralists (Sutter 1987; White 1990). Absentee herd owners may be able to bear this cost as they have interests in other income earning activities outside the pastoral sector. However, this inefficiency in tracking imposed by the nature of ownership and the lower commitment to pastoral production is an opportunity cost, as the same herds could be yielding a higher return under different ownership and with greater care.

Access to land. Perhaps the greatest constraint to efficient tracking is limited access to land, particularly to key dry season grazing resources. This constraint is being felt by nearly all pastoral peoples. Securing rights of access to land and water is perhaps the most important challenge for the future of pastoralism. Appropriate resource tenure regimes and associated institutional and administrative arrangements are key to increasing the efficiency of tracking (Lane and Moorehead; Swift; Sylla this book).

Borders, boundaries and conflicts. Efficient tracking very often requires access to large areas. Many pastoral populations straddle national boundaries or are resident in and around national parks or wildlife areas. To track an uncertain environment efficiently often requires access to areas across official borders or boundaries. Despite the ecological logic of flexible movement, this inevitably causes problems for state administrators who are obliged to defend the sanctity of lines marked on national maps. In some cases borders and boundaries remain notional and pastoralists can move uninhibited. Elsewhere, strong-arm tactics are employed when, for political or other reasons, it is deemed necessary to expel pastoralists from national parks or when a 'security threat' requires the state to prevent 'insurgent' pastoralists from crossing a national border (Hogg 1992; Homewood 1993). Local boundaries, within larger territories, are also the site for contests over access rights, particularly where key resource sites are limiting (Scoones and Cousins 1994). Appropriate forms of governance and legal measures are required at both international, national and local levels to facilitate mobility and improve tracking efficiency.

Information. Efficient tracking requires good information. Ideally this information should include predictions about future patterns of resource availability. At the minimum effective tracking requires the ability to respond to current conditions, with regular up dates, so flexible responses can continue. Pastoralists traditionally use complex weather forecasting techniques and networks of communication between different well sites, oases and outposts to be able to respond flexibly to variability. Such systems have proved very efficient under the conditions of poor electronic communication and low infrastructural development in most pastoral areas. Attempts to develop early warning systems using satellite technology, while technically feasible, have not been effective in the management of pastoral areas (Buchanan-Smith *et al.* 1992; Toulmin this book).

A number of issues combine to make satellite monitoring a poor solution to increasing tracking efficiency in most pastoral settings in Africa. First, flows of information from centralized satellite imagery processing facilities to pastoral areas are slow and inefficient. Second, the information, or more particularly the holder of the information (the local district administrator or animal development officer who is often not a herder or from a herding group), is often not trusted and most pastoralists are unprepared to risk their herds' survival and so their livelihoods on information from such a source. Third, the form of the information supplied may not be what the pastoralist needs. For instance, the scale of resolution of most fodder availability maps is so coarse that its utility for fine-tuned management remains limited. Although it is feasible to gain high resolution, high quality information, the processing costs and information overload implications are excessive. As a result, pastoralists tend to prefer information that is generated by them, rather than information generated by satellites and scientists. Finally, the costs of implementing (and sustaining the recurrent costs) of such a system are beyond the means of most national governments in Africa. While satellite images and image processing are becoming progressively cheaper, the administrative and bureaucratic costs of disseminating information remain high.[6] It is difficult to escape the conclusion that the use of such techniques is often driven by a need to find a use for the technology.

Service provision. The provision of services in pastoral areas can both constrain and support efficient tracking. Constraints arise when services are

---

[6] In Australia satellite technologies are used to good effect as a tool for range planning and management. The large size of ranch properties, the dispersed nature of the ranching community and the easy access to computer and telecommunication systems means that, in the Australian case, satellite, remote sensing systems provide an appropriate technological solution (Foran and Stafford-Smith 1991; Stafford-Smith and Pickup 1993). There is therefore nothing fundamentally wrong with the use of satellite systems, it is just that they are inappropriate for most African cases. However, in the future, localized satellite systems may be developed that are appropriate for pastoral settings in Africa.

provided in a way which either limits the ability to move flexibly or withdraws labour from herding and livestock management activities. Although approaches to mobile service delivery (schools, clinics, veterinary care) have been devised and in some instances implemented (Antenneh 1985; de Haan and Bekure 1991; Iles and Young 1991; Umali *et al.* 1992; Young 1992), conventional state service provision has concentrated on the provision of services assuming a sedentary life-style or identical transhumant routes each year.

When tracking fails

Efficient tracking may not always work. There are many barriers and there will continue to be. The experience of pastoral areas in the past two decades has not been a happy one. Conflict is increasing, very often involving bloodshed; levels of destitution are rising, with increasing numbers of people being forced to leave the pastoral sector with little prospect of a return; and major food deficits sometimes leading to famine continue to haunt dry Africa. The costs of this situation, particularly locally, but also internationally, are high, and escalating.

When effective tracking fails, other options are necessary. Safety nets that can help maintain livelihoods and avoid conflicts are critical components. Without such social security measures, the opportunities for a return to pastoral livelihoods and the efficient exploitation of a variable and hostile environment are lost, for some maybe forever.

Providing safety nets. Social welfare interventions may act to avoid destitution among pastoralists, reducing the ratchet effect of poverty. If livelihoods can be sustained through external intervention during periods of crisis, such as drought, there may be a greater chance of a return to a pastoral way of life following the crisis. The opportunity costs of doing nothing are potentially very high. Previous drought periods have seen pastoral populations driven to migrate to urban areas, often ending up in settlement camps with few prospects for the future. The social costs of such outcomes are high not only for the destitute pastoralists, but also for host communities and agencies obliged to intervene.

Strategic drought interventions. Welfare and development support can be strategically timed to offset the high costs of drought on pastoral livelihoods. Such interventions include:

○ Livestock price interventions to avoid mass sales;
○ Food aid or cash/food-for-work to avoid the necessity of further asset disposal or famine;
○ Livestock aid (fodder imports, anti-helminth control, etc.) to avoid excessive livestock mortalities.

These interventions are best implemented at a local level as part of a drought contingency plan where pre-planned actions are designed and actions implemented in relation to various 'warning' signals based on an understanding of pastoral livelihoods (cf. Buchanan-Smith 1992 for Turkana, Kenya; Davies 1992 for Mali). Too often drought interventions

22

have arisen through relief, resulting often in aid dependency and the loss of indigenous coping mechanisms, rather than long-term development responses. They have often been haphazard and uncoordinated, arriving too late and implemented in a poorly thought-out manner without analysis of the longer-term implications. In dryland environments 'crisis' events are, after all, 'normal'. Although unpredictable, they are certainly expected. Integrating relief with longer-term development activities is thus an important challenge.

Alternative livelihoods. Flexible exit and re-entry into the livestock sector are rare. The loss of a pastoralist's herd and flock during a drought may be permanent. Indigenous systems of stock redistribution (sharing, loaning, herding and stock associate relationships, raiding, etc.) are increasingly rare (Toulmin 1992b). Small-scale restocking operations initiated by NGOs and other development agencies (Oxby 1989; Toulmin this book) have had some success, but little impact overall. Wider interventions are required that allow opportunistic livelihood strategies that stretch beyond the pastoral sector. Providing alternative livelihood options during drought, which allow pastoralists some alternative to destitution, may provide a greater chance for re-entry into the livestock sector at a later date. Public works, cash-for-work schemes, assisted migration, pastoral reserve areas in high potential zones and provision of local income-earning alternatives may represent legitimate public investment priorities in pastoral areas (Teklu *et al.* 1991; Maxwell 1992; Webb *et al.* 1992).

Flexible resource tenure arrangements for variable environments

The conventional typology of resource tenure suggests a set of mutually exclusive property regimes. In the context of the pastoral development debate, the most common of these are private, communal and state property regimes.[7] Yet in pastoral areas, because of the extent of spatial heterogeneity and temporal variability in resources, different resource tenure systems co-exist and overlap. Different types of property regime may be more or less appropriate at different times and places. Empirical data from pastoral areas show no neat division between property regimes, but rather a complex set of overlapping rights that are continuously contested and renegotiated. These rights may shift over time and shift from place to place.

In uncertain environments the value of resources changes sharply over both space and time. This is why we see dynamic resource tenure systems in pastoral areas, with different levels of rent extracted from a resource, depending on where the resource is and the prevailing environmental conditions at the time. When rent extraction potential rises, the incentives increase to invest in managing that resource and exclude others, if at all possible. According to property rights theory, when the benefits derived

---

[7] One other non-property regime is open access settings where no rights, rules and regulations exist over use. Most areas that are seen as 'open access' are in fact state property, as the state very often holds the residual legal rights over pastoral land.

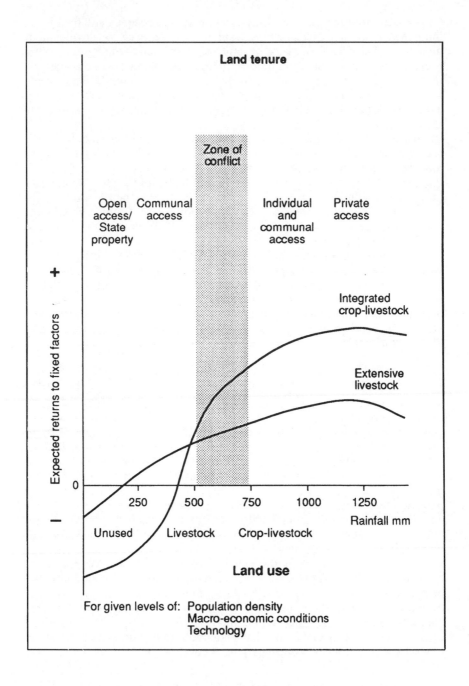

Figure 1 *The Swallow model (Swallow, Woburn workshop)*

24

from controlling access to the resource (as an individual or group) exceed the transaction costs of defending the resource from others and managing it, then we can expect a greater chance of more exclusive forms of property regime to emerge (Demsetz 1967; Behnke 1991, 1994; Bromley 1992; Lane and Moorehead this book). Put simply, if it pays to keep others out, then people will do so if they can. Whether such exclusive forms of tenure turn out to be private or communal will depend on particular circumstances. Local politics, social organization, assurance mechanisms and history (among many other things) may influence the emergence of new tenure settings in different ways in different places.

Expected forms of tenure can be expected to change along an environmental gradient, from drier zones where resources are generally of low value per unit area and environmental variability is high, to more humid zones where resources are of higher value per unit area and the environment tends to be more stable (Figure 1). A number of predictions follow from the property rights argument outlined above. In drier zones, more flexible forms of land tenure can be expected, involving few (co-ordinated access) or no property rights (open access). In wetter areas more exclusive forms of tenure can be expected (private property, exclusive communal tenure). In the semi-arid areas between, a more confused situation arises, with a greater range of options and a greater potential for conflict. With few exceptions, this is exactly what we see in practice (Lane and Moorehead this book).

Although the simple property rights model appears robust, there are a number of other important dimensions. The tenure situation described in Figure 1 is far from being static and must consider first, the implications of dynamic variability at a particular site; second, the implications of spatial heterogeneity; third, the implications of longer-term changes in land use across environmental gradients; and finally the social, political and historical context in each setting. These issues are examined below.

Interannual variability in resource productivity
In dryland areas fodder production varies enormously and unpredictably, as does its scarcity value. In dry years (or during the dry season) forage is at a premium, as livestock compete for the limited available fodder. In such situations the curve described in Figure 1 shifts upwards. Conversely, in seasons of relative plenty, the curve shifts downwards. As the demand–supply situation changes, so does the resource value and consequently the incentives to engage in defending resource rights. In other words, the type of resource tenure and organizational arrangements will depend on how good the season has been.

For instance, in the Darfur area of Sudan an increasing number of grazing land enclosures were seen during the dry years of the mid to late 1980s. Such areas provided restricted access grazing to particularly powerful kin groups of settled farmers in the El Fasher region. Simple thorn fences were used to exclude others, including migrant herders (Behnke 1985b; Curtis and Scoones 1990).

25

Spatial variability in resource value
Environmental variability also has a spatial dimension. The value of different resources within the pastoral landscape at any point along the curve described in Figure 1 is not the same. Usually a variety of patches of different quality (in terms of fodder production or forage quality) make up a heterogeneous fodder resource base. Small, high-value key resources (e.g. drainage lines or sinks, river banks, water points, salt-licks, strategic fodder reserves such as trees, etc.) may be highly contested areas, particularly in periods of drought, and are thus often areas where more exclusive forms of tenure emerge. This pattern is observed in western Sudan in wadi areas (Behnke 1985b), in Zimbabwe in *dambos* (valley bottom sites) (Cousins 1992; Scoones and Cousins 1994) and around boreholes and other water points (White 1992 for Botswana; Thébaud 1993 for Burkina Faso; Guèye 1993 for Senegal). In these cases, it has become worthwhile to exclude others, either because of drought, or because of increased population pressure or because of competition for a high-value resource.

Access to key resources is often central to the survival of the whole pastoral production system, because without access to such areas, livestock cannot survive dry periods. Removal of relatively small patches (through encroachment by agriculturalists or expropriation by state farms or other interests) can be highly damaging, inflicting major costs on the pastoral sector (Lane and Scoones 1993). It is for this reason that we see much of the conflict around resource use associated with such areas. This is particularly the case in the semi-arid zone, where such resources are especially valuable, since resource pressures are at their most intense with the competition between agricultural and pastoral uses of land. In many areas these pressures are increasing, resulting in greater contests for key resources, greater shifts in resource tenure and greater opportunities for conflict between land users.

In many pastoral areas a hierarchy of different tenure systems is seen within the same landscape: some areas are uncontested (effectively open access), other areas are managed communally according to locally negotiated rules (co-ordinated access, common property) and other areas are used exclusively (effectively private).[8]

Secular changes in resource pressure
A number of longer-term trends significantly affect the simple relationship described in Figure 1. Although the debate on global climatic change still rages, there appear to have been changes in some pastoral areas in Africa which have received progressively less rainfall with increased variability between years (Downing 1982; Hulme 1992). Substantial shifts in land use have occurred in the Sahelian region over the period from 1973 to 1988 when a decline in rainfall of 20–30 per cent was observed (Farmer 1986;

---

[8] There are important differences between the *de facto* and *de jure* situation in many pastoral areas. For instance some areas may be effectively open access although they are nominally state property. Similarly 'privatised' areas may not be strictly so because of a poorly functioning land market.

IUCN 1989). In particular, as the rainfall isohyets moved south, so did the pastoral herds. This brought them into increasing conflict with settled agriculturalists (Bayer and Waters-Bayer this book).

Such changes may be combined with shifts in resource value brought about by changes in resource pressure. Increasing human populations in most parts of Africa have resulted in greater competition for available resources. As populations have increased, new forms of resource management and tenure have arisen. The expansion of arable farming into grazing areas has meant that livestock management has had to adapt. Fodder intake is maintained by the increased use of crop residues with high nutrient content, the use of arable fallows rich in legumes, the establishment of fodder trees and the practice of 'pastoral gardening', where careful grazing between fields and along field boundaries makes maximum use of available fodder (Bayer and Waters-Bayer this book; Thébaud 1993). Adaptation to increased resource pressure requires new arrangements. These may involve negotiations between farming and pastoral groups or access restrictions during the cultivation season within agropastoral communities so that mixed crop–livestock farming can continue successfully. Whatever the case, increased resource pressure inevitably means heightened opportunities for conflict and an increasing need for negotiation and arbitration procedures.

Flexible tenure regimes
Overlapping claims to resources, shifting assertions of rights and continuous contestation and negotiation of access rules dominate tenurial arrangements in uncertain environments. The solution is not to impose particular tenure types on a variable setting; whether these are uniquely communal or private they are unlikely to work. Instead, the need for flexible tenure arrangements must be recognized. This is problematic for two reasons. First, flexible arrangements, by their very nature, are difficult to codify in law, and second, because of this lack of codification, tenurial rights are difficult to defend through formal legal processes (Swift this book). This is why effective pastoral institutions are important. In the past, stable social groupings, based on kin, clan and tribal networks, were able to deal with these uncertainties. Today, this is less the case and new institutions to manage environmental variability and flexible tenure regimes are required.

Two aspects of variability require attention. First, where variability is unpredictable, then no form of prescriptive legal (or other) arrangement is of much use, except in terms of broad principles. Customary tenure systems operate shared, overlapping forms of tenure rights in such settings as maintaining strict boundaries is usually untenable. However in highly variable environments the need for conflict mediation will be fairly constant (Behnke 1994). In such cases, a form of conflict resolution *process* can be specified in law and attached to formal institutions. Such a procedural framework would have to be designed to deal with a range of unpredictable contingencies, but would offer a flexible mechanism for

27

dealing with disputes (Vedeld 1993). This avoids the need to transform customary land rights into formal law.

Second, when variation is more predictable, as in the case of identifiable key resources, or when longer-term trends are evident, such as expansion of arable areas into pasture lands, then more-formalized measures may be taken to secure access rights and specify tenurial regulations. In such situations, policy-makers must decide on the relative social, economic and other costs of different options (e.g. between the use of a particular area for agriculture or grazing) and examine these trade-offs in the broadest sense. Clearly this represents a policy decision ultimately determined by political processes; processes in which pastoralists are usually at a major disadvantage. Resolution of such issues must therefore rely on an increased policy leverage and lobbying power afforded by more effective pastoral organizations (see below).

In all cases, the development of flexible tenure regimes will require the consideration of a variety of trade-offs. These affect rights and responsibilities, access to resources and the form of user group (see Box 2).

Institutional development for variable environments

Most management and policy prescriptions are not attuned to flexible responses and variable environments; instead they assume equilibrium and predictability. Each of the previous sections on planning, tracking and resource tenure draw the same conclusions with regard to institutional

---

Box 2 Trade-offs central to negotiating tenure arrangements

Rights

Communal vs. private rights
Historical vs. current rights
Ownership vs. stewardship vs. usufruct rights
Permanent vs. temporary rights
Negotiable vs. fixed rights
Restricted vs. unconditional rights
Primary vs. secondary/tertiary rights

Access

Access to all resources vs. selected resource access
Free vs. paid access
Seasonal access vs. year-round occupation

User Groups

Exclusivity vs. inclusivity
Inheritable membership vs. non-inheritable
Homogeneity vs. heterogeneity of resource users

---

development. In highly variable environments it is essential to develop solutions at the local level and not attempt to impose institutional and organizational[9] blueprints from above. In order to deal with complexity and variability in a flexible and adaptive manner, local institutions must be strong.

This section pursues this issue with a discussion of institutional development in variable environments. Two major themes run through this discussion, both of which are central to institutional and organizational arrangements for responding to the high variability and uncertainty typically found in dryland Africa. The first theme is the need for an effective hierarchy of institutional responsibility for resource management, that stretches from the local to the national and sometimes beyond. It is not simply a choice between 'bottom-up' and 'top-down' approaches as some of the populist rhetoric would have it. Since environmental variability occurs over different spatial scales, with events occurring with different frequencies, different types of institution will be appropriate for dealing with resource management and pastoral development issues at each level. Because of the uncertain and episodic nature of environmental variability, centralized and bureaucratic state institutions are generally poorly equipped for dealing with local level management issues. Centralized bureaucracies tend to aggregate, standardize and prescribe, rather than differentiate, fine-tune and adapt. It is in these latter qualities that local institutions have a comparative advantage.

Nevertheless, wider-scale institutions have important roles to fulfil. Providing a broad and enabling legal framework which offers principles and guidelines for resolving issues through local level processes is one key area. Governmental institutions may be important in resolving disputes or negotiating between parties, acting as a broker and arbitrator. Credibility, transparency, accountability and impartiality are necessary attributes currently lacking amongst government structures in many pastoral areas. Equally governments and large donor projects are best able to provide certain services in pastoral areas (roads, marketing infrastructure, basic health-care facilities, etc.).

The second theme concerns issues of conflict negotiation, mediation and arbitration. If institutional responses are to be flexible, there are always going to be points of contest where different parties disagree. The previous section's discussion of flexible tenure systems has already highlighted this. Effective tenure systems that allow mobility and flexible response to contingent events must be firmly rooted in institutional arrangements that allow for the negotiation of resource access and resolution of conflicts. The focus on flexibility and mobility switches attention from 'ideal' tenure types that may be prescribed (private, communal, etc.) to dealing with overlapping rights with greater or lesser exclusivity. As resource rights vary in space and time and between different groups of people, this requires

---

[9] An institution is a complex of norms and behaviours that persist over time by serving some socially valued purpose, while an organization is a structure of recognized and accepted roles (Uphoff 1986: 8–9).

a shift of focus to conflict resolution mechanisms and institutional approaches for dealing with these. A number of principles for institutional development in highly variable, unpredictable environments can be drawn from the discussion.

Subsidiarity. The principle of subsidiarity can be a guiding concept in thinking about institutional development and administration in pastoral areas (Swift this book). Subsidiarity implies that power and responsibility should be devolved to the lowest institutional level consistent with the provision of services and maintaining accountability. In practice this implies a shift in responsibilities away from attempts at extensive state provision in pastoral areas to decentralized, local control. Rather than the state attempting to provide legal frameworks down to the lowest level, the state would offer a broad framework and require local groups to negotiate access rights and resource management agreements among themselves, while maintaining certain responsibilities for adjudication and arbitration. Similarly in the area of service provision, state support for veterinary health care or range management would be limited to basic infrastructural support with other elements being locally managed (Swift this book).[10]

Building bridges between customary systems and formal law. Another principle that emerges is the need to build bridges between customary systems (both *de jure* and *de facto*) and formal law. Formal legal systems, frequently anachronistic inheritances from the colonial era, often run counter to customary arrangements. The result is major conflict between state-led intervention and pastoral populations, particularly surrounding access to land. If this is to be resolved, investment in building bridges between the two systems will be enormously important (Swift this book). Without this, emerging pastoral organizations at the local level will find it very difficult to operate, especially when such local level organizations come into conflict with the state.

Pastoral institution building must recognize diverse interests. Building pastoral institutions is not an easy task. Too often an idealized notion of 'community' is imposed on pastoral societies. In fact, pastoral groups are highly differentiated, and increasingly so. There are often a wide range of diverse interests within groups, including women, men, richer herd owners, poorer people, those who are temporary migrants, absentee herd owners and so on. Some groups are more visible and vocal than others. Each group may have different options for responding to environmental uncertainty, and therefore require different things from a pastoral organization. For instance, large herd owners may be able to split herds and carry out complex forms of transhumance, while poorer herders may be unable to

---

[10] The debate on decentralization and subsidiarity does not derive solely from the need to respond flexibly to variable environments. However, the ecological argument provides another angle to the argument for increased attention to local level management issues derived from debates about participatory development (Chambers 1993; Scoones and Thompson 1994), state–civil society relations and democratization (Clark 1991) and the retreat of state service provision under liberalization and structural adjustment (Mosely 1991; Mosely and Weeks 1993; Woodward 1993).

respond through mobility and may need 'safety net' support in order to avoid losing their animals in a drought. The differentiated nature of pastoral society requires a slow and patient institution building process, and a recognition of different types of groups appropriate for different tasks. For instance, permanent pastoral organizations may be formed around regular and common tasks or needs that are widely felt, while *ad hoc* organizations may be more appropriate for dealing with episodic events (e.g. negotiating resource access during drought) or with sectoral interests (e.g. product processing carried out by women) (Sylla this book). *Conflicts should be addressed explicitly, not ignored.* Conflicting interests are an inevitable consequence of dealing with complex resource management and development issues involving a diverse range of highly differentiated actors. Visible and expressed conflicts can be tackled through an early initiation of 'round-table' discussions and consultation with different actors to explore conflicting interests, the establishment of procedural legal frameworks for resolving conflicts when they arise and formalized institutional settings for conflict negotiation, arbitration and resolution.

Pastoral organizations should start small and help forge collective interests. The experience of pastoral institution building in all parts of Africa suggests that starting small and forging collective action around sets of common interests (e.g. marketing, health care) is the most likely route to successful organizational development. Attempting to deal with complex issues at the start, such as range management or resource tenure, usually results in failure (Sylla this book). It is best to start small, working from existing organizational arrangements and build up from there (Esman and Uphoff 1984).

Lobbying for pastoral interests at national and international levels is an important role for pastoral organizations. A variety of changes in policy for pastoral areas are required if the practical implications of the new thinking in range ecology are to be realized on the ground. Such policy changes (e.g. in respect of resource rights) will not come easily. Pastoral groups are politically marginalized in most African countries and access to the political decision-making process is limited. However federations of smaller pastoral associations may be able to make pastoral interests heard at a national level through lobbying and advocacy, exploring the definition of rights through the legal system and through links and alliances in international arenas. The experience of forming such federations is so far limited, but there is a growing experience in Central African Republic, Mauritania, Burkina Faso and Senegal (de Haan 1991; Vedeld 1993; Zeidane 1993). Successes in other areas, such as associations of wildlife producing districts in Zimbabwe (Zimbabwe Trust 1991) or farmer organizations in many parts of the world (Uphoff 1992b; Bebbington 1991) suggest that the shift from the local level to political change at the national level is probably the only effective route to long-term policy change.

Extension support needs to shift from technical provision to institution building. Conventional extension at the local level has concentrated on technical advice on range management and animal health. While this is still needed, there is perhaps a more pressing need, that most fieldworkers (both

31

state and NGO) are ill-equipped to supply—support to institutional development. Skills required of 'institutional organizers' (cf. Uphoff 1992a,b) as organizational facilitators, development catalysts, brokers of information and conflict mediators are not part of the 'normal professionalism' of most rural development workers (Korten 1980; Chambers 1993). Investment in retraining for such challenges is a key task for the future.

New roles for different actors: projects, programmes and investments in the pastoral sector

Pastoral development is plagued by an 'equilibrium of low expectations' (Uphoff 1992b: 359). What are the conditions of breaking away from this, making things happen and exploring possibilities, rather than accepting the probability of failure?

Rural development 'successes' appear to rely on a good fit between the needs of beneficiaries, the organizational competence for decision-making and implementation at the local level and the programme's outputs and requirements (Korten 1980). Achieving such a fit must be high on the agenda of programmes in pastoral areas. This requires that attention be paid to the context and the relationship between the project and the supposed beneficiaries. In addition, attention needs to be paid to the building of local capacity to diagnose and solve problems through institutions that are able to sustain activities (Korten 1980; Chambers 1983; Uphoff 1992a).

Researchers, planners and administrators must interact closely if learning is to be encouraged. An action-oriented implementation, monitoring and assessment approach is central to adaptive management. This must be done in close contact with people on the ground, preferably with most tasks being carried out by them. Uncertainty, error and conflict must also be embraced in a learning process approach. Optimal intervention may be very limited where resource productivity is low, as in most dry rangelands. The costs of planning, administration and management must therefore be kept low, avoiding the tendencies for over-collection of data, excessive precision and zealous intrusion from outside (Behnke 1994).

Donors and other development agencies are increasingly adopting the rhetoric of participation and flexible, open-ended planning approaches. However, the establishment of effective adaptive management in practice is more elusive than the rhetoric suggests. There remain fundamental contradictions between declared purpose and actual procedures due to the reluctance to abandon rigid planning frames, commitments to strict procedures, the need to disburse money according to target deadlines and the desire to see quick returns from capital investment, rather than long-term returns from human capacity building. As a result very few large development agencies can legitimately claim to have effectively evolved an adaptive planning approach.

This is an important lesson in itself. Maybe large development agencies are structurally incapable of being flexible and able to learn adaptively.

They do, nevertheless, have an important role to play through taking the lead in policy analysis and institutional development at a national level, funding of capital development projects and supporting intermediary organizations working with local groups. Large development bureaucracies in pastoral areas should probably concentrate on simple, capital investments (roads, marketing facilities, basic infrastructure), while state agencies provide a certain number of regulatory, assurance functions (provision of legal frameworks, adjudication of disputes, securing of land access rights, etc.). Pastoral institutions, perhaps supported by intermediary NGOs, are better suited to carry out local level adaptive planning and management, although they may need support for policy-level initiatives (Hogg 1992). Intermediary organizations (federations of pastoral groups or other NGOs) may then act to channel funds and provide support for local level action (Pretty and Chambers 1993; Wellard and Copestake 1993; Farrington and Bebbington 1994). Some principles for project or programme design in pastoral areas are outlined in Box 3.

Conclusion: new directions in pastoral development in Africa

The new thinking in range ecology suggests a redirection of investment in the pastoral sector. The large livestock projects initiated in Africa

---

Box 3 Some principles for project and programme design in uncertain environments

○ Long time frames are needed for iterative planning with the involvement of pastoralists. Successful planning and intervention may take 15 years or more.

○ Start small and build up, focusing on institutional capacity at a local level.

○ Resist unrealistic disbursement targets.

○ Projects are learning experiments: change course if necessary. Do not get stuck with out-dated or irrelevant project plans.

○ Learn from experience, especially occasional episodic events. Monitoring and evaluation mechanisms need to be geared to the rhythm of learning in variable environments.

○ Institutional and organizational flexibility are important to allow responses to unexpected events. Bureaucratic project structures and procedures will stifle innovation.

○ A diversity of different organizations may be appropriate to tackle complex challenges found in pastoral areas. Pastoral organizations, service NGOs, producers' federations and government all may have roles. Do not get stuck with one organizational model.

○ Local level development will be affected by macro-level policy. Tackling these wider issues through support to legal cases, policy advocacy and lobbying is directly relevant to local level pastoral development.

Table 2 Comparison between the 'old' and the 'new' thinking about pastoral development

Area	'Old' thinking	'New' thinking
Objectives	Focus on commodity production: livestock development	Focus on livelihoods: pastoral development
Range management	Open range improvement (legumes, fodder trees, rotations) Paddocking and restrictive movement: fences	Focus on key resources: improvement, rehabilitation, creation Mobility and flexibility: no fences
Planning	Blueprint development planning	Flexible, adaptive planning, with local involvement and a recognition of uncertainty
Drought	'Normal' year development and drought relief separated Focus on production issues in 'normal' years	Drought 'proofing' and safety net provision integrated Focus on tracking: de/restocking, supplementary feeding, etc.
Tenure	Fixed tenure regimes: privatization (or exclusive communal) Conflict issues largely ignored	Flexible tenure: complex mix of overlapping and integrated regimes Focus on conflict negotiation, mediation and arbitration
Institutions and administration	Service delivery package through centralized extension services Extension worker for technical delivery	Pastoral organizations for local management issues Extension workers as institutional organizers

during the 1970s and whose offspring are still highly influential both among national planners and donors were characterized by several elements (Sandford 1983; this book). These included: boreholes and water points, veterinary support, technical range management, ranches, abattoirs and market infrastructure. How would this suite of investments change if the implications of the new thinking in range ecology were taken seriously?

Table 2 offers a summary of some of the issues highlighted by chapters in this book, contrasting 'old' with 'new' thinking. Obviously such simple contrasts over-simplify; very often the 'new' is not so new and the 'old' is quite rare. The aim is, however to capture the essence of the debate, rather than the detailed nuances, and to stimulate some reflection on the practical implications for development projects, programmes and investments.

Seven major shifts in pastoral development strategies are suggested by this analysis (see also Sandford this book). These are:

○ In highly dynamic, non-equilibrium environments land degradation is not the major issue it was once assumed. Therefore boreholes and water points should continue to be a priority in areas where water is a limiting factor. The cost of bare 'sacrifice' zones immediately surrounding each borehole is usually far outweighed by the benefits of more efficient fodder use and higher livestock populations (Hanan et al. 1991). However, very high densities of boreholes in arid environments may ultimately result in a decreased resilience of the system as the patchy nature of the environment is destroyed. Changes in resource access following borehole investment also remains a concern (cf. White 1992 for the Botswana case).

○ Maintaining the size and health of animal populations through investment in veterinary care also remains a priority. High populations do not necessarily impose long-term environmental damage, and healthy animals are able to track environmental variations more effectively. Conventional veterinary support, through vaccination campaigns, needs to be complemented by decentralized animal health services and the indigenous knowledge of herders themselves.

○ Conventional range management in dry areas is of limited value. Technical support should be focused on particular niches where productivity increases are most likely. Investment in the improvement or creation of key resource patches, for instance, deserves attention from technical experts. Breeding programmes using exotic breeds should be abandoned in favour of improving the physiological tracking capacity of indigenous breeds.

○ So-called 'traditional' pastoral systems have higher returns than ranches under comparable conditions (see Table 1). The ranch model for livestock development in dryland Africa therefore should be abandoned in favour of support for existing systems.

○ To make systems more flexible, pastoral institutions will have to be particularly strong. Greater emphasis needs to be paid to institutional capacity building. 'Institutional organizers' working with local pastoral associations provide opportunities for supporting the development of local institutions. This will require major retraining of field-based extension staff.

○ Investment in marketing and infrastructure still has a role. The need to secure livelihoods through cash sales of animals remains an imperative in pastoral areas. Good access to market facilities and information permits more effective tracking. Investments should focus on improving tracking abilities in order to sustain pastoral economies, rather than simply focusing on red meat production. Instead of investment in large abattoirs or freezing facilities, investment in basic infrastructure, including roads, will remain important in pastoral areas.

○ Policy analysis and reform need much greater attention. Instead of simply focusing on boosting meat production from pastoral areas, policies are needed to ensure the economic viability of pastoral communities and their contribution to the national economy. This means examining policy options that allow flexible planning and development, enhanced capacity for tracking, secure but flexible resource tenure systems and the development of effective and strong pastoral organizations at both local and national levels.

2. Climate variability and complex ecosystem dynamics: implications for pastoral development[1]

JIM ELLIS

Uncertainty can arise from many causes. One of the most pervasive, powerful and unalterable sources of uncertainty impinging on African pastoral and agropastoral systems is climate variability. Climate variability is characteristic of all drylands, but in Africa it is particularly potent. Over the long-term, African climate variability has had a critical role in human evolution and in the creation of biodiversity (Eldredge 1985; Vrba 1992; Coppens 1994). Today, climate variability exerts a major influence on human life-styles and land use patterns (Ellis and Galvin 1994). So, in attempting to develop technologies, reform institutions or frame policies for Africa that are capable of accommodating uncertainty, it is crucial to understand how and where climate variability promotes uncertainty in African ecosystems.

Non-equilibrium theory: its application to dryland ecosystems and African pastoralism

There is a high degree of uncertainty in the behaviour of many African ecosystems. This makes it difficult or impossible to predict the levels of production that the system might yield from one year to the next, or how ecosystem structure may change over time. Systems which demonstrate this sort of behaviour, be they physical or biological, are sometimes categorized as non-equilibrium systems and the behaviour typical of these systems is called complex or non-linear dynamics (Prigogine 1961).

As used in ecology, the term equilibrium connotes an ecosystem or community where populations are more or less in balance with resources, other populations or external forces like climate. They are

[1] The research upon which this chapter was based was supported by grants from the US National Science Foundation (BSR 9007303, BNS-9100132). Thanks to Russ Kruska for the African rainfall GIS map; to Mike Coughenour and Jim Tucker for analysis and data presented in the NDVI analysis (Figure 1); and to Joyce Olds for assistance with the figures.

equilibrial in a cybernetic, but not in a thermodynamic sense (Schneider and Kay 1994). Non-equilibrium ecosystems are those where populations or other components are not in long-term balance with other elements of the system; thus they are unpredictable and sometimes undergo complex dynamic behaviour.

Non-equilibrium ecosystems, the complex dynamics they manifest and the resulting uncertainties, arise because of amplification or positive feedback within systems, or due to external forcing (de Angelis and Waterhouse 1987; Nicolis and Prigogine 1989; Berryman 1991). In the case of dryland ecosystems, external climate forcing is the primary cause of complex dynamics. Severe droughts devastate plant communities and decimate animal populations. Where droughts are frequent, population fluctuations prevent plants and herbivores from developing closely coupled interactions, ecosystem development and succession are abbreviated or non-existent and ecosystems seldom reach a climatically determined equilibrium point. Uncertainty abounds.

The theory of non-equilibrium dynamics and complex behaviour is relatively new in ecology. Holling (1973) was among the first to apply the emerging concepts of complexity to ecological systems. His early theoretical work focused on the relationships between resistance, resilience and stability. Subsequently, Weins (1977) interpreted avian community structure and competition as a demonstration of the prevalence of non-equilibrium conditions in grassland ecosystems. Walker and colleagues (Walker *et al.* 1981; Walker and Noy-Meir 1982) recognized the relevance of these ideas to arid savannas and applied these approaches to the highly dynamic ecosystems of southern Africa.

Somewhat later, a series of analyses pointed out that existing rangeland management practices were based on equilibrium concepts, whereas dryland ecosystems in Africa and Australia are often distinctly non-equilibrial, with complex dynamical patterns of behaviour (Caughley *et al.* 1987; Ellis and Swift 1988; Westoby *et al.* 1989; Mentis *et al.* 1989). This work called for a new approach to the management of rangeland ecosystems.

Ellis and Swift (1988) specifically addressed the question of economic development of African pastoral systems. They concluded, as Sandford (1983) had earlier, that traditional pastoral strategies of flexibility and opportunism are the bases upon which development interventions should be built in highly variable ecosystems. Shortly thereafter, the studies of Scoones (1989b, 1990, 1993) explored the applicability of the non-equilibrium paradigm in southern African agropastoral systems, while Behnke and Scoones (1993) conducted a wide-ranging review of the implications of non-equilibrium perspectives for pastoral development.

Empirical explorations of climate variability and complex ecosystem dynamics

Interest in the theories of chaos, complex dynamics and non-equilibrium systems has grown rapidly in the last decade (for example, Glieck 1987; Nicolis and Prigogine 1989; Logan and Hain 1990; Solbrig and Nicolis

38

1991). But empirical assessment of non-equilibrium dynamics is challenging, requiring long-term data collection. Nevertheless, some broad-based studies have analyzed ecosystem responses to climate variability and the results have been generally consistent with emerging non-equilibrium theory.

The arid and drought-stressed rangelands of eastern Australia are grazed by sheep and kangaroos. Caughley et al. (1987) analyzed interactions between climate variability, plant production, plant species composition and kangaroo populations during a multi-year study in Menindee District, New South Wales. Rainfall averages 200–300mm per year, but is unreliable. With a coefficient of interannual rainfall variation (CV) of 45 per cent and rainfall departures from the mean, either above or below, exceeding 50 per cent in three years out of ten, the effect on pasture and herbivores is substantial. Pasture biomass fluctuated by two orders of magnitude during the study and plant species composition changed dramatically with rainfall patterns. Kangaroo population densities ranged from a high of 50–60 per km^2 during a drought recovery phase, to a low of about 15 per km^2 following a drought. Analysis of long-term regional climate records showed that these rainfall variations were not unusual and long-term records of sheep populations demonstrated 'much short-term fluctuation in response to variable weather' (Caughley et al. 1987:5).

The investigators concluded that in this system measurements of rainfall variability have more significance than the mean. They suggest that such strong climate variability induces a centrifugal, chaotic aspect to system behaviour. The effects of grazing upon the system, although weak, nevertheless add an element of 'centripitality', reducing the chaotic tendencies of system dynamics. Caughley and his colleagues judged that the threshold, where a system becomes dominated by variability more than by average conditions, occurs when rainfall CV nears or exceeds 30 per cent. They also suggest that where CVs are below 20 per cent, animal populations will remain relatively stable and strong feedback will develop between herbivores and plants. The study thus describes the range of climatic conditions that may discriminate equilibrium from non-equilibrium ecosystems.

The South Turkana Ecosystem Project (STEP) was a long-term interdisciplinary study of nomadic Turkana pastoralists and their arid ecosystem in northern Kenya. Ellis and Swift (1988) synthesized the results of many components of that study and arrived at conclusions similar to those of Caughley et al. (1987). Rainfall in the South Turkana region averages around 200–300mm per year, but CVs are near 50 per cent and reach 60 per cent in nearby central Turkana. Droughts occur on average every four to five years; severe multi-year droughts, which decimate livestock populations, happen about once a decade. The STEP study witnessed one such multi-year drought (1979–80) where roughly 50 per cent of monitored livestock herds died and upwards of 20 per cent of the human population temporarily emigrated from the drought area. In contrast, a single year drought (1984) caused no livestock mortality (McCabe 1987; Ellis et al. 1987).

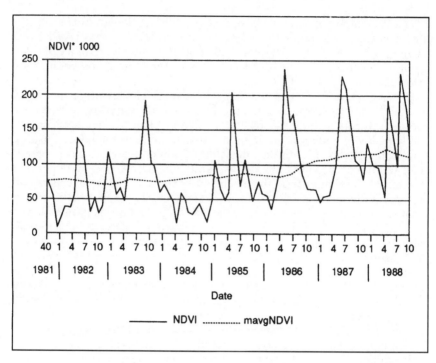

Figure 1. *Monthly and running mean NDVI values (normalized difference vegetation index) for Nysonyoka territory, Turkana District Kenya (Source: C.J. Tucker, GSFS, NASA. Analysis courtesy of M.B. Coughenour)*

Plant biomass in the region was greatly influenced by rainfall variations. Wet season biomass, as indexed by AVHRR remote-sensed vegetation index values (NDVI), was low during the drought year 1984 (Figure 1). However the running mean NDVI increased steadily over the period 1981–88, from 0.05 following the severe drought of 1979–80 (not shown) to about 0.125 by 1988. The index, and presumably green biomass, more than doubled over this period. This trend indicates that plant biomass was in a recovery phase for at least eight years following the multi-year drought of 1979–80. Since droughts occur every four to ten years, it seems probable that this vegetation community is in an almost constant state of flux in response to these droughts; vegetation seldom reaches an equilibrium with 'average' climate conditions.

The dynamic nature of the Turkana ecosystem fits the non-equilibrium paradigm. Under these conditions, the effect of erratic rainfall on plant biomass is likely to be much greater than the effect of livestock grazing. Turkana livestock were estimated to remove on average only about 7 per cent of above-ground primary production annually. Thus concerns of severe overgrazing by pastoralists are unlikely to be realized in non-equilibrium ecosystems like the Turkana region (Coughenour *et al.* 1985;

40

Ellis and Swift 1988). However, specific concerns about overgrazing and general approaches to economic development have been predicated on assumptions of stable or equilibrium conditions. Clearly these assumptions are inapplicable in systems that exist under highly variable climates.

Since the early part of this century, overgrazing has been alleged to be responsible for a southern advance of the Sahara desert into the Sahelian zone (Stebbings 1935). During the 1970s and 1980s, at the height of a 20-year drought, a desertification control programme was implemented by the United Nations, to try to halt supposed human-induced degradation and the expansion of the Sahara. However, analyses of a decade-long record of remote-sensed data and ground truth studies suggested that the desert was not advancing at all, or at least not at a rate that could be detected over a 10-year period. Instead, researchers found that the Sahara–Sahel boundary is very dynamic and moves both north and south in response to annual rainfall variability; no long-term directional trends were evident and no evidence of massive human-caused degradation was found (Hellden 1988; Tucker et al. 1991). As in the two previous examples, these patterns are consistent with those expected in non-equilibrium ecosystems.

Recent studies of agropastoral systems support the conclusions that climate variability is of crucial importance in regulating African livestock-based economies. For example, analysis of a 60-year record of cattle populations in Zimbabwe suggested that density-dependent factors may regulate both birth and death rates when populations approach equilibrium densities; but cattle populations in southern Zimbabwe seldom reached these densities due to droughts, disease or destocking (Scoones 1993).

Under the more equilibrium conditions of southern Ethiopia, however, where droughts occur about once in 20 years there is ample time between droughts for Borana livestock populations to build up to levels which negatively affect vegetation. Periodic heavy grazing might therefore combine with infrequent but severe droughts to induce shifts in vegetation, from grasslands to bush-dominated communities (Coppock 1993).

The results of all these recent analyses show that dryland ecosystem dynamics often differ from those patterns expected in stable, equilibrium ecosystems. The primary cause of non-equilibrium conditions (rainfall variability) has been identified, but many questions remain about the occurrence and magnitude of climate-induced instability and the impact on ecosystems, livestock and people.

Models of instability

The empirical analyses reviewed above, plus numerous other observations, have discredited the traditional equilibrium approach to rangeland management for regions with highly variable climates. This traditional approach, embodied in the range condition and trend model, was initially proposed 70 years ago (Sampson 1923) in North America where, for the most part, it remains an appropriate and effective model (Dodd 1994). The range condition and trend model is derived from the Clementsian theory of succession (Clements 1916). It assumes that range–livestock systems

41

operate in environments that are stable or equilibrial in nature, where climate variability is not important.

The realization that equilibrium conditions are not met in many ecosystems derives from studies like those discussed above. This has led to the non-equilibrium model and the state and transition model (Westoby *et al.* 1989), both of which recognize that equilibrium conditions may be rare or non-existent. The non-equilibrium model is concerned with the dynamics of populations under conditions of environmental uncertainty, while the state and transition model focuses on the concept of multiple stable states (Noy-Meir 1975 1978 1982; Walker and Noy-Meir 1982) and emphazises the probabilities and causes of how herbivores and unusual climate conditions or other events (e.g. fire) might combine to drive an ecosystem from one state to another. These models of instability emphasize thresholds in state changes, irreversibility of change and critical levels of variability as key concepts for understanding dryland ecosystems, in contrast to the static, linear models of range condition and trends based on successional concepts.

Domains of uncertainty in Africa

Just how widely applicable are these concepts of instability, non-equilibrium and climate-induced uncertainty? Is all of Africa so affected? Are only the most arid zones influenced by these sorts of dynamics? Where are we most likely to encounter non-equilibrium ecosystem dynamics?

A critical nexus in non-equilibrium ecosystem dynamics is the interaction of drought with mortality rates, reproductive rates and the generation time of resident organisms (Scoones 1993). If the generation time of herbivores is very long, as in the case of elephants, then even very infrequent but severe 'killer' droughts could have large order consequences that might include transitions in ecosystem state. For sheep or goats, generation time is short and population recovery from drought is rapid. So a drought frequency/severity regime that would induce a long-term shift in the interactions between elephants and trees, might have a much more transient effect on sheep and their forage plants. Cattle or medium-sized wild ungulates, with intermediate-length generation times, would probably respond differently than either elephants or sheep. In this regard, we might expect that with larger organisms, more severe but less frequent droughts could cause non-equilibrium dynamics; with smaller organisms, droughts of greater frequency and less severity might suffice.

Predicting the likelihood that non-equilibrium dynamics or state transitions will occur in a particular ecosystem is thus a formidable analytical task. It requires a detailed analysis of drought patterns and the responses of principal plants and herbivores to drought. However, in the absence of these analyses, we can get some crude idea about where drought-driven domains of uncertainty may exist, simply by exploring rainfall variability patterns.

The STEP study and the Mendinee kangaroo analysis provide clear evidence of non-equilibrium ecosystem dynamics. In both cases, the rainfall variability is very high (CV=45–60 per cent) because droughts are both frequent and severe. But non-equilibrium dynamics may become apparent at considerably lower levels of variability (30 per cent, Caughley *et al.* 1987; 33 per cent, Ellis and Galvin 1994). What do these measures of rainfall variability really imply about drought frequency and severity? The coefficient of interannual variation is an integrated measure of the magnitude and frequency of departures of annual rainfall from the long-term mean. Thus CVs around 30–33 per cent may occur if positive or negative departures from the mean are frequent, but not too large, or large but not too frequent; if both frequent and large, then CVs may be as high as those observed in Turkana and Menindee. We are concerned here with droughts which are severe enough to cause mortality in herbivore populations by reducing plant production to the point that herbivore nutrition and health is seriously impaired. Figure 2 shows that a frequency of one drought every three years is sufficient to give a CV of 33 per cent if the average negative departure from the mean is about 40 per cent. However, if drought frequency is only one year in 20, then the departure must be near 100 per cent to yield a CV of 33 per cent. These are idealized values; experi-

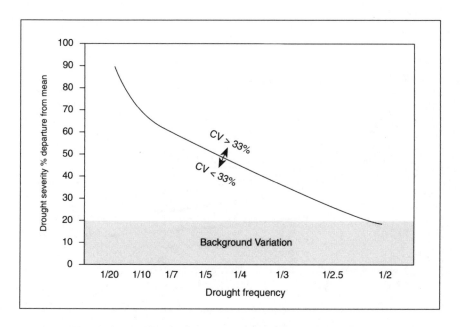

Figure 2. *Hypothetical relationship between drought frequency and severity, yielding rainfall CVs of 33 per cent. Drought frequency portrayed as one drought in 20 years, one drought in 10 years, etc. Relationship assumes a background rainfall variation of 20 per cent, unrelated to drought.*

43

ence shows that even very severe droughts may not induce herbivore mortality if the drought persists for only a single year, whereas multi-year droughts are often lethal (Ellis and Swift 1988). So the most important criterion for drought-caused herbivore mortality is probably the length of the period over which large negative departures from the mean continue. Nevertheless, Figure 2 provides a possible indication of the drought patterns necessary to cause non-equilibrium ecosystem dynamics, if in fact 33 per cent is the critical value or threshold for non-equilibrium conditions.

Dry ecosystems are more unstable than wet ones because rainfall variability is inversely correlated with total rainfall. The lower the annual rainfall, the greater the coefficient of rainfall variation (Conrad 1941). However, dry equatorial systems are among the most variable on earth

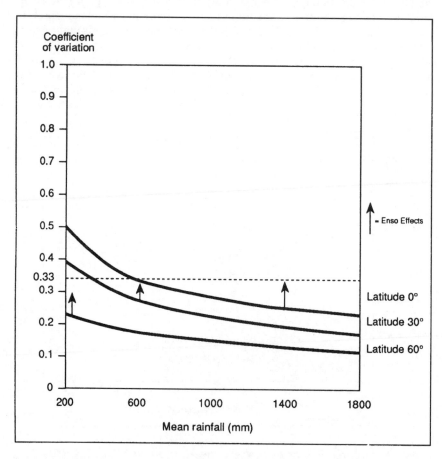

Figure 3. *Empirically derived relationships between coefficient of interannual rainfall variation (CV) and total rainfall, latitude and ENSO effects. Modified from Nicholls and Wong (1990). Dotted horizontal line = CV of 33 per cent; hypothetical threshold for non-equilibrium dynamics.*

44

because rainfall variation is also negatively correlated with latitude. Variation also increases in regions influenced by sea surface temperature anomalies associated with El Niño–Southern Oscillation (ENSO) patterns. Nicholls and Wong (1990) developed a relationship which integrates the effects of total rainfall, latitude and ENSO on interannual

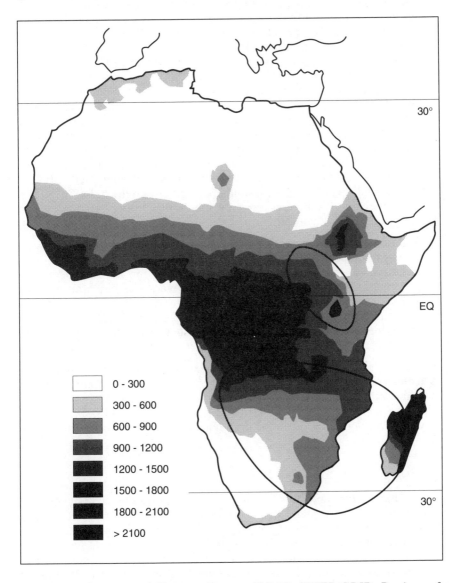

30°

EQ

30°

0 - 300

300 - 600

600 - 900

900 - 1200

1200 - 1500

1500 - 1800

1800 - 2100

> 2100

Figure 4. *African rainfall zones. Source: ILRAD, UNEP/GRID. Regions of ENSO influence from Ropelewski and Halpert (1987); indicated by bounded regions in eastern and southern Africa.*

45

rainfall CVs. Their analysis suggests that at latitudes near the equator, CVs of 33 per cent or greater will occur at rainfall levels of about 600mm or less (Figure 3): in other words, we can expect the non-equilibrium dynamics in equatorial regions with less than about 600mm rainfall. However, where ENSO effects prevail, then CVs of 33 per cent might be found even where rainfall levels are as high as 1400mm. At higher latitudes ENSO effects are much less potent and CVs are lower for any given level of rainfall, than near the equator. Thus at 30 degrees latitude, CVs of 33 per cent or greater are likely at about 350mm rainfall or below, if there are no ENSO effects. With ENSO effects, 33 per cent CVs could occur up to 600 mm rainfall (Figure 3). At 60 degrees latitude, CVs are unlikely to reach 33 per cent, even at rainfall levels as low as 200mm (Nicholls and Wong 1990).

Most of Africa lies between latitudes 30 degrees north and 30 degrees south and a significant portion of the continent receives 600mm rainfall or less per year (Figure 4). El Niño effects are prevalent throughout most of southern Africa and in the east African equatorial area (Ropelewski and Halpert 1987). In east Africa, ENSO effects result in positive departures from normal rainfall levels, so while variability is increased, drought frequency and severity is not. In southern Africa by contrast, ENSO effects result in negative departures, thereby increasing drought frequency and severity. Based on this information it seems reasonable to hypothesize that:

o Rainfall CVs might exceed 33 per cent anywhere in Africa with 600mm or less rainfall per year;
o In areas of southern and eastern Africa, where ENSO effects are prevalent, CVs may surpass 33 per cent, even where rainfall exceeds 1000mm per year.
o Non-equilibrium dynamics and state transitions are likely to occur even in the higher rainfall semi-arid zones of southern Africa, where ENSO effects are associated with drought.

If CVs of 33 per cent do mark the critical value where non-equilibrium dynamics begin to emerge, then it would seem that only the humid and sub-humid core of the continent is totally immune from the potential effects of climate variability, drought and non-equilibrium dynamics. Domains of uncertainty may indeed span the drylands of the African continent (Figure 4).

Challenges

The challenge for ecologists is to determine the reality of these hypotheses and better to describe and define patterns of non-equilibrium ecosystem behaviour under different regimes of drought frequency and severity. The challenge for social scientists is to define and describe viable patterns for coping with this climate-driven uncertainty, where it occurs. The challenge for all of us is to help design and implement strategies which enhance people's welfare in the pastoral areas of Africa without compromising the resilience and diversity that aeons of climate variability have helped to bestow upon African ecosystems.

3. New directions in range management planning in Africa

GREGORY PERRIER

This chapter examines the consequences of environmental variability on planning for pastoral development. Planning is an exercise by which problems and opportunities are identified, goals are determined and a strategy to achieve goals is formulated. This strategy is then implemented through a set of activities. In Africa, two general types of pastoral sector planning take place: formal planning by government, donors and other organizations; and planning by pastoralists. In formal planning broad goals are determined at the national level and expressed as policies. Technical specialists then plan strategies at the field level to achieve these policy objectives. In parallel to formal planning, pastoralists set production and management goals and develop strategies to achieve these goals. The objectives of this chapter are to examine previous approaches and offer new directions both for formal planning and for support of planning by pastoralists.

Policy-level formal planning

Policy-level planning is concerned with the question of how resources are being allocated to development and what are the expected outcomes of such resource allocations. The goal of planning at this level is to determine broad goals for pastoral development.

Previous approach
In the past policy planning for pastoral development has been top-down (Baker 1975; Sandford 1983), with economic and political influences dominant (Perrier 1991). Policies have often been designed to benefit politically dominant sectors of the national society or economy (Doornbos and Lofchie 1971). Planning has been founded on three assumptions: that the pastoral sector does not contribute its fair share to the national economy (Vedeld 1992); that pastoral production goals and practices are irrational and need to be replaced (Livingstone 1977); and that pastoral livestock management systems are environmentally destructive (White 1992). These

47

assumptions have often provided justification for the allocation of resources to uses other than traditional pastoral production.

From these assumptions a common set of policies emerged. To increase the contribution of the pastoral sector to the national economy, policy planners proposed an increased volume of pastoral livestock in formal markets (de Haan 1990). Pastoralists were to focus on cattle and sheep, the main export animals. Pastoralists were to adopt a 'modern and scientific' commercial ranching approach based on 'rational' western models. To conserve the range resources, policies often called for determining grazing plans and optimal stocking rates. These policies were justified by macro-economic analysis based on estimated (often over-optimistic) increases in market volume. The resultant increased income of the pastoral sector was expected to improve the quality of life for pastoralists and to facilitate the development of pastoral regions.

There were other motivations for resource allocations to the pastoral sector, not related to the welfare of pastoralists. Increased sales at low prices would provide inexpensive meat to the urban population, many of whom were poorly paid civil servants. Increased exports would provide hard currency for the central treasury. Ranches would reduce the mobility of pastoralists, often an objective of government security services, and allow the provision of social services using the standard sedentary model. One result of water development was the movement into the pastoral region of government officials, traders and farmers, with settlements being developed around public boreholes. Development policies have frequently led to the expropriation of pastoral land for government ranches (Sandford 1981, 1983), for private ranches and wildlife parks (Homewood and Rodgers 1991) and for cropping (Vedeld 1992; Niamir-Fuller 1993). During the colonial era, stocking rate controls were expected to force pastoralists to sell more animals. Similarly, veterinary health policies were used to limit pastoralists' access to livestock markets in Kenya due to the fear that they would reduce market prices for European producers (Kerven 1992).

Given these other agendas, it is no wonder that pastoralists often view government policies as a burden rather than assistance (Howze 1989). Many policy planners viewed pastoralists and rangelands as a resource to aid the national economy. Pastoralists would incur the costs of production, but receive few benefits from sales or foreign exchange earnings. When pastoralists failed to oblige, they were labelled 'conservative', 'backward' and 'difficult to work with'.

Pastoralists, however, are now increasingly seen as important economic actors in both the formal and informal sectors (Kerven 1992; Holtzman and Kulibaba this book). Studies have shown that pastoral systems are as productive as commercial ranches in similar environments, though less stable (de Ridder and Wagenaar 1984; Breman and de Wit 1983; Scoones this book). However, because the pastoral sector is not focused solely on commercial meat production, but rather has multiple goals (e.g. milk, traction, capital accumulation, manure and so on), pastoral production is at odds with the production priorities of government. Many of the benefits flow directly to pastoralists or through informal markets where they cannot be monitored or taxed.

Pastoral production systems are generally well suited to highly variable, non-equilibrium environments (Livingstone 1977; Coughenour *et al.* 1985; Behnke *et al.* 1993). They often focus on milk production, the most efficient pathway for converting forage to human food. They tend to store wealth in large ruminants, which are more metabolically efficient users of forage than small ruminants, are more mobile, and generally have lower disease risk. Ecological studies have shown pastoral system characteristics, such as multiple livestock species, multiple goals, mobility, opportunism and diversity to be critical factors for survival in arid and semi-arid areas (Breman and de Wit 1983; Sandford 1983; Coppock *et al.* 1986; Behnke and Scoones 1993).

The environmental destructiveness of pastoral systems is also being questioned. In non-equilibrium environments stocking rates rarely reach levels that degrade resources (Ellis and Swift 1988; Ellis this book). Many cases of degradation are the result of the weakening or destruction of traditional mechanisms of pastoral resource use by government policies or actions; others are the result of cropping or tree cutting (Manger 1994). Some observed changes in vegetation are natural transitions between states (Westoby *et al.* 1989; Friedel 1991; Laycock 1991), rather than a result of high stocking rates. Finally, claims of overstocking are frequently the result of a difference in production priorities between pastoralists and technicians (Bartels *et al.* 1990).

New directions

The assumptions on which the old approach was based must now be rejected. Policy-makers need to see pastoralists as legitimate contributors to the economy, to see pastoralists' goals as rational in their context, and to understand better the complex relationship between stocking rate and degradation. Successful development requires policies that enhance the survival of pastoralists in highly variable environments. New directions in research and training are required to achieve this change.

With very few exceptions, formal training programmes in Africa in livestock production and range management have been established and taught by people with a strong bias for western models of livestock production and range management. They have failed to recognize the uniqueness of the western case (Gilles 1993). Their bias has been transferred to generations of technical specialists who often see pastoralists' goals as irrational and pastoral systems as something to be replaced, rather than understood. New curricula are required for training in livestock production and range management in Africa which provide an understanding of the production goals and strategies of African pastoralists in highly variable environments and explore the interface between traditional systems and conventional, technical interpretations.

A holistic approach to planning analysis is required. Such an approach requires a sound understanding of production goals, system variability and contingency strategies. It would consider incentives and constraints

49

operating at the management decision-making level, usually the household in pastoral systems. It is at this level that the adoption of proposed behavioural changes and technology innovations will be decided. Successful planning requires adequate information and an adaptive management approach to sequential learning (Holling 1978; Walters 1986; Scoones this book). If properly implemented, pre-project studies are good mechanisms for the acquisition of this information. Such an approach facilitates the determination of the systemic effects of proposed innovations, helping set up monitoring systems to allow continuous feedback during policy implementation.

Another fundamental change required is an increase in pastoralists' participation in the policy development process. This will only be achieved by an increase in the political influence of the pastoral sector. In all governments, policies are likely to benefit most those with the greatest political influence. With only a few exceptions, pastoralists in Africa are politically marginal. Although there are non-pastoralists who are genuinely concerned about pastoral development in Africa, their good will alone is not sufficient to counter the increasing demands by other sectors for scarce resources (Galaty 1993a,b).

Pastoral demands can come through military action, as recently happened with the Tuareg in West Africa; or they might arise through the establishment of indigenous NGOs with effective lobbying power (Sylla this book). The broadening of the political process, now taking place across Africa, might offer possibilities for empowerment and greater access to the policy-making process (Swift this book).

Strategic-level planning

The goal of strategic-level planning is to develop a plan to achieve policy-level goals, in the form of a list of resources required and a system for linking goals to specific activities.

Previous approach
Although donors and ministry officials remain very influential at this level of planning, the influence of technical specialists and local administrators greatly increases. Pastoralists, however, usually remain outside the formal planning process. At the strategic level, the importance of production, management, economic and conservation considerations increase and the importance of political factors generally decline relative to the policy level.

With few exceptions, conventional, mainstream strategies propose replacing the existing pastoral systems with a western ranch model. These efforts have met with little success (IDA 1980; Goldschmidt 1981; Sandford 1981; de Haan 1990; Perrier 1991). Part of the problem has been the western bias of range and livestock management disciplines: a commercial meat-and-fibre focus, private land tenure, fenced livestock, a pre-eminence of cattle and sheep, low human density and so on (Perrier 1990). African pastoral systems differ radically—in exploiting diversity, being opportunistic, lacking boundaries, having multiple goals, accumulating capital in livestock, using communal lands, herding livestock and having high human densities and layered decision-making structures (see below).

A study of three large bilateral aid projects in Africa revealed nearly identical 'off-the-shelf' strategies, developed practically independently of the local context (Perrier 1991). Communal grazing lands were divided up into bounded areas and a rotational grazing plan developed. This plan frequently required water development to allow all pastures to be used during the dry season. Technical specialists determined 'carrying capacity' and proposed an optimal stocking rate for meat production. All pastoral households using an area were grouped into a grazing association. An artificial structure was created for the association, with an 'executive committee' functioning as the main decision-making body, ignoring traditional resource use decision-making structures. The executive committee was to see to the implementation of the grazing plan and enforce the optimal stocking rate. The projects focused on cattle and to some extent sheep, ignoring other indigenous stock. The projects usually provided improved veterinary care, breeding programmes and marketing infrastructure. Finally, the projects provided credit, while complaining about the large amount of capital stored in livestock.

The response of pastoralists was mixed. They seemed most interested in legal title to their grazing lands and improved veterinary care. They failed to implement the grazing plans or limit livestock populations to the 'optimal' stocking rate. Across projects, livestock-focused innovations were received better than range management innovations, indicating that the grazing management and stocking rate recommendations were inappropriate.

Why was there such a poor response to range management recommendations? By being mobile and herding livestock, pastoralists have a high level of control over grazing factors such as intensity, frequency, grazing pressure, time of grazing, livestock species mix, grazing in relation to watering points, and the selection of forage species, grazing sites, plant communities and ecological zones. Pastoralists herding livestock can manage grazing much more intensively than is possible with pastured livestock (Perrier 1988; Niamir 1990); the rotational grazing systems recommended by projects are often crude by comparison.

Range technicians have assumed that they can determine a 'carrying capacity' for a given range area, a limit that becomes the optimal stocking rate. They ignore the fact that an optimal stocking rate is an economic decision determined by production goals (Workman 1986). They also fail to consider that it is doubtful that 'carrying capacity' is a meaningful concept for the non-equilibrium systems of arid and semi-arid Africa (Ellis and Swift 1988; Behnke et al. 1993), that it can rarely be accurately measured (de Leeuw and Tothill 1993), or that stocking recommendations so derived can be enforced by external agents (Bartels et al. 1990). In fact, range science has not yet determined what stocking rate means in unbounded systems. Rather than adjust the number of animals, pastoralists

51

tend to adjust time, season and area of use to manage stocking rate (Gilles 1988).

Many planners believe that if only adequate market infrastructure and livestock prices were present, then pastoralists would adopt western approaches, maintaining stocking rates optimal for meat animal production and sustaining high commercial off-take rates. This assumption totally ignores the multiple goals of pastoral systems, the relatively high densities of people in pastoral systems and the effects of capital accumulation in livestock on production and marketing strategies. Expected increased market volumes and destocking levels are thus seldom realized (Holtzman and Kulibaba this book).

In addition, conventional blueprint planning usually ignores the high variability of arid and semi-arid rangelands (Scoones this book). Rare events, such as very severe drought or fire, can move such range ecosystems quickly from one state to another (Westoby *et al.* 1989; Friedel 1991). Furthermore, pastoralists are continuously adjusting production strategies and practices to reflect ecological, economic and political events.

Pastoral development strategies have tended towards unintegrated component approaches, assuming homogeneity, of both social groups and landscapes. By planning for averages, diversity is unaccounted for (Lawry 1988). It is often this diversity that allows pastoral systems to sustain themselves (Coughenour *et al.* 1985). Households vary in their available resources, production goals and production strategies, allowing different production niches to be filled. There is a complex patchiness to landscapes, with many different grazing sites that vary in productivity and nutritional value (Scoones 1994). There are also special-use sites, such as watering points, trekking trails and so on. The relative value of these different landscape components can vary seasonally and annually. At regional levels, there are major differences between ecological zones, with their relative value highly seasonally dependent (Breman and de Wit 1983).

New directions

If government, or any external agency, is to assist pastoral production systems in Africa, the western ranch model has to be abandoned. Pastoralists are the actual managers of the resources: livestock, land, water, labour and capital. It is only reasonable that their complex and highly adapted production and management strategies form the foundation of any pastoral development strategy. Pastoral societies have complex and flexible decision-making structures for production and resource management. As recent experience in West Africa has demonstrated, successful development assists pastoralists to build on the strengths of existing pastoral institutions (Vedeld 1993; Sylla this book).

Successful pastoral development focuses on providing pastoralists with clear title to key resources (resources critical to the sustainability of the production systems) through traditional or newly formed associations (Lane and Moorehead Sylla this book). Control of these resources allows effective management of much larger areas. On the other hand, the loss of these resources, usually the most productive sites, can have devastating effects throughout the whole production system. Some key resources, such as drought reserves, might only be used occasionally, and therefore be hard to identify in normal years. Pastoral participation in strategy development and understanding of indigenous knowledge systems becomes vital to identifying this environmental complexity. Given the high enforcement cost in Africa, only by focusing on group management of key resources can effective communal land management be economically feasible (Behnke 1991; Lane and Moorehead this book).

Pastoral systems are dynamic, changing in response to social, political and ecological factors. Sound planning must reflect the dynamics and variability of pastoral systems and develop contingencies for action under different probable situations (Coppock 1994). This can only be achieved with detailed knowledge acquired through working together with pastoral communities.

Social equity is also a consideration in strategic planning. No society is truly equitable, and pastoral societies are no exception (Bekure *et al.* 1991; Sutter 1987; Behnke 1987). Social equity considers the degree that a strategy assigns costs among groups in relation to the benefits each group receives. The objective is to avoid placing costs on one group and providing benefits to another. Unfortunately, pastoral development strategies frequently do this. For example, development interventions often ignore the role of women in livestock management, assuming that men make all the important functions and decisions (Oxby 1983). Diversity within pastoral groups means that most innovations will only be appropriate for a specific subset of households or individuals within a group (Lawry 1988). The identification of these subsets is critical to the prediction of innovation adoption and the determination of the benefit and cost allocations within groups.

The approach to development planning is also important. In highly variable environments, successful development strategies will evolve from an iterative dialogue between government, technicians and pastoralists (Korten 1980). Adoption of this framework will require major changes in institutional values, incentive structures and norms of operating. Current strategic planning processes facilitate the administration of development, but often constrain actual development (Mickelwait *et al.* 1979); benefits tend to flow more to donors, ministries and contractors than to targeted beneficiaries. There are strong vested interests in maintaining the status quo. NGOs usually operate closer to the field level than donors or ministries and, if allowed, will likely play an increasingly important role in pastoral development (Cullis 1992; Manger 1994).

Planning by pastoralists

For pastoralists, planning takes place within complex social contexts, requiring multi-layered decision-making structures (Hoben 1976; Hogg 1990; Akabwai 1992). Which decisions are made at which level varies among pastoral groups. Individuals, households and groups all set their specific goals and strategies. Most daily management decisions are made by individuals living together in households or household clusters. Watering decisions are often made by a larger group sharing a common water point. Decisions on access to communal grazing lands are usually made by an even larger group, such as a clan. Within this structure decisions tend to be made by consensus. Planning at all levels is strongly influenced by the biophysical, social and political environment and by available resources, experience, knowledge, skills and culture. Government policies and actions are additional factors that pastoralists must incorporate into their planning.

Goals and strategies in pastoral systems

Pastoralists' survival depends on the production of children and of goods and services to support those children. These goods and services have traditionally been primarily livestock and livestock products, but they are increasingly wage labour, cropping and so on. Pastoralists are also concerned about the survival of a larger social group of which they are members and upon which they are often dependent in times of crisis.

There are three general goals common to pastoral systems: risk reduction, system productivity and the conservation of resources upon which production is dependent. Each of these goals is associated with specific strategies.

Risk reduction.

In highly variable environments risks are high and diverse. Pastoralists mitigate risks through strategies that enhance diversity, flexibility, linkages to support networks, self-sufficiency and wealth. Diversity is crucial to pastoral survival in dryland Africa. Pastoralists generally keep a diverse mix of livestock in terms of species and class (Jahnke 1982). This allows them to exploit better different niches in the environment, resulting in multiple pathways of energy flow (Coughenour *et al.* 1985; Coppock *et al.* 1986). This also allows them a better match of labour, grazing and water resources to livestock demands (Jahnke 1982). Pastoralists use a diverse mosaic of grazing sites, exploiting seasonal and annual variability in forage quality and quantity on a local and regional basis. Pastoralists have a diverse mix of goals for livestock production including milk and meat production, animal transport, traction and capital accumulation. Failure at one goal is buffered by returns from others. Pastoralists reduce risk by diversifying their economic activities into cropping, wage labour or commerce (Swallow 1994; Thébaud 1993).

Flexible responses to a diverse resource base allow further reductions in risk. Multiple grazing sites allow for complex grazing strategies. For example, within a grazing area a household can place its livestock on patches with the highest forage value, with the relative value of patches changing daily (Perrier 1988). Spatial mobility is a key element of this flexibility (Swallow 1994). Multiple livestock species and goals allow pastoralists to adjust the relative emphasis of production goals to match the current resources available and economic conditions. Diversity and flexibility thus give rise to opportunistic management, management for

54

current conditions, rather than for long-term means or for rare events such as extreme drought (Sandford 1983).

Household links to larger social groupings are vital to survival. Within groups these links provide support networks that assist households in times of crisis. Pastoral households can also reduce risk by being self-sufficient in food, especially in more arid areas. This allows them to be very opportunistic in their movements and management practices, but they have to balance maintaining self-sufficiency with using government services and integrating into wider social networks.

In pastoral systems, wealth in livestock provides a buffer against crisis. Households with high livestock to human ratios can absorb high drought-related livestock mortality rates and frequently provide milk sufficient for the household's needs during dry periods (Coppock 1994). As livestock to human ratios drop there is an increased risk of not being able to survive during dry periods or of being forced out of livestock production during droughts. From a risk perspective, there is a strong motivation to maintain large herds.

Productivity.
Pastoralists are economically rational, maximizing returns per unit of scarce resources (livestock, labour, forage and water). For these resources pastoral groups frequently have well-developed regulations and management strategies. Livestock constitute the critical resource, the other limiting resources become important when they constrain livestock production. In some pastoral areas land is in surplus, so it has low value. Under such conditions pastoralists do not manage for the stocking density, but rather manage for the ratio of livestock to other limiting factors (e.g. labour or water). However, under other conditions land, or at least particular 'key resources' within the landscape, may be limiting. In this case there will be greater incentives to establish exclusive forms of tenure and regulate the stocking rate (Behnke 1994; Lane and Moorehead this book).

What strategies and practices do pastoralists use to enhance livestock productivity in relation to labour, forage and water? Evidence from the Maasai (Bekure *et al.* 1991) and Fulani (Sutter 1987) show that households with high labour-to-animal ratios achieve very high levels of productivity per animal. These poor families basically consume or sell everything the animals produce. Productivity per animal quickly declines as household labour to animal ratios decline, indicating that the per-animal labour demands for very high productivity are hard to sustain at larger herd sizes.

By dividing a herd, labour can be used more efficiently. Small stock are frequently herded by children and women, and nursing animals are often intensively cared for by women. Lactating animals are kept near the household, usually herded by men and milked by women. Large herds are often split with dry animals herded by young men far away from the household. Pastoralists thus can manage animals to enhance grazing efficiency. By checking milk yields and rumen extension, grazing is assessed daily (Perrier 1988; Oba 1993).

The labour efficiency of watering is also an important issue. During the dry season many pastoralists adopt alternate-day or every-third-day watering. The reduction in livestock productivity in growth and milk yield is offset by the savings in labour spent lifting water and the ability to use grazing sites distant from water. Reduced water intake also reduces forage intake, helping to conserve dry season grazing resources (King 1983; Bayer and Waters-Bayer this book).

Conservation of resources.

In uncertain environments livestock populations are limited by mortality associated with frequent droughts, frost and so on (Ellis and Swift 1988; Behnke *et al.* 1993; Ellis this book) and only cause degradation when purposely concentrated. In less variable systems pastoral strategies have mechanisms designed to keep stocking rates below levels that can cause range degradation. The practice of placing livestock on sites with the best forage tends to rest an area previously heavily used. When possible, pastoralists keep livestock densities low by spreading out (Stenning 1957). Nevertheless degradation definitely occurs, particularly in areas with more stable environmental conditions (Coppock 1993). However, there is ample evidence that, with appropriate policy support, pastoralists can properly manage common grazing resources (Swift this book).

Serious rangeland degradation problems develop when the conservation components of pastoral strategies break down (Niamir-Fuller 1993). This can occur when traditional decision-making structures are weakened or replaced by government services with insufficient resources to enforce regulations or when all land is taken by the state, destroying existing associations between pastoral groups and grazing resources and the ability of those groups to control those resources (de Haan 1990; Lane and Moorehead this book). Public boreholes reduce the effectiveness of using private water points to control access to grazing land. Pastoralists, aware of this, resisted borehole development in Somalia (MASCOTT 1986). Other problems result from actions to limit mobility, thereby disrupting traditional seasonal movements (Oba 1993). Commonly, large areas of grazing land are expropriated for government ranches, national parks or cropping, thereby quickly increasing the stocking rate on communal grazing areas (Niamir-Fuller 1993; Homewood 1993). All the above are common aspects of government policies and practices in pastoral areas.

New directions

Across Africa, pastoral systems are facing a crisis as the increasing human population places a growing demand on shrinking resources. Addressing this crisis will be a major challenge for pastoralists and for pastoral planning mechanisms. The area available for livestock grazing is declining due to crop expansion and the expropriation of grazing land (especially key sites) for other public and private uses (Winrock 1992; Bayer and Waters-Bayer this book). Except in truly non-equilibrium systems, there is a potential for livestock populations to place a demand on the forage resources greater than those resources can sustain. With the traditional institutions for resource control weakened, if not destroyed, appropriate mechanisms to form a foundation for enhanced control of grazing lands are often absent. In order for pastoralists to obtain control of communal grazing areas and develop or re-establish decision-making structures to conserve the resource base upon which they are dependent, effective pastoral associations and secure land tenure are essential (Lane and Moorehead, Sylla this book).

A future for pastoral areas will be difficult without the development of investment and employment opportunities outside livestock production. As livestock-to-people ratios decline, social networks are unable to assist those families that fall below self-sufficiency. Pastoral planning must address this issue and develop strategies that allow poor households or individuals to move successfully between livestock production and other economic activities (Jahnke 1982; Swift this book).

Conclusion

Several common themes emerge from this analysis. The western ranch approach is inappropriate for pastoral development in highly variable environments in Africa. Because the goals, management strategies and production practices of pastoral groups are adapted to high environmental variability, there needs to be a strong integration of formal planning with pastoralists. Policies for pastoral development need to facilitate the dynamics, diversity, flexibility, mobility and opportunism of pastoral systems. Policies and strategies need to focus on assisting the pastoral sector, rather than on its exploitation. Planning therefore needs to promote the participation by pastoralists in their own development through the use of participatory tools for development planning (for instance, participatory rural appraisal and related approaches; Chambers 1992; Cornwall *et al.* 1993; IIED 1994).

These proposed changes are not new (IDA 1980; Casimir *et al.* 1980). Most ministries and donors have failed to enact them, however, because these changes run counter to conventional organizational and administrative norms and interests (Chambers 1993; Wallich and Holloway 1993). A major challenge is how to break down these institutional and political barriers to improved planning for pastoral development in arid and semi-arid Africa.

4. Forage alternatives from range and field: pastoral forage management and improvement in the African drylands[1]

WOLFGANG BAYER AND ANN WATERS-BAYER

Recent research has shown that fluctuation in yields of natural forage in dryland areas is affected far more by variability in rainfall than by grazing pressure (Warren and Khogali 1992; Behnke *et al.* 1993) and that, because of rainfall variability, some ecosystems are in constant disequilibrium (Ellis *et al.* 1993). In these uncertain environments, opportunistic range-land exploitation is more advantageous than a conservative approach (Sandford 1983).

Nevertheless, it cannot be denied that grazing has an impact on vegetation. Range generally consists of both annual and perennial herbaceous plants, often also trees and shrubs. Where annuals predominate, such as in the Sahel with a unimodal rainfall pattern, grazing pressure has little effect on range yield in subsequent years. In areas with higher or bi-modal rainfall, where more herbaceous perennials grow, high grazing pressure can lead to replacement of perennials by annuals. This may not mean that less forage is produced in a given year but, as annuals respond more slowly to rainfall and disappear faster in the dry season, annual fluctuation in forage availability may increase with higher grazing pressure.

The yields of deep-rooted woody species generally vary less than those of herbaceous plants, but are still affected by water availability. Although some woody species are well adapted to severe defoliation, most trees and shrubs do suffer under heavy browsing and cutting. Where they disappear as a result of intensive use, the total yield of woody species will indeed be affected in subsequent years. Thus, the theory of range ecology at disequilibrium (Behnke *et al.* 1993; Ellis this book) applies much less to woody species than to herbaceous plants.

To cope with the fluctuation in forage yield resulting from climatic variability, pastoralists have developed a variety of survival strategies.

[1] Financial support for preparation of this theme paper was provided by the German Agency for Technical Co-operation (GTZ).

Persistence strategies, where the herd's forage demand is adjusted to the variations in forage supply, include:

○ Maximizing herd size during favourable periods so that animal losses during drought do not reduce herd size below a viable level;
○ Using adapted breeds and taking advantage of animal physiological processes which make lower demand on forage during periods of low supply;
○ Adjusting herd composition in terms of dry versus lactating females and young versus adult animals, so that animals with lower nutrient requirements are kept during dry periods;
○ Keeping herds with a mixture of animal species which feed on different components of the vegetation.

These strategies can be applied in both sedentary and nomadic herds, but, because they give little scope for counteracting large fluctuations in forage supply resulting from variable rainfall, most pastoralists also pursue strategies involving mobility, such as:

○ Opportunistic movement of herds to track sporadic rainfall events within the arid zone;
○ Opportunistic or regular movement of herds to use more productive key forage resources, such as wetlands, together with less productive upland range in the same agro-ecological zone;
○ Regular movement of herds between different agro-ecological zones.

In addition, many pastoralists deal with fluctuations in forage supply by seeking links with crop farmers and by diversifying their own activities into cropping, trade, migrant labour, etc. These efforts all form part of their wider strategy to ensure family survival (Perrier this book).

This chapter examines pastoralists' strategies in using natural forage and the potentials and limitations of crop–livestock integration to counteract fluctuations in range yield resulting from annual variation in rainfall.

Forage use strategies involving persistence

Maximizing herd size
Pastoralists' attempts to maximize herd size are rational in a highly variable environment (Sandford 1983), but there is an upper limit to how many animals can be handled in a herd. This will depend, among other things, on topography, vegetation structure and animal watering methods. Moreover, animal performance, such as weight gain, milk yield, reproduction and thus herd growth, is affected by stock density (Jones and Sandland 1974; Coppock 1993).

Stock density also influences the frequency of feed shortage: the higher the density and thus the level of forage use, the more frequently will rainfall variation result in insufficient forage. Even if high grazing pressure does not affect vegetation yields in subsequent years, stock density does affect animal performance per head and per unit area and, thus, the capacity of the livestock to meet human needs.

Using the physiological traits of adapted breeds

Certain physiological processes can help ruminants cope with feed shortage. Basic metabolism and maintenance requirements depend on the level of feeding; for example, the fasting metabolism of undernourished zebu cattle can be up to one-third less than the normal maintenance metabolism level. The level of feed intake can be managed by controlling access to water. Ruminants watered every second or third day consume less feed and, when their diet is changing to sub-maintenance level, they reduce their basic metabolism faster than those watered daily (Finch and King 1979). Animals with a nitrogen-deficient diet also appear to use the nitrogen more efficiently when access to water is restricted (Payne 1990). As long as the animals survive the dry season or the transition from dry to wet season, weight losses in the dry season are largely compensated by rapid growth in the wet. This compensatory growth favours opportunistic management of forage resources in seasonally dry areas.

Breeds differ considerably in their fasting metabolism; the higher the genetic potential of an animal to grow or produce milk, the higher the basic metabolism. Animals with lower genetic potential fare better with feed of poor quality or low quantity. They can still have a positive nutrient balance when animals with higher genetic potential are already in a negative balance and are losing weight. Tropical breeds, such as zebu cattle, can adapt their basic metabolism faster to sub-maintenance conditions than high potential breeds (Frisch and Vercoe 1977).

Adjusting herd composition

Herd composition can be adjusted to reduce feed requirements when feed is scarce. Dry females and adult males require less feed than pregnant or lactating females or young stock and can therefore better survive periods of shortage. A herd's forage demands can be reduced seasonally by disposing of young stock not needed to replace breeders and by drying off milch animals to keep only a reproduction herd. Mating can be timed so that lactation does not coincide with dry seasons, where these are fairly predictable. This strategy is most suitable for meat-producing herds. In dairy herds, it results in great seasonal variation in milk supply and can therefore be used only during severe drought, but not for coping with normal seasonal variation in forage supply.

Keeping multiple-species herds

Pastoralists are better able to maintain a viable herd in a given area if the herd includes several species which eat different components of the vegetation. Herbaceous plants grow rapidly after the rains start, but dry out quickly in the dry season. Quantity and quality of herbaceous forage therefore fluctuate greatly between seasons. Leaves and fruits from trees and shrubs can even out some of this fluctuation. Such forage may be viewed as unconventional by scientists, but is well known to African herders. About three-quarters of all woody species in sub-Saharan Africa can be used as feed (Wickens 1980), not only for camels and goats, but also for cattle and sheep. Given the choice, however, the latter generally prefer grass, whereas camels and goats prefer browse (van Soest 1982). With a multiple-species herd, a larger spectrum of the vegetation can be used and the balance between woody and herbaceous species can be manipulated.

Keeping several species also permits faster rebuilding of herds after drought, as the feeding habits and physiology of camels and goats allow them to survive droughts better than cattle or sheep and, afterwards, small ruminants recover in number more quickly than cattle and camels.

Forage use strategies involving mobility

Tracking rainfall by moving herds
Rainfall in arid areas is scattered and sporadic. When herds are moved opportunistically to 'follow the rains', they gain access to a more balanced forage supply than if they were kept in one place (Swallow 1994). This is a strategy not only of traditional herders but also of ranchers, who trek or truck animals to leased pastures far from the home ranch when local rainfall and therefore pasture is insufficient (Lühl 1992). Tracking of rainfed forage lacks a regular pattern because the amount and geographical distribution of rainfall is irregular.

Movements to key resources
In arid and semi-arid rangelands, variation in soil type and topography can result in very patchy pasture production (Swallow 1994). Highly productive patches are most likely to be found in low-lying wetlands, which are key resources for grazing management. They still provide good fodder when the upland range has declined in quality and quantity with the advance of the dry season. They thus reduce seasonal variation in forage supply (Scoones 1989a; Marsh and Seely 1992). They may also reduce annual variation, as their forage yield is likely to vary less between dry and wet years than that of upland range. However, as wetlands are attractive for expansion of cropping, they can become focal points of competition between farmers and herders.

Movements between different agro-ecological zones
Inter-zonal movements of herds are normally more regular than movements within a zone. Seasonal transhumance between lowlands and highlands is practised in parts of east Africa, whereas the most common pattern in West Africa is transhumance between drier areas during the wet season and more humid areas during the dry season (Wilson *et al.* 1983; Grayzel 1990). As a rule, the quality of herbaceous forage in arid areas is higher and shows less seasonal variation than in wetter areas (Penning de Vries and Djitèye 1982). However, its sparseness and its disappearance through natural decay in the dry season severely limit grazing. Lack of water for animals also limits dry season access to arid range. Wetter areas provide a higher

and more constant supply of forage and better access to water. During the wet season, however, ticks and biting flies can increase disease risk and animal discomfort to such a degree that pastoralists bring their herds into these areas only during the dry season.

If herds are moved seasonally to use forage in both drier and wetter zones, more animals can be kept than if nomadic herds grazed solely in the drier zone and settled herds in the wetter zone (Breman *et al.* 1982). Inter-zonal transhumance also provides more opportunities for links between pastoralism and cropping, and gives herders better access to markets.

Links between pastoralism and cropping

In arid and semi-arid areas with large seasonal and annual variation in rainfall and forage yield, specialized livestock husbandry is hardly possible without links with cropping areas. Animal keeping and cropping can interact via (McCown *et al.* 1979):

o *Food links.* Crop products make up an important part of the diet of almost all pastoralists, including nomads (cf. White 1990; Wilson *et al.* 1983); animals and their products are often sold to buy grain;
o *Forage links.* In many pastoral systems, crop residues and fallow fields are used as fodder and pasture;
o *Manure links.* Animal dung is used to fertilize fields and home gardens;
o *Draught links.* Animals are used for traction in cultivation and transport of farm inputs and products;
o *Investment links.* Income from cropping is used to buy animals, and animals are sold to finance cropping operations;
o *Employment links.* Herders are hired to tend farmers' animals, and farm family members to help pastoralists in herding or cropping.

These links help reduce risks of animal keeping in the drylands and broaden the base for securing a livelihood. With a view to managing pastoral herds, the forage, manure and investment links are of particular interest.

Forage links
Expansion of cropping diminishes the area of natural range, but not necessarily total forage availability. During the growing season, cropped areas yield little forage: only some weeds, thinnings and lower leaves stripped from crop plants. After harvest, however, crop residues can provide valuable feed. The straw of cereals and grain legumes provides up to 20 per cent of cattle diet on a year-round basis in sub-Saharan Africa, and up to 80 per cent immediately after crop harvest (Sandford 1988).

Assessing the feed value of crop residues is difficult, as digestibility and nutrient content differ greatly between plant parts. Assessed on a whole-plant basis, sorghum and millet straw barely cover the maintenance requirements of zebu cattle. However, the animals generally select only the better parts. In Nigeria the digestibility of millet residues eaten by cattle was up to 10 percentage points higher than that of all plant parts combined, and its nutritional value was higher than that of natural grass at the same time of year (Powell 1986).

Most crop residues in sub-Saharan Africa are grazed *in situ*. This allows the animals to select among not only the residues but also the weeds. In Nigeria about 20 per cent of the bites by cattle in stubble fields were on weeds (Powell 1986). Depending on the species, the availability of weeds can enhance the role of crop land in grazing management. *In situ* grazing also allows crop regrowth on residual moisture, for example, in low-lying areas, to be used as forage.

More data comparing yields of crop residues and natural range are needed to judge whether oscillations in forage supply from crop land reinforce or dampen those from range. As soil preparation for cropping improves water infiltration, the plants are likely to make better use of scarce water and produce relatively more biomass than on non-cultivated range in years of low rainfall. As nutrient availability can limit plant growth where annual rainfall is as low as 250mm in the Sahel (Penning de Vries and Djitèye 1982), fertilizer application to crops also increases the likelihood of more reliable forage yields from crop residues than from non-fertilized pasture. However, because of food preferences, market demand and other economic factors, farmers may choose to grow crops that are less drought resistant and use water less efficiently than natural grasses. In such cases, grain and residue yields will show higher annual variation than natural range.

To see whether the use of crop residues as forage stabilizes revenues from crop land itself, Sandford (1988) compared variability in yields of grain and residues in various parts of Africa but found no clear differences. However, in dry years in the Sahel when total dry matter yield is low, grain yields tend to be more depressed or even zero, whereas straw is still produced (van Duivenboden 1992). Thus, use of crop residues can even out some of the variation in yield and revenue from crop land in dry years, although extreme drought may lead to total crop failure.

Another forage link between livestock and crops is the use of fallow land as temporary pasture. Whether fallows produce more or less forage than range is not clear. In the sub-humid zone of Nigeria, fallows provide more herbaceous dry matter per unit area than natural savanna (Powell and Waters-Bayer 1985). Vegetation yields from fallows in semi-arid Mali are equal to or greater than from range (Hiernaux *et al.* 1983) and include more legumes, which provide more nutritious forage than grasses (Penning de Vries and Djitèye 1982). In the Ethiopian highlands, however, young fallows contain many plants not palatable to animals and provide only about one-quarter as much forage as natural range (Sandford 1988).

Manure links
Manure generally benefits rangeland only indirectly, but can greatly benefit crops and their residues. Only a small part of what animals eat is converted into meat or milk; most goes back to the soil as faeces and urine. The passage of plant matter through an animal's stomach makes the nutrients more easily available to crops. In Niger it was found that the nitrogen in

millet residues used as mulch and organic fertilizer was immobilized in the straw in the early wet season and was released only later in the season, whereas nitrogen from cattle manure was released when the crop needed it for establishment and early growth (Powell and Ikpe 1992). This quick recycling of nutrients means that, in years when rains are unusually short, crops will benefit from dung to a much greater extent than from plant matter used as organic fertilizer.

The importance of manure for crop production is well documented (cf. Powell 1986; Toulmin 1992a). Its importance in semi-arid areas also became evident after the Sahel drought in the mid-1980s, when grain yields remained low even after rainfall increased. This was attributed to low animal numbers resulting from the losses during the drought, leading to low manure production in subsequent years (Powell and Williams 1993).

In West Africa, farming areas are still relatively lightly stocked during the growing season and there is a substantial influx of herds after cereal harvest. A large amount of manure is available during the dry season and very early wet season (when manure is particularly rich in nutrients), before the herds depart to graze range in drier areas. The most common way to manure land is to kraal herds on fields overnight. This demands little labour and allows the soil to be fertilized by the faeces as well as the urine (Powell and Ikpe 1992). However, the relative number of cattle being kept in mobile herds in sub-Saharan Africa is declining, while a growing number are in settled herds. As fewer animals can be kept year-round in arable areas than can be kept in mobile herds which graze in drier areas during the wet season, the increase in sedentary animal keeping and decrease in nomadism will mean that less manure can be produced in the dry season for wet-season cropping. It is true that settled herds produce manure in arable areas year-round, but they also graze or are fed cut-and-carry fodder year-round from the nearby non-cultivated land. The more intensive nutrient extraction from this land may lead to its degradation in the long-term (Swift et al. 1989).

Investment links
Investment by farmers in livestock is a widespread practice. Animals serve as a means of saving and accumulating capital and as a productive asset, providing not only meat, milk and manure but also draught power. Farmers who adopt animal traction can expand the area under crops by 25 per cent or more (McIntire et al. 1992). In areas where rainfall is highly variable, farmers invest in animals also to hedge against risks of crop failure. As cropping expands further into drier zones, the risks increase. In years of low rainfall, farm households cannot grow enough grain and must sell stock to meet their needs; they are therefore unlikely to accumulate large herds. It is among farmers in better endowed areas, who can cover their food needs from crops, that accumulation of livestock as a savings account is most pronounced (Grayzel 1990).

Substantial investment in animals is also made by non-farming people such as traders, government employees and urban-based entrepreneurs. According to a six-year study in Lesotho, investing in cattle earned the equivalent of a 10 per cent interest rate, while a bank account lost 10 per cent because of inflation (Swallow and Brokken 1987). Conditions in many other African countries are probably similar. In some Sahelian countries, it is estimated that non-pastoralists already own half the cattle (Grell 1992), which are kept in a more extensive way than those of pastoralists (Toulmin 1992a). This shift in stock ownership from specialized herders to farmers and non-farming people means that more capital is locked into livestock and fewer animal products reach the market. Especially where the non-pastoral stock owners can obtain land-use rights according to 'modern' law, traditional herders have less access to forage resources, and their herds suffer even more than before from natural fluctuations in forage yield.

Diversification by pastoralists into cropping

Although specialization in either animals or crops brings clear advantages in terms of labour productivity (Delgado 1979; Toulmin 1992a; McIntire et al. 1992) and cost-effective use of information and knowledge, diversification of economic activities is a safer strategy for a rural family in view of the climatic and economic uncertainties in the drylands. One way in which herders can reduce risk is to do some cropping themselves. Cropping by pastoralists, even nomads, is not new. In arid areas the Bedouins, for example, have long practised 'chance cropping'. Plots in run-on areas are cultivated and drought-tolerant cereals sown. Usually no weeding is done; the sowers (and their animals) return only to harvest. If enough rain falls, grain can be harvested and fewer animals have to be sold to buy cereals; even if no grain forms, the stubble still provides forage. However, if 'chance cropping' is too widespread, it reduces ground cover and promotes erosion, as can be seen in the Halfa grass steppe in the Maghreb countries. Another form of cropping by herders in the arid zone is gardening in oases or around water points. As this requires considerable labour, some family members must remain at the garden sites year-round.

In the arable parts of the semi-arid zone, both rich and poor pastoralists may diversify into cropping. Some richer ones invest in cropping by renting or buying land and hiring farmers to work it. Very rich pastoralists may settle in towns to manage their affairs better and exert political influence, while relatives or hired herders continue to move with the animals. Poor pastoralists take up cropping out of necessity. According to van Raay (1975), a pastoral family needs at least five head of cattle per person to secure subsistence from animal produce alone (consumed and traded). Those with fewer cattle need an additional source of income. If they grow their own crops, they need not sell so many animals from their small herds to buy food grain. Without the means to hire labour for cropping or herding, they are obliged to reduce herd movements and become settled or semi-settled.

Farming may remain a side-line activity or become the major occupation of settled pastoralists. Settlement may also be only temporary. In central Nigeria, settled Fulani who had built up large herds started to migrate again between dry season range in the 'home' farming area and wet-season range in less densely populated areas (Bayer and Waters-Bayer 1991). Increased mobility after building up herds is also reported from Sudan (Haaland 1972). Herds above a certain size threshold cannot be kept year-round in a farming area. In Mali, herds with more than 100 cattle are taken on transhumance during the cropping season, irrespective of whether they belonged to Fulani herders or Bambara farmers (Grayzel 1990). The size threshold will depend on cultivation density: the higher the proportion of land under crops, the more herding labour will be needed to avoid crop damage.

Relations between pastoralists and farmers

The links between livestock and crop husbandry greatly influence the relations between herders and farmers. Among the various resource use arrangements between the two groups, herding contracts and agreements to exchange crop residues and manure are particularly important. In some cases, these arrangements develop into longer-term alliances which serve to secure access to resources which can compensate for variability in the livelihood base in non-equilibrium environments.

Herding contracts

It is common for pastoralists to care for animals not owned by household members. Animals in the herd may belong to relatives who live and work elsewhere, such as in town or in the army, or to a married daughter who has left her stock with her father until she feels confident in her marriage. Animals are exchanged between pastoral households to reduce the risk of losses: if one herd is affected by disease or drought, other herds may survive and a household will lose some but not all of its assets. Animals are also loaned to other pastoral group members who suffer misfortune.

In addition, young herders used to work for farmers, traders or richer pastoralists for some years in order to build up their own herds. However, the extent and terms of herding contracts have changed in recent years. For example, before the drought in the 1970s, hired Wodaabe herders in Niger received milking rights, as well as some of the offspring of the 'contract animals'. As many pastoralists lost their herds during the drought, the number willing to enter into herding contracts increased. By the mid-1980s, contract herders were given only milking rights and, instead of keeping a few contract animals with their own, many herders were tending only contract animals. The contracts no longer gave them an opportunity to reconstitute their own herds by earning offspring (White 1990).

Herding contracts have considerable implications for herd management. A family with its own animals not only consumes and sells milk, but can also sell animals. A contract herder who can use only the milk must care for a larger number of animals to secure family subsistence. He is also likely to milk more intensively and leave less milk for the calves, leading to higher calf mortality in a contract herd than in a herd managed by its owner. Contract arrangements also limit the extent of herd movement. The owners want to 'keep an eye' on the herders and are therefore loath to allow long migrations (Toulmin 1992b). In turn, contract herders are less inclined to invest a great deal of labour and thought into herd management.

Forage arrangements
Arrangements for forage use between herders and farmers range from open access to stubble fields, to the sale of grazing rights or crop residues to particular herders. Where grazing territories are clearly delineated, temporary grazing rights may be given by one pastoral group to another. Throughout West Africa, arrangements between herders and farmers for stubble grazing are common. Where stock density is low in relation to cropped area, for instance in central Nigeria, few formal arrangements for use of crop residues are made; access is free to all herders, whether settled or migrant, although farmers' permission may have to be sought. In the more densely settled zone in northern Nigeria, herders gain rights to stubble grazing by paying in cash or kind or by helping farmers with the harvest (Perrier 1983). Here, there is competition between herders and farmers, who store some of the crop residues for their own animals or for sale.

Similar trends are obvious in eastern Sudan. Whereas access to wetter areas was free until the mid-1980s, after recent droughts farmers were able to change the terms of forage arrangements. Herders now have to buy rights to use crop residues. This puts those with small herds under considerable pressure, since animals have to be sold to finance access to dry season forage (Pflaumbaum 1993, pers. comm.).

As gaining and maintaining access to crop residues is crucial for forage management in many seasonally dry areas and as outside interventions can have serious implications for the forage links between herders and farmers, it is of utmost importance that the existing arrangements and their dynamics be well understood by researchers and policy-makers.

Manuring arrangements
While forage arrangements are crucial for animal keeping, securing manure is crucial for cropping in many parts of sub-Saharan Africa. With the expansion of cropping and the decline in fallowing, measures other than long-term fallowing are needed to maintain soil fertility. Manure is removed from pastoralists' kraals and sold to farmers, and arrangements are made for keeping herds overnight on fields to deposit manure.

For example, farmers in central Nigeria pay Fulani herders in cash or kind to camp on their fields in the dry season, particularly where the cash crop ginger will be grown. There is a generally agreed 'normal' price for manuring fields but actual payment is often less. The settled Fulani regard the income as less important than the function of manuring agreements in maintaining good relations with the farmers, who hold traditional land rights and give the Fulani permission to build temporary homes, use some land for cropping and graze stubble fields. In times of high demand (e.g. when chemical fertilizers fail to arrive or when ginger prices are very high), farmers may offer more than the 'normal' price for manure or the Fulani can be particularly 'generous' in order to secure good relations.

67

Manuring contracts are also arranged via access to water, such as in the millet zone of Mali, where farmers have private wells dug to attract pastoral herds to their fields in the dry season (Toulmin 1992a). Thus, through manuring contracts, the herders gain access to a vital resource for livestock keeping in the drylands. In view of the importance of manuring contracts for good herder–farmer relations and in view of the close link between manuring and forage arrangements, these must be well understood before any interventions are made which could weaken these arrangements, and every opportunity should be sought to find ways to strengthen them.

Coping with conflict.
The relations between herders and farmers oscillate between conflict and co-operation. In parts of Africa where many pastoralists are Moslem, while many farmers are Christian, ethnic and religious conflicts, often imported from urban areas, sometimes cause tensions over and above those which arise from conflicts over natural resource use.

Local conflicts often arise over crop damage. Herder–farmer relations may be tense during the growing season but ease after grain harvest, when farmers are eager to obtain manure for their fields and herders to gain access to crop residues for their animals. One advantage of transhumance is that herds are taken away from cropping areas during the wet season, thus decreasing the danger of crop damage. Changes in cropping patterns, such as the introduction of cash crops like cotton or the expansion of dry season gardening in lowlands, can restrict access of herds to stubble grazing and increase the conflicts over crop damage (van Raay 1975; Delgado 1979).

Many indigenous groups try to preserve their own rights to resources and to maintain their identity by placing tight limits on outsiders. They may welcome herders on a temporary basis but oppose their permanent settlement, as found by Toulmin (1992a) in Mali. Immigrant herders wanting to maintain good relations with farmers have learned to respect this. For example, Fulani pastoralists have lived in farming areas in central Nigeria for several generations, yet many of the richer ones continue to inhabit grass huts to suggest that their presence is not of a permanent nature.

Farmers who invest in large-scale cash cropping are less likely than traditional small-holders to seek good relations with herders. Commercial farmers' exclusive land use rights, gained according to modern law, deny herders access to valuable grazing resources. A particularly stark example recently occurred in Senegal, where the state allocated 45000 ha to a religious sect, which ousted Fulani herders from the tree savanna area they had used for seasonal grazing and some subsistence cropping. The area was completely cleared to grow groundnuts, with substantial short-term profits (Schoonmaker-Freudenberger 1991). The extension of this type of cash cropping not only reduces the space and options for pastoralists but also precludes small-scale farming systems of a more sustainable nature.

In another part of Senegal, herders and farmers have joined forces to prevent the intrusion of commercial farmers and to maintain the traditional links between crops and livestock (Guèye 1993). However, the conventional paradigm in formal agricultural education and the popular notion of 'modern' farming makes it difficult for such crop–livestock integration to gain official backing. Traditional land-use systems are still regarded as backward and in need of being replaced, ostensibly to 'feed the nation'. This attitude may be partly due to ignorance among policy-makers, but may also be displayed to justify actions which benefit the new African élites.

Herder–farmer interaction versus mixed farming

A recent review of animal agriculture in sub-Saharan Africa (Winrock 1992) concluded that human population growth will lead to mixed crop–livestock farming and that mixed systems are more efficient than specialized ones. Mixed farming largely avoids conflicts between herders and farmers. As the fields can be manured by the farmers' own animals, manuring arrangements are no longer necessary. Even if farmers' animals produce less than those in pastoral herds, they serve as a buffer against risk, as long as labour availability permits both operations within one farm.

The analysis, however, overlooks a number of factors. Although animal density may increase with human population and cropping density (McIntire et al. 1992), the livestock wealth will not be evenly distributed. Many farmers will have only few, if any, animals. For example, in densely populated Ovamboland in Namibia, already half of the rural households own no cattle (Tapscott 1990). As most of the land is cropped, even those with cattle cannot keep them near the homestead (Jensen 1990) to provide a means of transport or manure for cropping. It is doubtful whether mixed farming will be an option for poor farmers in many densely populated areas.

Another disadvantage of mixed farming is that farmers tend to invest less labour than pure pastoralists in animal keeping and put less value on animal-related skills. Pastoral herds are tended mainly by young men, whereas the animals of many mixed farmers are tended only by children, if at all. Animals in transhumant herds also enjoy a longer herding day and, given the same access to grazing resources, their productivity is higher than that of settled livestock (van Raay 1975; Bayer 1986a).

Good herding is a highly skilled activity. Transhumant movements also demand considerable organizational capacity and diplomatic skills to negotiate passage rights and access to water, crop residues and so on. These skills are seldom appreciated by development agencies and educationalists. Is there any formal training institution in which herding skills and managing a transhumant cycle are taught? If pastoralists become settled mixed farmers, the 'art of herding' (Müller 1991) will be lost. To maintain the present level of livestock productivity in the drylands, expensive technology and external inputs would have to be introduced to substitute for herders' indigenous knowledge and management skills.

Further expansion of farming into drier areas and an increase in mixed farming would have severe implications for rangeland use. Farmers' animals graze mainly near the farms, using forage resources already in the wet season which transhumant herders traditionally used only in the dry season. If this 'intensification' of resource use continues unchecked, over-all animal production in sub-Saharan Africa will decrease. In the Sahel, 20–30 per cent fewer animals could be kept if the present integrated use of arid range and savanna farming areas by transhumant herders breaks down (Breman *et al.* 1982). Since mixed farmers are less likely than pastoralists to sell animals or to use the milk, the decline in food consumption from local stock would be even greater.

Disintegration of transhumant use of forage resources not only dimin-ishes national food production. The reduction in total number of animals which can be kept also destroys the livelihood base of many herders, who must then find other sources of income. It is often difficult or impossible for them to gain access to crop land, because of prevailing land rights and population growth among farmers. As specialized herders have little formal education and are poorly equipped for urban life, they can find work—if at all—only as casual labourers or night watchmen. This is in sharp contrast to their previous, highly skilled animal husbandry work.

Forage production and use

In view of the high variability in yield of natural forage in the drylands, forage production—either in mixed farms or for sale to pastoralists—is often proposed. Research over several decades has shown that many plants used for forage production elsewhere in the tropics can also be grown in sub-Saharan Africa. However, there are several reasons why forage cropping in the conventional sense has not been widely adopted:

○ Price ratios between crop and livestock products in sub-Saharan Africa do not favour intensification of ruminant production;
○ External requirements for forage improvement (fertilizer, seed, fencing materials) are expensive and difficult to obtain;
○ Crop residues already play a prominent role in African livestock sys-tems; these can largely assume the role of improved forage, but their value is not yet fully appreciated by researchers and policy-makers;
○ As the emphasis on increased production does not take into account the more complex aims of small holders and pastoralists, research has produced few technologies which fit into their livestock keeping systems.

Few animal experiments with improved forage have been carried out in sub-Saharan Africa. As animal production responses are site specific, it is difficult to extrapolate results from elsewhere. For example, replacing natural range with a grass/legume pasture can double the rate of animal growth and increase production per hectare six times or more in tropical Australia (Mott *et al.* 1981), but similar on-station trials in Africa showed only a 40 per cent increase in weight gain per animal and less than 200 per cent increase per unit area (Clatworthy 1984). As the controls in these trials did not include traditional techniques of crop residue grazing and using patches of different vegetation types, even these increments are likely to be over-estimates if compared with the actual livestock systems in Africa. One reason for the small increment from improved forage is the nature of the vegetation. The Australian range has been grazed by large ungulates for only about 100 years, whereas the African range has been grazed for thousands of years—time for a vegetation to evolve which can withstand high grazing pressure. In fact, many grasses recommended for pasture improvement in tropical Australia come from Africa (Skerman and Riveros 1990).

Economics of growing fodder
Feed has a value only if it is converted by animals into useful products. The economics of growing forage or feeding supplements depend on the cost of acquiring the extra feed and the value of the additional animal products. If cattle are fed grains, then the conversion ratio of grain to liveweight is about 8:1. However, the price ratio of grain to liveweight in sub-Saharan Africa is usually far below the threshold which would render grain feeding economic (McIntire *et al.* 1992). The ratio of conversion from cultivated forages to liveweight gain is much more variable and usually much poorer than in the case of grain.

McIntire *et al.* (1992) summarized available data about fodder prices in sub-Saharan Africa and concluded that legume feed is cheaper than grass-based forage, crop residues are normally cheaper than special forage crops and dual-purpose legumes (e.g. cowpeas, groundnuts) are the cheapest feed supplements. However, consideration must be given not only to the costs of the feed but also to the season when it is available. Cheap supplements in the early wet season, when natural pasture is abundant and of good quality, will have less positive economic effects than more expensive feed which is available when other forage resources are scarce or of poor quality. Calculations based on trials in Togo suggest that it is not economic to grow forage to fatten cattle (Doppler 1980). However, as the case study from Nigeria shows (Box 1), it may pay to grow forage for survival feeding.

Box 1. Fodder banks in Nigeria

In a three-year researcher-managed trial in central Nigeria, small sown-legume pastures (fodder banks) were superimposed on traditional forage resource use and grazed in the late dry season for part of each day. In the first year, the cattle with access to improved pasture lost 12kg on average, or 30 per cent less than the weight lost by animals under traditional management in the control group. In the second year, no difference between the two groups was found. In the third year, however, when the wet season ended unusually early, weight losses in the dry season exceeded 20 per cent of bodyweight in the control group, but were halved by giving animals two hours daily access to improved pasture. Moreover, half of the control animals died, whereas all animals with access to the fodder bank survived (Bayer 1986b). In trials managed by the Fulani, 'survival grazing' of the fodder bank cut calf mortality from 28 to 14 per cent and reduced emergency sales of adult animals to such an extent that the costs of establishing the improved pasture could be recovered within 2–3 years (Taylor-Powell 1987).

Survival feeding may justify high costs. It is an open question which strategy is better: sowing forage or buying feed when required. In years when survival feeding is necessary, ranchers in northern Australia commonly buy hay and grain which is transported over long distances. Although the price per unit of feed is higher than that of forage grown on-farm, many ranchers prefer buying feed, since costs for the extra feed occur only when it is really needed, the benefits of feeding are quickly visible and feeding can be stopped easily as soon as conditions improve. By contrast, growing forages requires investment well in advance of the time of need, the benefits can be gained only after one or more growing seasons and the forage may not be needed every year.

For pastoralists it is attractive to grow forage only when severe feed shortages occur regularly. This may become more frequent when herd movements are severely restricted, or when herders lose access to key forage resources because of increased cropping and animal keeping by farmers. If feed shortages are irregular, it is better to buy feed—if available—and to externalize the risk of not needing extra forage. Since forage growers face the risk of producing something they cannot use or sell, dual-purpose crops are more suitable as a potential source of survival feed.

Limits to forage production in drylands

Herbaceous forage plants are subject to the same environmental constraints as field crops. As a rule of thumb, at least 500mm per annum is needed for rainfed production of forage legumes in the tropics. A few grass species (e.g. *Cenchrus ciliaris*) can be cultivated with as little as 350mm but, below this level, irrigation is needed to grow forage. Forage cultivation and pasture improvement in the African drylands are limited by several factors.

○ Investment in land preparation and seed is economic only if yields are reliable. As vegetation yield in drylands varies greatly between years (Le Houérou 1989; Hiernaux 1993), yields of sown forages, like food crops, are unpredictable.

○ Sown forages require care if they are to contribute substantially to total forage yields. They respond well to fertilizer application; without it, they may quickly disappear. Fertilizer is scarce and expensive in Africa and, if available, is more likely to be used on food and cash crops.

○ Pastures with some introduced legumes, such as *Stylosanthes* spp., require grazing during the wet season for good legume establishment. Cattle and sheep prefer grass in the wet season; this reduces competition and creates better growing conditions for the legumes (Gillard and Fisher 1978). However, keeping the animals there to improve pasture establishment must be weighed against the advantages of moving them to high-quality natural pasture elsewhere in the wet season.

There are similar climatic limits to planting fodder trees. Most cultivated browse species require more water than is available in the African drylands, where only one truly dryland species is widely promoted: *Faidherbia* (formerly *Acacia*) *albida*. As naturally occurring browse is much more diverse than the cultivated species (Le Houérou 1980; von Maydell 1986), encouraging the natural regeneration of selected local species offers greater promise than planting browse trees.

Cultivating forage, whether herbaceous or woody, is likely to limit the mobility of pastoralists, as the forage plots may have to be guarded to ensure that the investor can reap the later benefits. Where herd mobility is already being limited by external conditions, cultivating forage can offer animal keepers an opportunity to balance the forage supply. As a rule, however, this will be possible only in areas where arable food cropping is also possible.

Storing fodder

Another way of balancing the forage supply is to conserve and store forage for times of shortage. However, the value of this strategy has been questioned (Humphreys 1991), in view of the following:

○ Alternative ways of balancing the forage supply, such as seasonal movements of herds, may still be possible;
○ It is often more economic to let the animals go through a natural cycle of building up body reserves during favourable periods, mobilizing them during times of feed shortage, and capitalising on compensatory growth when conditions improve;
○ Considerable technical difficulties have been encountered in conserving tropical forages;
○ Withdrawing land from grazing to conserve forage can have a negative effect on the performance of grazing animals;
○ Effects of hay feeding are small, because hay often tends to substitute for natural forage, rather than supplementing it (Minson 1990).

Forage conservation can involve setting aside pastures as forage reserves; storing crop residues as hay; or cutting, transporting and conserving natural or sown forage as hay or silage (Pearson and Ison 1987). As silage making requires considerable technical inputs and investment and is not a realistic option for most herders, we focus here on reserving pasture and hay-making.

Range enclosure

Areas of range set aside for standing hay may consist only of natural vegetation or may be oversown with improved forage species. Reserved grazing areas were components of some traditional pastoral systems, where particular pastoral groups managed the land as common property (Niamir 1990). More recently however, range in sub-Saharan Africa has been enclosed by individual stock owners and government agencies. Such enclosures take the form of:

○ Holding grounds and feed-producing areas for market stock (Reusse 1982);
○ Small dry season pastures in agropastoral areas, where some animals can

be grazed while most are moved to distant pastures; this enables the pastoralists to keep some milch animals close to home to supply the family in the dry season (Behnke 1985b);

o Large dry season pastures, where owners of large herds—often business-men without opportunities to draw on traditional grazing rights—try to gain exclusive rights over tracts of land (White 1992);

o Enclosures decreed or supported by the state, such as group ranches, or induced by projects, such as grazing schemes (Cousins 1993; Galaty 1993a,b).

Often, enclosure follows privatization of crop-land or general privatization of land. Under these conditions, range enclosure by pastoralists is an attempt to secure at least some land for themselves. Enclosures are used seasonally or for special purposes. Generally, communal land is grazed during the wet season and enclosed land during times of feed shortage. Whereas such arrangements are very favourable for the owners of the enclosures, they decrease the availability of forage for the animals of herders who have no access to the enclosed areas.

Hay-making
Hay-making is not widely reported from sub-Saharan Africa. Crop residues may be stored, often in trees, and are also sold, particularly near towns (Dugué 1985). Storing crop residues offers possibilities for dry season feeding of smallholders' animals. For large pastoral herds, the amount which can be stored is usually too small to have an appreciable impact on the nutrition of the entire herd. However, small amounts of stored crop residues are useful for sick animals, calves or a few milch cows kept close to home while the main herd is on transhumance.

Fluctuations in forage supply between wet and dry seasons can partly be evened out by making hay from natural grasses. In Ethiopia, where Borana women traditionally collect grass in the dry season for calf feeding, hay-making during the wet season was encouraged (Coppock 1991). The amounts collected by the women were small (up to 300 kg per house-hold), but still facilitated calf feeding in the following dry season. It is too soon to tell whether this is a viable option in years of extreme drought. Fulani men, co-operating with a non-governmental organization in northern Burkina Faso, are also making hay in years with good to average rainfall, but can collect little or no hay in drought years (Bühlmann 1993, pers. comm.). Where rainfall is highly variable, hay yield suffers the same large fluctuations as range yield. Hay-making can reduce annual variations in forage supply only if relatively large quantities of hay can be stored for more than one year.

Importing feed

In the African drylands there is little experience with importing feed from wetter areas to compensate for fluctuation in forage supply. Emergency schemes during recent droughts were costly and seldom effective (Toulmin this book); experience elsewhere is also not encouraging. In Australia forage transport was subsidized when drought was declared, which could be done even by a local government. It was striking that certain local governments declared drought much more often than adjacent ones, although this could not be explained by differences in rainfall or soils. Within a district, those who were the first to apply for drought relief were those who maintained a much higher stocking rate than their less 'drought-prone' neighbours. Drought relief in this form rewarded poor forage management.

Facilitating feed imports into African drylands could create similar problems (see the case study from the Maghreb in Box 2). Subsidizing feed only during drought can also encourage the build up of herds and, as the frequency of situations experienced by stock-keepers as 'drought' is influenced by stocking rates, feed subsidies may become a permanent feature of the dryland economy. Furthermore, feed subsidies favour large herds, often owned by people outside the traditional pastoral sector.

Box 2. Subsidized feed in the Maghreb

In North Africa, grain is cheap because of government policy to subsidize basic foods. At one point, the price ratio of sheep liveweight to grain in Algeria exceeded 20:1 (Grell 1993, pers. comm.). Considerable amounts of hay and grain for feeding are traded in all Maghreb countries. In semi-arid central Tunisia, small-holders buy 40 per cent of feed needed in normal years and up to 70 per cent in dry years (Johnson et al. 1988).

Although various feeds are available, most livestock are not stall-fed. Range still offers the cheapest feed, meat quality is improved if animals have exercise and grazing requires less investment than stall-keeping. It is not uncommon to see stock in good condition on almost bare range. If the animals had to rely solely on range vegetation, most would be long dead but, since part of their maintenance requirement is covered by grain, they survive to graze the last blade of grass on the range. As much of the original vegetation is perennial, the high grazing pressure affects range yield in subsequent years. In view of the high stocking rates, the range can cover an appreciable part of the forage needs only when rainfall is unusually high. Since the heavy grazing reduces soil cover, heavy rains tend to cause greater erosion than previously.

Availability of cheap feed favours the keeping of larger herds. Small herds have restricted mobility, having to graze near water points, where pastures are poor and animals must be sold to buy feed: in one shepherd's words, the herd 'eats itself'. As large herd owners can transport water by truck, they can use better pastures further from permanent water. Their transport capacity also gives them easier access to subsidized feed. They can buy up the animals which smallholders must sell, speeding up the process of concentration of stock ownership in a few hands.

Conclusions and policy implications

Policies to support strategies of persistence
Pastoralists' strategies to persist in the drylands by adjusting forage requirements to forage supply include using adapted animal breeds, keeping multiple-species herds and changing herd structure, either seasonally or during drought. Policymakers can do little directly to improve these strategies. Indirect support can be given by revising university and college teaching so that the merits of the present practices are recognized and processes of animal adaptation to environment are given more attention (Sandford this book).

As African breeds have undergone centuries of natural and deliberate selection, there is little scope for improving their adaptability to existing conditions. But there is great scope for improving the breeding policies of governments and donor agencies, which often still advocate introduction of temperate breeds or selection of superior local animals under artificially improved conditions. Only under very favourable natural (e.g. highlands) and economic conditions (e.g. cheap concentrates and high prices for animal products) would such breeding programmes be appropriate in sub-Saharan Africa.

Marketing interventions are often proposed to facilitate adjustment of herd composition to fluctuation in forage supply, particularly severe drought. However, direct market interventions have had little positive effect, whereas providing infrastructure, such as roads for easier transport, has improved pastoralists' possibilities to buy and sell animals (Kerven 1992; Holtzman and Kulibaba this book).

Policies to support strategies of mobility
Most government policies discourage tracking forage growth, the seasonal use of key resources and movements between agro-ecological zones. International borders have cut across traditional transhumance routes. Government administrations are keen to settle pastoralists so as to have some control over them. Herd mobility and lengthy administrative procedures, especially when crossing borders, do not mix well. There is a need to strengthen pastoralists' control over the resources they traditionally use, so that they are better able to react quickly when decisions about herd movements have to be made (Lane and Moorehead this book). The extent to which herd movements can balance seasonal and annual fluctuations in forage supply depends on the distances covered. Movements between agro-ecological zones can help to cope with not only seasonal fluctuations and short-term drought, but also multi-year droughts, as long as mobility is possible without major obstacles (Toulmin this book).

Policies to support crop–livestock links
Use of crop residues reduces seasonal fluctuations in forage supply, and use of manure helps maintain crop productivity in those areas where there is sufficient water for cropping. However, animals and crops also compete for

land, especially key resources in lower-lying areas in the drylands. Mixed farming may offer the possibility of balancing the risks of cropping and animal keeping within one enterprise but, where specialized herders and farmers complement each other, there are advantages in terms of labour productivity and overall production of maintaining separate enterprises. Subsidizing 'modern' farming with high levels of external inputs, such as commercial feed concentrates and chemical fertilizers, can jeopardize the alliances between specialized herders and farmers. Agricultural policy should include public recognition of these positive interactions and should focus on creating or strengthening mechanisms to manage the conflicts which inevitably occur when different groups use the same natural resources.

Crop–livestock interactions within an ecological zone, and especially across zones, permit higher total production per unit area of land. More people can be supported than would be possible without these interactions. Promoting links between cropping and animal keeping should therefore be a high priority for governments trying to accommodate human population growth.

Policies concerning forage production
Forage production appears to be of greater interest to research and development agencies than to pastoralists. The climatic limits for growing the proven forage crops correspond largely to the limits for food crops. The price ratios between external inputs and animal products, and between crop and animal products, do not favour intensification of animal production in most parts of sub-Saharan Africa. However, strategic use of sown forage for survival feeding, particularly dual-purpose crops for both food and feed, deserves attention. Range enclosures to reserve forage may help even out seasonal variations in forage supply, but policymakers must be aware that enclosures increase the pressure on communal range and thus disadvantage those herders who do not have access to them. Storage of hay, mainly from crop residues, is worth promoting in smallholdings with few animals and in pastoral herds for strategic feeding of particular classes of animals. As the price ratios between inputs, livestock and crop products are not likely to change substantially in the near future, the role of sown and stored forage will be limited to special purposes and should not be over-estimated by policymakers. Dual-purpose crops should be given higher priority in research and development than solely forage crops.

Policies concerning feed imports
Subsidized feed imports into the drylands are often proposed to alleviate the impact of drought, but experience shows them to be questionable (Toulmin this book). Not only do they create dependencies and encourage overstocking, they also tend to favour richer pastoralists to the detriment of those with small herds. Importing feed into dryland areas has a potential for ensuring survival during a limited, critical period but, with present prices and costs, it is unlikely that imported feed can maintain herds for more than a couple of months. Subsidizing feed imports should be restricted to short periods of extreme stress only.

Policies supporting pastoral strategies
Pastoralists normally combine several strategies to cope with fluctuations in forage supply. They must react not only to climate-related variability, but also to increased population pressure and detrimental administrative policies. The continued survival of at least some pastoral groups under these conditions suggests that their strategies have worked fairly well. Political support for these strategies would not only promote sustainable use of the drier parts of sub-Saharan Africa for food production from animals; it would also help to assure more people a livelihood base.

As strategies such as tracking forage and arranging crop–livestock interactions involve land which is used by several groups, a balance of different interests between pastoral groups, as well as between pastoral and farming groups, has to be maintained. This means that emphasis in agricultural development policy must be placed on mechanisms and institutions for balancing these interests. Interventions which would support pastoral strategies include (see also other chapters in this book):

o Convincing political decision-makers of the advantages of transhumant systems and of farmer–herder interactions in terms of overall productivity of the drylands;
o Initiating or improving contacts between government officials and pastoralists;
o Giving legal advice about proposed and actual changes in formal land laws so that pastoralists are better able to defend their interests;
o Giving legal support to herd mobility, for example, by recognizing traditional transhumance routes and seasonal grazing areas;
o Introducing university and college courses about the advantages and constraints of pastoral systems, including the art of herding and managing transhumant herd movements, in order to improve the standing of these skills in the eyes of present and future political decision-makers;
o Critically examining the impact of proposed agricultural intensification of key resource areas used by herders; this would involve limiting any interventions which would prohibit pastoral use of such areas at vital times of the year, and supporting negotiations between farmers and herders about the shared use of such areas.

5. Livestock marketing in pastoral Africa: policies to increase competitiveness, efficiency and flexibility[1]

JOHN S. HOLTZMAN AND NICOLAS P. KULIBABA

This chapter identifies approaches to support livestock producers affected by climatic and price instability, and the implications for livestock marketing. With an examination of the failure of government measures to control livestock marketing, the chapter identifies an appropriate public sector role in support of competitive and efficient markets. The chapter also proposes interventions designed to improve livestock marketing during crisis periods, as well as considering the potential costs and benefits of such interventions.

Two fundamental problems underlying livestock marketing in arid and semi-arid zones are supply and price variability. Climatic variability, particularly the spatial and temporal distribution of rainfall, affects livestock production systems profoundly through its impact on forage and water resources (Behnke et al. 1993). When feed and water resources decrease, livestock struggle to maintain weights and the incidence of malnutrition and disease rises. To avoid morbidity and mortality, producers sell off non-essential and weakened stock at low prices. Since producers over a wide geographic area may be affected simultaneously by drought, they offer livestock on the market at the same time, and so depress prices. While livestock prices fall, cereal prices rise, as do the prices of other staple foodstuffs. Terms of trade between products that livestock owners sell and the goods they buy worsen and livestock producers' real incomes decline.

The impact of expanded supply is the flooding of rural, urban and nearby export markets with cheap animals and meat. Livestock traders may initially benefit from low purchase prices for livestock, but they are likely to face low sales prices as markets become glutted. Hence, alleged windfall profits by traders may be an ephemeral phenomenon. Because producer

[1] This paper draws on work carried out by the USAID-funded Agricultural Marketing and Improvement Strategies Project (AMIS), with field studies in Burkina Faso, Mali, Côte d'Ivoire and the Niger–Nigeria corridor. The views expressed should not, however, be attributed to USAID or Abt Associates.

incomes drop during drought periods, they lack the resources to purchase livestock in order to reconstitute herds in post-drought periods. Producers also do not sell animals after droughts. As marketed surplus collapses in post-drought periods, traders have trouble procuring animals even at high prices. Trader margins are eroded during these periods, as the prices they receive for livestock are held in check by substitution possibilities between red meat and other commodities (fish, poultry, pork, dairy products). When the supply of animals is lowered and substitution possibilities are limited, consumers suffer, paying higher prices for red meat and dairy products during the post-drought, herd reconstitution period.

Without ways to control supply, non-equilibrium, opportunistic pastoral systems are plagued by market disequilibria. Significant, non-marginal shifts in supply, following the cycle of drought and recovery, play havoc with livestock prices, marketed surplus and producer incomes, not to mention consumption patterns for livestock products. Given the inherent instability of supply, governments and private traders under-invest in livestock marketing infrastructure and facilities.

The key issue underlying African livestock marketing is not supply control, but rather strategic public sector interventions that contribute to competitive, efficient and flexible markets. Such markets will generate the most broad-based benefits for producers, livestock traders, consumers and government agencies. The exact distribution of benefits depends on the bargaining strength of the different players, as well as the distributional impact of government interventions. Most governments are interested in increasing national herd productivity and offtake through slaughter and exports, while assuring the sustainability of the resource base. In unusual cases, where drought forces herders to destock swiftly, greatly diminishing the national herd, governments, with assistance from donor agencies, can intervene to minimize hardship and to ease the transition of poorer, marginal herders to other means of earning a livelihood (Toulmin this book).

Livestock traders are interested in free markets and the absence of interventions which distort market incentives. Livestock traders and producers are typically supposed to have opposing interests, though both benefit from reliable access to market opportunities and infrastructure. Producers and consumers are also assumed to have differing interests, although there is often considerable overlap. Consumers are interested in reliable supplies and high quality, not merely the lowest possible cost livestock products, as is often supposed.

Many economists, government planners and donor agency officials focus on the end products of livestock production systems in Africa—red meat, hides and skins. They are preoccupied with increasing productivity, defined in terms of offtake and red meat production. Much of the economic analysis of livestock production and marketing systems in Africa has focused on how to expand slaughter and exports. But most African livestock producers think of their livestock enterprises less as end products and more as economic units capable of generating a stream of benefits or use values over their economic lifetime (Perrier this book). Hence, livestock are only sold when they no longer generate a stream of benefits (such as cull cows), when they are non-essential to the herd (such as culled males) or when the alternative to timely sale is either mortality or heightened risk of mortality.

This chapter explores the key policy issues and economic factors that are critical to ensuring an efficient, flexible livestock marketing system which is able to respond to price and supply instability. The themes covered in the following sections are:

○ The role of private traders;
○ The failure of government intervention to control producer livestock or consumer meat prices;
○ The relative efficiency of parastatal or private livestock traders in highly variable market settings;
○ Appropriate kinds and levels of infrastructure;
○ Public sector roles;
○ The capacity of markets to absorb high but temporary levels of off-take; and
○ Pastoral welfare support.

Opportunistic traders

Private livestock traders behave as opportunistically as the shrewdest of pastoralists. During drought periods, they procure animals at very low prices, knowing that producers are strapped for cash (to buy grain and other necessities) and that marketed surplus has burgeoned. Low trader offer prices are in part protection against the higher risk of animal mortality during drought periods. Underweight, weak animals are far more susceptible to disease and to accidents or mortality during transport, regardless of whether trekking, motorized transport or rail is used.

While some traders may not serve livestock producers well, this does not necessarily imply conspiratorial, clan or class-based conflict (as Aronson argues regarding Somali livestock traders, 1980). It is true that buyers and sellers have diametrically opposed interests, particularly if they are buying on open, spot markets and mutual trust between buyer and seller does not build up (Williamson 1979, 1985). Yet despite the fact that traders strive to procure animals from producers at the lowest possible prices, studies of returns to livestock trading enterprises typically show that net returns are modest (Staatz 1979; Holtzman et al. 1980; Herman 1983; Holtzman et al. 1992).

Furthermore, the majority of livestock traders involved in the trade between the Sahel and the West African coast have regional, ethnic or kinship ties to livestock producing communities. The complementarity of economic roles between livestock producers and traders in some segments of this community are often comprised of social relationships that span several generations. What appear from the outside to be excessive profits often mask a simultaneous 'commerce' in social goods and services of benefit to both parties. The numerous instances of child

81

fostering, marriage and other relationships observed between pastoral producers and their trader 'patrons' in terminal markets are evidence of this phenomenon.

During some periods returns to livestock trading enterprises are negative or zero. Reasons why livestock traders continue to trade, even when returns to livestock trading enterprises are negative, are that money is tied up in trader credit to wholesale butchers, or that traders make their money by importing consumer goods or foodstuffs on return trips.

Some livestock traders possess a competitive edge in the form of superior market information, thus introducing localized market imperfections in some of the more isolated livestock-producing zones. Eliminating these imperfections is best done by enhancing competition, rather than by controlling prices or mandating sales through livestock marketing parastatals. The critical policy question, then, is how to increase competition in the most cost-effective manner.

Credit programmes may be one route to expand entry into livestock trading. But formal credit programmes have a dismal record in most African countries (Meyer et al. 1992). Among the key problems in larger Sahelian and coastal livestock markets are the unrestrained use of supplier credit, the prolonged repayment schedules by urban traders and high rates of loan default.

Why government intervention to control prices does not work

Controlling live animal prices is generally not feasible in sub-Saharan Africa. In African livestock marketing systems, live animals are rarely weighed prior to bidding and sale. Range-fed livestock are not used to being enclosed in weighbridges, and trying to force them onto scales may lead to fractures, bruising of animals or to market-place disruptions. In many 'improved' livestock marketing facilities in Africa, weighbridges have been abandoned (if they were ever used at all), and traders and butchers estimate carcass yield based on visual inspection of animals offered for sale.

Given the difficulty of weighing range-fed livestock, government attempts to fix animal prices have not been based upon liveweights. Instead price controls have been imposed at the retail level. Generally, these controls are ineffective. In most cases they are evaded by butchers who offer consumers less than a true kilogram of meat (Holtzman 1988). Alternatively, butchers will offer lower quality meat by mixing red meat with bone or offal. In cases where price controls are enforced, butchers have either gone on strike or greatly reduced slaughterings, as in Senegal in the mid-1980s (Holtzman et al. 1989). In most urban areas where there are nominal price controls in place, enforcement is lax and haphazard. Efforts by butchers to by-pass regulated pricing are overlooked or encouraged by poorly paid officials only too willing to accept bribes.

Government attempts to set retail prices are invariably based on incomplete calculations of butcher costs and returns. Typically, these calculations fail to account for the cost of capital, losses (failure of animals to pass veterinary inspection; losses due to next day sale of meat) and any unofficial marketing costs. Wholesale butchers in urban areas complain bitterly about retail price controls. They point out the incongruity of controlling prices at one level of the livestock marketing system (i.e. the retail level), while allowing wholesale transaction prices to vary according to market conditions. When wholesale prices (butchers' procurement prices) rise, yet retail prices remain fixed, butchers' margins are squeezed.

One option for controlling wholesale live animal prices is to establish price ceilings for different age–sex categories of livestock. This has proven to be very difficult and costly to operate, given the heterogeneity of animals even within the same age–sex category. In Burkina Faso collection of detailed prices for different age–sex categories was discontinued as the data-collection task was too complex and costly, and the price information was not used by livestock traders.

Some governments have attempted indirect efforts to manage prices. In Côte d'Ivoire municipal authorities limit the number of licenses issued to butchers for the purpose of ensuring that only qualified practitioners enter the trade. The consequences have had the opposite effect: licensed butchers 'rent' protection to all comers. The proliferation of 'apprentices', many of whom are unqualified, has created a situation of hyper-competition, high turnover among practitioners and a market-place where credit sales and high default on repayments are characteristic.

Governments should refrain from setting fixed, floor or ceiling prices. Governments usually lack the capability to enforce prices, as well as the financial resources to defend them. Furthermore, administrative controls are typically accompanied by rent-seeking behaviour on the part of officials overseeing enforcement. More importantly, supply and demand conditions change seasonally, cyclically or secularly so that prices would need to be adjusted continually to reflect changes in supplies and marketing costs, not to mention geographic variations in market conditions. Because most African governments lack the data collection and analysis capacity to track changes, prices are typically not allowed to vary. As a result, control prices do not accurately reflect the interplay of changing supply and demand conditions for livestock products and changes in livestock marketing costs and services.

Parastatal and private livestock traders in highly variable market settings

Given the difficult macro-economic conditions and fiscal stringency prevailing in most African countries under structural and sectoral adjustment programmes, expanding existing parastatal agencies or creating new ones are not viable options. Many parastatals are being dismantled, including Somalia's Livestock Development Authority, the Kenya Meat Commission and Mali's Office Malien du Bétail et de la Viande. Parastatals that remain are liquidating assets and shifting certain commercial functions to the private sector, or contracting out some operations, such as transport or storage.

As real incomes fall in many African countries, parastatals face the increasingly thorny problem of ceilings on salaries and rigid schemes of service, which undermine incentives for good performance. Improving parastatal performance is a difficult challenge in institutional design, which requires flexibility in employment policy, pay scales and non-salary incentive schemes.

The performance of government marketing boards, with the exception of a few export-oriented parastatals, has been uneven in most of sub-Saharan Africa (Woodward 1992). Even once-praised multi-purpose boards, such as ADMARC of Malawi, have come in recently for extensive criticism. Rather than consider creating new public organizations for livestock marketing, the focus needs to be on what the public sector can do to support, strengthen and facilitate private sector marketing to be responsive to variable supply and demand conditions.

Appropriate types and levels of infrastructure

Livestock trekking infrastructure
Livestock trekking is an important transport mode for animals moving from isolated rural markets to larger market towns on paved roads or at rail-heads. Once trekked animals reach such market towns, they are invariably transferred to trucks or railcars. While the cash outlay for trekking on to the final destination may be smaller than truck rental or rail shipment, trekking has declined in importance as a long-distance transport mode since the mid-1970s in West Africa. A key reason for this is that trekking takes too long and scarce capital is tied up for long periods (see Box 1). A second reason is that trekking has become increasingly risky and treacherous. As farmers have encroached on trek routes formerly reserved for the livestock trade, conflicts with farmers and fines paid by trek bosses have mounted. Furthermore, the risk of theft and predation from corrupt authorities is greater while trekking.

While trekking is likely to continue to decline in importance, it will still remain the primary mode of transport for moving livestock from rural markets to market towns in much of pastoral Africa. In more densely populated and cultivated areas, public investment in upgraded trek routes and watering points should be a priority. Traders may be willing to pay for well-maintained routes that help to keep their animals in good condition. However, this will depend upon assurances of security, as well as adequate forage and water along trekking routes.

Livestock trucking and rail infrastructure
As the share of export livestock trucked from the Sahel to coastal West Africa has increased significantly since the mid-1980s (Holtzman *et al.* 1992), the need to upgrade roads has risen. However, the existence of road infrastructure in pastoral production zones does not necessarily ensure

84

Box 1. Costs and returns from trekking: evidence from West Africa

While trekking retains its place as the principal means of conveying livestock through various stages in the marketing chain, in West Africa's Central Corridor it appears to do so only by default. Alternative means for bringing livestock to collection and redistribution markets rarely exist for cattle and, where they do, are generally prohibitive in cost.

The principal advantages of trekking are the economies of scale generated for large herds. For example, present costs for trekking a herd of 60 cattle from any of the major markets in southern Burkina Faso to Lomé, Togo are roughly identical to the costs of trucking livestock along the same route. However, the comparative advantages of trucking begins to diminish with herds comprising more than 60 head. While delivery time for trucked livestock in the Burkina–Togo example is not likely to exceed 48 hours, a trekked herd would require seven or eight weeks to complete the journey. The opportunity costs of tying up capital for such long periods is also compounded by delays in return on investment due to interest-free credit sales which are characteristic of larger urban markets in the region.

Enhanced communications between most northern Sahelian zones and coastal markets now provide livestock traders with current market information. This allows them to ship by rail or truck during periods when prices are highest and when they can easily recover motorized transport costs. The arrival of trekked herds, however, cannot be as easily timed to take advantage of favourable market conditions. While traders frequently withhold livestock from markets during price slumps, daily grazing and guardian fees add to their costs, limiting the time period during which animals can profitably be held off the market.

access to suitable vehicles or competitive transport charges; the incorrect 'mix' of goods and passenger vehicles can, in effect, isolate pastoral producers, even when traffic counts suggest increased access to markets (Kulibaba 1991).

Regional transport policy is an issue of considerable importance where multi-country agreements regulating the allocation of freight shipped from coastal ports to interior countries serves as a driving force in transport costs and availability of suitable vehicles. This affects the supply of trucking services, including the availability of truckers willing and able to transport livestock on Sahel-to-coast back-haul routes. Transport in West Africa is highly regulated and maintains high trucking prices. Regulation also invites rent-seeking behaviour in countries with limited capacity to supervise the enforcement of regulations, and it may reduce the supply of transport serving interior-to-coast routes.

Truck transport is generally more economic and flexible than rail transport. However, the financial costs of rail shipment of livestock may be lower than truck transport (Holtzman *et al.* 1992). Along some itineraries, where rail lines exist, rail shipment of livestock may represent a cost-effective alternative to trucking. The rail line from Ouagadougou, Burkina

Faso to Abidjan, Côte d'Ivoire is one such case. Despite lower financial costs, more cattle and small ruminants are trucked from Burkina Faso to Côte d'Ivoire than sent by rail, because of poor railway management and inadequate rolling stock.

Communications
Timely communication is a high priority for livestock traders, particularly those involved in exporting. One reason for Somalia's dramatic loss of market share in the lucrative Saudi Arabian market during the second half of the 1970s and early 1980s was the poor communications within Somalia and between Somalia and the Arabian peninsula (Holtzman 1982a). Large-volume Saudi importers based in Jeddah expressed frustration with their inability to communicate with Somali exporters in a simple and timely manner (Holtzman 1982b).

A good domestic telephone system improves market efficiency and competition. Reliable telecommunications links with exporting countries are also key to maintaining a competitive position in increasingly saturated regional and international markets. Where adequate telecommunications exist, networks of information linking production and consumption markets are important in ensuring a flexible and responsive marketing system.

Livestock marketing facilities
The highest priority livestock marketing facilities are generally the actual market-places and water points. The conditions of some large urban livestock market-places, such as the Port Bouet market in Abidjan, are appalling. Although Port Bouet is the largest livestock market outside Nigeria in West Africa, it is a small, poorly drained facility without water, forage or feed supplies. Accidents involving cars and cattle are common, given the high density of settlement around the market and the fact that many traders keep their animals outside the fenced-in market-place. None the less, the facility is a valuable source of revenue for local government; this has led to extensive rent-seeking and the diversion of collected fees and taxes, and the failure to provide even minimal funds for maintenance and sound operation.

Infrastructural investments must be tailored to actual marketing operations and the needs of market participants. In cases where this is not done, such as with the installation of weighbridge scales or the construction of modern refrigerated slaughterhouses, the results are usually unsatisfactory. In the late 1970s the World Bank funded the construction of abattoirs in Yaoundé and Douala, Cameroon (Holtzman et al. 1980). Slaughter and dressing-out charges per animal were far higher at the new facilities, which were capital-intensive and employed hired labour, than at older, less modern abattoirs. Many urban butchers chose to use the old facilities, rather than pay the higher processing cost at the new abattoirs.

A related problem has emerged with refrigerated facilities, particularly where slaughter, storage and transport capacity are not complementary. A legacy of inoperative or loss-making facilities of this kind throughout

86

pastoral Africa suggests that the impulse toward modernization, rather than feasibility, has been the driving force in their construction. Where consumer preference for chilled or frozen meat does not exist; where premiums for such products cannot be captured in the market-place; where transport vehicles and tariffs are not economic; and where the maintenance of quality cannot be preserved during transport, such facilities are almost certain to require large subsidies.

Export marketing facilities
For countries exporting to international markets, investment in export marketing facilities is essential to ensure compliance with international animal health regulations which include requirements for quarantine and vaccination.

Despite becoming a major exporter of live animals to Gulf countries during the 1960s and 1970s, Somalia was never able to establish a functional, cost-effective and well-managed set of export marketing facilities. Holding grounds were invariably poorly designed, constructed and maintained. Forage production was typically inadequate and water sources were not always reliable. Furthermore, livestock traders never accepted that they had to put their animals in holding grounds for quarantine. Some traders feared mixing their healthy stock with other traders' diseased stock; others preferred simply to graze and water their export herds on the open range.

In addition, temporary holding facilities are usually required near ports. At Berbera in northern Somalia, the port through which the largest numbers of export stock passed, the temporary veterinary holding facility was never large enough or well enough managed to accommodate trade herds, particularly during the pre-*hadj* period of maximum export volumes. A major logistical problem is moving herds from distant holding grounds to temporary holding facilities at ports. In Mogadishu, herds were trekked at night to the port to await loading the following day. While this resolved potential traffic problems, it meant that trade animals were packed into penned areas that were inadequate in size and not provided with enough shade, water or feed. Physical stress on livestock immediately prior to shipment led to a worsening of condition and high in-transit mortality. Saudi importers reported that they had to recondition animals imported from Somalia on private holding grounds-cum-feedlots before they were ready for market.

Appropriate public sector roles in livestock marketing

Donor agencies are encouraging African governments to focus increasingly on limiting the public sector role to a restricted set of strategic interventions that provide needed public goods, are likely to have positive externalities and help to catalyse private sector investment and enterprise.

Consistent policies and regulations
Policies, regulations and programmes affecting the livestock subsector are formulated and implemented by numerous agencies. The Ministry of

Finance is usually the key mover in macro-economic and fiscal policy, determining what economic activity should be taxed and at what rates. Trade regulations and many aspects of trade policy affecting livestock originate typically in Ministries of Commerce. The Ministry of Livestock (or Agriculture) focuses on programmes and regulations affecting animal health and animal production. Other government agencies intervene in planning and implementing policies and regulations affecting livestock marketing, including Ministries of Industry (slaughterhouses), municipal governments (retail price controls; management of urban market facilities), and Ministries of Public Works (road construction and maintenance).

Given the number of government players taking actions or administering programmes which affect the livestock subsector, it is no surprise that some policies and regulations work at cross-purposes. The effectiveness with which policy and regulatory reform is implemented also varies greatly. Line officials working outside capital cities are often charged with interpreting and enforcing regulations that they do not understand or that they oppose. The capacity and political will of central offices to monitor and evaluate implementation of policy and regulatory reform in sub-Saharan Africa is typically very weak.

While the concept of creating an enabling environment has entered conventional wisdom, it is none the less true that private sector economic

---

Box 2. Some requirements for a positive policy environment for livestock marketing

o Minimal yet necessary taxation, which is used to maintain and enhance livestock marketing infrastructure.

o An exchange rate set by market forces rather than by fiat. Also easy convertibility of both the domestic currency and currencies of key trading partners is imperative.

o Banking regulations which allow for simple transfer of funds from export markets to the exporting country.

o A modest and rational tariff structure, where imported inputs into livestock marketing (vaccines, veterinary medicines, trucks, fuel and lubricants, railway equipment, etc.) are not heavily taxed.

o No export surcharges which penalize livestock exports in increasingly competitive regional markets.

o Simplified export registration and certification procedures, as recently developed in Niger, Burkina Faso and Mali in the form of *guichets uniques* (one-stop export processing windows).

o Simple, well-understood and consistently applied veterinary procedures for marketing and export.

o Greater transparency in policy formulation and implementation and in the management of public facilities serving the needs of producers and traders.

activity will not flourish without complementary policies and regulations. Some requirements for a positive policy environment for livestock marketing are listed in Box 2.

Taxation of livestock marketing

Governments face a basic dilemma: they need to raise funds to pay for needed facilities and services, yet they do not wish to penalize trade in livestock and other agricultural commodities and force operators into the informal sector. The governing principle should be to levy user fees on livestock producers and traders for visible, tangible services and for maintenance and upgrading of marketing facilities. There needs to be a direct relationship between payment of fees, the provision of services and improvement of facilities. All too often government agencies charge relatively high fees for control 'services' which do little if anything to improve livestock marketing, but which generate rents for the state. Funds collected end up in revenue collectors' pockets or in general municipal revenue pools; they are typically not used to upgrade facilities or improve services. As a result, livestock producers, traders and butchers resent these fees and evade paying them. Furthermore, these private sector participants begin to view government agents as illegitimate extractors of fees or rents, rather than public agents committed to serving private producers and traders.

Provision and maintenance of trek routes and water points

Governments need to provide and maintain trek routes and water points as private operators will be unlikely to find opportunities for commercial gain in such service provision. Setting user fees is problematic since trek routes are not turnpikes where livestock herds periodically pass toll booths. Livestock traders are thus likely to regard trek routes as free, public resources under government stewardship. Fees must probably be levied at market-places or through the sale of livestock movement certificates. Fee levels will need to be raised in order to recover the costs of maintaining trek routes and associated water points.

Provision and maintenance of marketing infrastructure

National transport infrastructure is a public good which has to be provided and maintained by government agencies. Such infrastructure includes roads, railways, ports, airports and waterways. User fees are directly levied for use of all of this infrastructure except roads. Charges for road use are collected indirectly through high levels of taxation of fuel and trucks, and licences, registrations and permits. Whether direct or indirect user fees cover infrastructure maintenance requirements is doubtful in much of sub-Saharan Africa, where heavy use of transport infrastructure has degraded roads and railways (Heggie 1991).

Provision and maintenance of export-specific marketing infrastructure, such as holding grounds and quarantine stations, must be financed out of user fees. Initial construction or significant upgrading is more likely to be financed by governments and donor agencies, especially if such facilities remain public. One way to obtain private finance for such facilities is to set them up as privately owned and managed operations. In northern Somalia in the early 1980s, several traders proposed establishing privately run holding and quarantine facilities (Holtzman 1982a,b, 1984). However, similar facilities would have to be closely supervised by government veterinary agents in order to meet animal health requirements for export. Governments would be wise to limit the numbers of such private facilities in order to minimize supervision costs. Groups of livestock traders could be encouraged to collaborate in establishing private facilities of sufficiently large scale. The owners could then charge other livestock traders user fees that reflected actual investment and operating costs.

Market information for key terminal markets

Many livestock marketing information systems in sub-Saharan Africa are overdesigned, unwieldy and do not serve potential users. In many francophone countries in West Africa, livestock ministries collect primary data on livestock prices and numbers of animals offered for sale for a large number of cattle and small ruminant age–sex categories. While officials readily admit that the quality of the data is dubious, once issued, even inadequate statistics acquire a sacrosanct character in government operations. Furthermore, there is typically little or no analysis of the data. Prices are simply reported by animal category and not examined in time series or in any comparative perspective.

Potential users of livestock marketing information are producers, traders and wholesale butchers. Producers are interested in knowing how the prices they are offered by traders compare with prices in other areas. Traders are keenly interested in information on market conditions in terminal markets (volume of animals sold, rapidity of sales, import data for arrivals from non-African suppliers) and price movements. Actual price levels are less relevant because of the heterogeneity of livestock. Wholesale butchers are interested in wholesale and retail prices at terminal markets. In a few cases, wholesale butchers-cum-traders may be interested in live animal prices in assembly markets.

Satisfying the diverse needs of these potential users of market information is no easy task. In establishing a system, it is advisable to choose one price transaction level and report price data in a consistent manner. Retail prices are good enough proxies for underlying wholesale prices (either for live animals or carcasses) and are also easy to collect. However, producers are not likely to be well served by retail prices, unless they monitor markets closely and understand the correspondence between prices at terminal markets and prices in rural assembly zones. Furthermore, since there is a lag between shipment of livestock from collection markets to terminal markets, there is an imperfect correspondence between retail and producer price.

Given the expanded imports of non-African meat, principally of European Community origin, into West African coastal markets during the second half of the 1980s, and continued significant levels in the early 1990s even after imposition of variable levies, a number of market participants are likely to be interested in price and supply information for chilled and frozen meat of non-African origin.

Supply and demand factors affecting the capacity of markets

Supply patterns from pastoral areas are characterized by occasional large peaks of usually low-grade meat as pastoralists destock during drought periods. The capacity of domestic and export markets to absorb such supply variations depends on a range of demand factors. Supply levels are also affected by the dumping of meat of non-African origin on local markets. This in turn affects the ability of markets to absorb supply variations from pastoral zones.

Domestic demand factors

The capacity of the domestic market to absorb additional animals may be quite limited. In trying to forecast the consumption behaviour of urban households, it is important to identify the commodity characteristics precisely: which group of urban consumers is likely to purchase the commodity, and what are the group's income, demand propensities and preferences?

The income elasticities of demand for animal products are high on aggregate in sub-Saharan Africa (meat 0.79; milk 0.68; eggs 1.05) (Sarma and Yeung 1985; Winrock 1992). As incomes increase, consumers seek to diversify their diets and buy more meat, fish, fruit, vegetables and dairy products. Rising urbanization expands total demand for red meat, but increasing numbers of low-income urban households will represent a drag on demand shifts. As poor urban consumers comprise a greater proportion of total urban consumers, demand is likely to become increasingly segmented. Wealthier consumers will buy certain types of higher-grade meat, dairy products and eggs, while lower-income consumers will purchase lower-grade meat and offal.

The lower meat prices that prevail in the event of a large increase in meat supply, brought on by a drought, increase the real income of low-income urban consumers at the margin. How they choose to use this additional income, however, is unclear. They may use it to purchase more grain or tubers, cooking oil or other household goods. The consumption behaviour of different income groups of households will depend upon the income elasticity of demand for different types of animal protein, as well as cross-price elasticities of demand among these products. Middle- and upper-income consumers in urban Africa are less likely to buy significantly greater quantities of low-grade beef and small ruminant meat than poorer consumers. Wealthier consumers are meeting their calorific and protein needs; they are not likely to buy a lot more low-grade meat simply because it is cheaper. Thus expenditures need to be disaggregated by type (and, if possible, grade) of livestock product for different socio-economic groups.

The impact of international trade and dumping

European Community (EC) dumping of low-grade, industrial beef, pork and offal on coastal West African markets during the second half of the

91

1980s depressed demand for Sahelian fresh beef and small ruminant meat in key terminal markets such as Abidjan, Côte d'Ivoire. Many Sahel-based exporters lost money during this period as coastal wholesale butchers could not pay for shipments of livestock procured on credit. In recognition of the damage done to local markets, Togo and Nigeria imposed outright bans on non-African meat imports, and Côte d'Ivoire and Cameroon imposed variable levies to offset EC export subsidies.

An important event to consider in international trade, likely to affect livestock export opportunities for some African livestock-exporting countries, is the signing of the General Agreement on Trade and Tariffs (Uruguay-round GATT) and its impact on the EC Lomé agreements. Key questions for African countries and livestock producers are:

o To what extent will EC export incentive schemes be curtailed?
o To what extent will African exporters, such as Botswana, continue to have preferential access to the European market?
o What will be the effect of CFA franc devaluation on the competitiveness of African livestock exporters to other African countries? What will the impact of CFA devaluation be upon the structure of incentives facing livestock producers and traders in francophone African countries?

Pastoral welfare interventions

Government interventions to assist livestock producers in distress, such as purchase of weakened stock at a support price, should be regarded as a form of social welfare and be explicitly accounted for as an income transfer to herders. Making such a subsidy transparent is critically important as governance, management and financial accountability have come to dominate discussions of the public sector's role in economic development. The costs of government procurement of drought-stressed livestock at above market support prices could be borne in some African countries by taxing exports of non-livestock commodities where export performance has been strong. Such cross-subsidization is usually only recommended in countries where indebtedness is not a large government burden, and where governments do not run large budget deficits. Given the fiscal stringency of IMF-funded adjustment programmes, subsidies to livestock producers are not likely to be viewed favourably.

Any scheme designed to subsidize the income of poor livestock producers is very difficult to administer. How would poor herding households be identified? How many animals would an individual household be allowed to sell? Would the number be calculated on the basis of household size or income, size of the household's herd or the number of animals sold in a prior period? Support prices would have to be set at levels that encourage poor households in risk of losing their stock to sell, but not so high as to induce wealthier producers to sell when they otherwise would withdraw from the market, bearing the cost of supplementary feeding. Finally, disposal of weakened stock would lead to heavy financial losses. Slaughter for processing (canning, refrigerating) would require costly investments in physical plant and transport. Processed red meat would be sold at a loss on both domestic or regional African markets, where consumers prefer fresh meat, and on international markets, where demand for canned meat is limited and where there is stiff competition among suppliers of low-cost chilled and frozen red meat.

Drought cropping is one way of removing excess stock from the range during periods of drought in order to avoid animal losses (World Bank 1978). This requires rapid transport of animals out of drought-afflicted zones or the ability to slaughter stock on the range and move carcasses quickly to market. Carcass meat, of course, needs to be chilled, requiring refrigeration. The capital investment requirements are high, making such a strategy economically unviable.

Small field abattoirs require modest investment compared to typically over-designed urban slaughterhouses. But since red meat demand is limited in production zones, the fresh meat still requires transport to an urban market. Some return can be salvaged, however, whereas trekking to markets would result in considerable mortality or weight loss. Yet some government intervention would be required to subsidize such a scheme. It is likely there would be a significant wedge between prices paid to producers, set at levels to try and maintain producers' terms of trade, and sale prices to private traders and butchers who would transport meat to urban markets. Alternatively, a government agency could operate a network of rural abattoirs and urban distribution centres at a loss, although this would undercut livestock traders. In sum, drought cropping and field abattoirs must be viewed primarily as social welfare schemes with limited commercial viability. Low-grade meat would not command any premium on domestic urban or international markets and a subsidy would be necessary to offset the significantly higher marketing costs (especially transport costs).

Regional projects or NGOs may be able to play a positive role in administering pastoral welfare schemes. For example, during the drought of 1993 the EC facilitated destocking in northern Kenya by purchasing livestock through a local project. The EC also provided loan funds to the Kenya Meat Commission (KMC) to can the meat from the purchased livestock. This meat was later distributed by UN agencies to a large number of Somali refugees camped in the area (Kerven 1994, pers. comm.). The scheme faltered when the KMC did not repay the EC the loan advanced for canning, but EC-funded purchases of livestock did help to bolster prices at a critical time.

Despite these difficulties, the costs of policy inaction in the pastoral zone may be high. Failing to intervene on behalf of livestock producers facing drought, forced destocking and adverse terms of trade may lead to longer-run destitution of pastoralists. As individual herds are decimated or reach such a low level that they cannot come close to sustaining a pastoral livelihood, livestock producers will be forced to settle in urban areas or take up alternative occupations, such as irrigated agriculture or off-farm employment. One way to counter such shifts is to provide herders with food aid during droughts (and perhaps for some time afterward) and with breeding stock on (most likely subsidized) credit during post-drought rehabilitation (Toulmin this book).

Conclusions

Ensuring the efficiency of opportunism requires flexible and responsive marketing systems for livestock. The most effective way of reducing price and supply instability is to improve marketing efficiency. This requires less attention to intervention in the regulation of supply through government price support, parastatal marketing boards and subsidized marketing costs, but more attention paid to improving market competitiveness and the efficiency of private marketing operations. This requires a public policy and investment focus on improving market infrastructure, ensuring effective communications and deregulation to encourage increased competition. Investments in market infrastructure must be tailored to actual marketing operations and the needs of market participants, rather than a zeal to modernize. Government roles thus are focused on ensuring a positive marketing environment, while maintaining standards (particularly for the export trade) and providing safety nets in its social welfare role.

6. Tracking through drought: options for destocking and restocking

CAMILLA TOULMIN

This chapter aims to examine strategies for dealing with the effects of drought on the pastoral sector. It begins by describing the broader context within which the pastoral sector must operate, which sets the constraints for dealing with drought effectively. It then examines patterns of pasture and livestock productivity, and relative prices of livestock and grain, at different stages in the cycle of drought and recovery. Tracking measures to destock and restock herds, to mirror changing patterns of pasture productivity, are described within this framework of change. The chapter concludes that the range of options available for mitigating drought depends greatly on the circumstances of people and place, and the extent to which there is some slack within the system. Drought is but one of numerous risks faced by the small-scale pastoral producer (Perrier this book). Other areas of policy intervention also require urgent attention if the sector as a whole is to survive the adverse trends of recent decades.

The pastoralists of dryland Africa demonstrate a diverse range of adaptations to the risk and uncertainty they face in daily life. Adaptation and risk avoidance are possible through maintaining mixed herds containing different animal species, being mobile and developing other forms of income to supplement herding, such as farming, woodcutting and trade. At the same time, people's adaptations change as conditions alter, so that a snapshot of pastoral life today is but one in a sequence of moving images.

Several longer-term forces provide a background against which are set these processes of continual adaptation and change. Such forces include ecological and climatic trends, political and economic marginalization of pastoral communities, widespread alienation of areas formerly used for grazing, and substantial shifts in animal ownership patterns (NOPA 1992). Such rapid and far-reaching changes are already having a major impact on how pastoral systems operate in dryland regions. Policies of neglect and of inappropriate project interventions within pastoral areas have further weakened the capacity of such systems to operate effectively and yet, this chapter contends, mobile transhumant patterns of livestock production remain the most environmentally benign and effective means for using the highly variable grazing of dryland areas.

95

Attention must urgently be paid by national governments and donor agencies to the costs of continued neglect, in terms of the economic, environmental, social and cultural losses sustained by pastoral communities across the continent. Such losses will continue to sap the ability of the pastoral sector to deal with drought, until decisions are taken to address positively the particular needs of these producers.

An opportunistic tracking strategy for dealing with drought

Little control can be exercised over the instability of non-equilibrium grazing systems. Hence, policy and interventions must work to make best use of such variability, by maximizing use of resources in good years and minimizing costs in years of low rainfall. Such a policy orientation has been termed an opportunistic management strategy (Sandford 1983) and it clearly approximates to what herders try to achieve themselves.

A tracking strategy aims to match changes in animal numbers with changes in the availability of grazing. Figure 1 presents a typical drought sequence, in which rainfall failure leads to a fall in pasture production and a collapse in the number of livestock able to be supported. In subsequent years, as rainfall improves, pastures recover their former productivity fairly rapidly. In contrast to vegetation, when herd losses have been substantial, it may take a long time for animal numbers to re-establish themselves. As a result, much grazing will be wasted, and considerable hardship suffered by those whose living depends on pastoral production.

Strategies aimed at timely destocking and restocking of livestock numbers have the dual advantage of taking animals off the land sufficiently early in a drought to avoid causing long-term damage to vegetation and soils, and of reconstituting the livestock economy in the post-drought period. However, as will be shown below, the mechanisms for destocking and restocking effectively are complex, and programmes attempting to intervene in this field have had mixed experience. Design of such programmes must tackle questions of equity, and how to transfer livestock entitlements from the drought period to the recovery period. They must also examine the broader political economy of pastoral production in the region, including issues of resource tenure (Lane and Moorehead this book) and livestock marketing opportunities (Holtzman and Kulibaba this book).

Re-establishment of pastoral herds in the post-drought period is particularly difficult because of the typical pattern of animal price movements over the drought cycle (see Figure 1). While prices tend to plummet as the drought lengthens, and as herders try to salvage something from emaciated beasts, once conditions improve the relative scarcity of animals ensures that they command a good price.

Breeding stock are in particularly high demand. At the same time, in each of the recent African droughts, livestock have been bought up increasingly by absentee herd owners, who invest in animals as one among a number of assets. The broad base of their income and wealth enables them to withstand more easily the impact of drought, since they can fall back upon other resources. Drought crises also provide an opportunity for

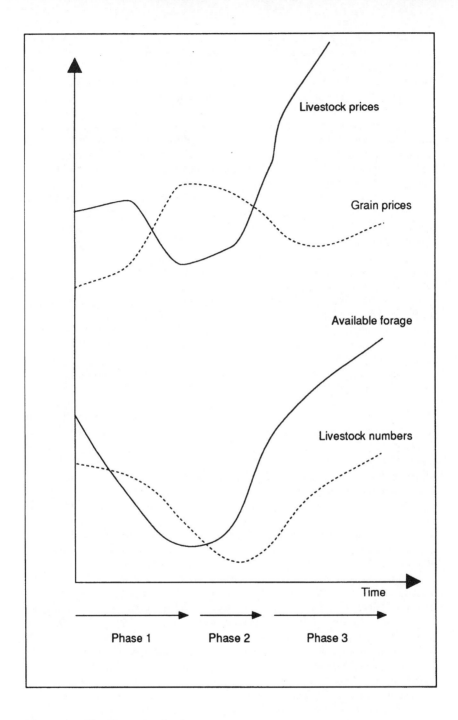

Figure 1: *The Drought Cycle*

investors to buy up stock at cheap rates, where they have the means either to maintain these animals through supplementary feeding, or to transport them for sale at a profit elsewhere. Hence, the recovery of pastoral communities post-drought is often slow, and increasingly hindered by the economic strategies of other livestock-owning interests.

In the case of West Africa, there is the additional problem faced by Sahelian producers of substantial in-roads having been made into their traditional coastal meat markets, by frozen meat imports, particularly from the European Community. Highly subsidized, these imports have undercut prices, and greatly reduced returns from livestock sales (Madden 1993; Holtzman and Kulibaba this book).

At the same time, the classic cycle of herd accumulation, drought, impoverishment and a rebuilding of herds characteristic of many pastoral systems (Dupire 1962; Haaland 1977) no longer seems to operate so effectively. Taking a Sahelian example, Dupire's description of cyclical wealth accumulation, followed by severe drought-induced impoverishment, followed by hard work and subsequent herd reconstitution, depends on a degree of flexibility and slack being present within production systems (Dupire 1962). Due to pressures on land and other resources, and persistently low rainfall since the late 1960s, such a passage from wealth to poverty to wealth is no longer so easy. Today, impoverishment among pastoralists seems to lead more assuredly to further privation, rather than a return to viability.

As each drought occurs, patterns of pasture and animal management and ownership change further in a manner which will constrain future development options. For example, where there is a significant number of absentee herd owners with major investment in animals, they will themselves constitute a powerful political force aiming to influence decisions in their favour. This is likely to be particularly true in the case of changes to resource tenure rules. Attempts may be made to block or subvert reforms where these would lead to a tightening of rules of access to pasture and water that would prevent easy access by 'outsiders' to grazing resources. As noted by a recent review of pastoral associations in the Sahel, the presence of substantial numbers of absentee herd owners can seriously damage an association's ability to identify common interests and enforce decisions regarding natural resource management and use (Shanmugaratnam et al. 1992; Sylla this book).

Neglect by government and donors of drought-related issues and the implications for pastoral society, livestock ownership and herd management, will likely lead to further growth in animals owned by those outside the small-scale sector. The probable consequences will be:

○ Growing impoverishment amongst those periodically hit by drought and rendered increasingly unable to re-enter the pastoral economy, with the consequent loss of their skills and numbers to pastoral society;
○ Weakening of many pastoral households' ability to make ends meet, and their need to adopt strategies which are themselves likely to produce negative consequences for herd and pasture productivity (as when there

are substantial outflows of migrant labour during the dry season to earn cash, at a time when intensive labour is needed to water and pasture animals); and

o A decline in the confidence, cultural cohesion and overall capacity of pastoral society to reproduce itself.

Ultimately, a position will be reached where the small-scale pastoral sector is no longer able to be reconstituted, since it will have been damaged— economically, socially and culturally—beyond repair.

Interventions within the drought cycle

The options for moderating the impact of drought on the pastoral sector can usefully be discussed by dividing the drought period into three phases. Levels of and trends in pasture production, livestock numbers and productivity, cereal availability and relative prices all constrain what can be achieved within each phase, as is shown in Figure 1.

In phase one, drought brings about a fall in available forage throughout the system. It is assumed here that drought conditions are sufficiently harsh and widespread for extensive movement to be unable to compensate for falling fodder availability. Livestock numbers start to fall, through sales and deaths among the most vulnerable. However, despite such animal losses, there remains an overall imbalance between livestock numbers and available fodder. As drought hits harder, bringing failure of cereal harvests and deteriorating animal condition, grain prices rise while livestock prices fall. These relative price movements provide an increasingly tight squeeze on herders' ability to raise cash to buy the food needed by their families. Thus, herders may be forced to sell animals far in excess of those required to bring animal numbers into balance with fodder available, and thus compromise their ability to reconstitute a viable pastoral existence in the post-drought period.

In phase two, herd numbers continue to fall, as sales and deaths continue, despite the levelling off and gradual improvement in fodder availability. Shortages of grain continue to keep food prices high, although these levels will be somewhat moderated where food aid is delivered in substantial quantities (Coles 1989). Meanwhile, there is continuing pressure on herders to sell further stock in order to purchase food.

In phase three, with improved rainfall, fodder production starts to recover, yet livestock numbers remain well below the level which could make effective use of the available grazing. Some households may still be under pressure to sell stock, due to food shortages. A few lucky ones may be able to start reconstituting herds. As pasture conditions improve and post-drought harvests start coming in, a rapid inversion of relative grain to livestock prices takes place. Cereal prices fall, while the price of animals starts to rise rapidly, given the shortage of animals and the greater likelihood of their survival now that grazing is available. Since many herders would like to reconstitute their herds, the demand for animals—particularly young breeding stock—is very high, pushing up prices.

Given these various trends in pasture availability, livestock numbers and relative price movements, a range of interventions can be designed to moderate the effects of drought within the particular constraints encountered within each phase of the drought cycle. Early warning systems attempt to monitor these trends in order to prompt interventions appropriate to the circumstances faced (see Box 2).

Phase one: the initial crash

The main imbalance to be addressed in this phase is the excess of animal numbers over fodder availability. Thus, either animals can be taken out of the drought-affected system, through slaughter and movement elsewhere, or fodder can be brought in to permit the survival of certain animals.

Destocking options
There are basically two destocking options open to pastoralists. These are:

○ Animals can be sold, while still in good shape, either for meat or to another owner who has better access to fodder.
○ Where animals are already in very poor condition, some value can be salvaged from them through slaughter and sale of meat and hides.

Where meat markets are well developed and there is sufficient slaughter and cold storage capacity, large numbers of stock can be taken off the range relatively quickly, enabling farmers to minimize losses from death and declining weight and condition. Receipts from commercial sales can be banked for subsequent reinvestment when conditions have improved. Such cases are found for the commercial farm sector in African countries such as Zimbabwe, Botswana and Kenya. Here, however, there are usually restrictions on the grading of cattle which can be accepted, as well as disease controls, which may prevent access to such market outlets for many small-scale herders.

In countries such as Australia, computer models have been developed for commercial sheep farmers facing drought conditions to help them think through the implications of different destocking options. The main parameters within these models include costs of supplementary feed, livestock price trends and possibilities of hiring in land elsewhere, given alternative assumptions about the possible duration of the drought and consequent risks to stock. Over a period of several decades, the best strategy developed by the models maintains high stock densities, with rapid and substantial destocking as soon as pasture conditions worsen substantially. However, there will be some years when cash flow is substantially negative with this approach. A more conservative stocking regime brings fewer risks to cash flow, but lower aggregate returns over several decades. The models conclude that it is usually very damaging to adopt a 'wait-and-see' policy (Stafford-Smith and Foran 1990; Foran and Stafford-Smith 1991).

Voluntary destocking by small-scale herders in Africa is not well documented. Partly, as noted above, they tend not to have access to formal marketing channels capable of absorbing large numbers of animals at reasonable prices. Instead, they must rely on opportunities at local and more distant markets, weighing up price differentials, costs of moving animals from one to another and risks of substantial loss from moving weakened animals long distance (Holtzman and Kulibaba, this book). In a comparison of strategies pursued by pastoralists in the droughts of the 1970s set against the 1980s, recent research has found evidence of a far greater willingness to sell animals early in the drought cycle in the latter period, than was evident earlier (FAO 1992). This suggests that many herders learned from the earlier droughts that holding on to animals as drought conditions intensify may not be the best way of ensuring their own survival.

Policies for forced destocking from the small-scale sector, practised mainly in the colonial period, as a means of reducing the perceived problem of 'overgrazing' within pastoral areas, provoked great resistance (Tignor 1976). More recently, certain projects have attempted to impose tight limits on livestock numbers, but usually with an overall range management objective, rather than specifically in relation to drought mitigation (such as the GTZ-funded sylvo-pastoral programme in the Ferlo region of Senegal and the Hado project in central Tanzania (Kerkhoff 1990)).

Evidence from several cases can be found of organizations trying to support herders desperate to gain something from emaciated animals, by buying and slaughtering them. In northern Mali, in the mid-1980s, Vétérinaires sans Frontières bought animals in the Léré area for slaughter and subsequently dried the meat for use in emergency feeding camps. Similarly, Oxfam in Kenya supported the purchase of animals from Samburu communities in 1984–5, among a series of measures aimed at mitigating the effects of drought upon these pastoralists.

Movement of livestock
The traditional response of herders to fodder shortage in times of drought has been to move elsewhere. This continues to be a crucially important mechanism for transferring grazing pressure from areas of deficit to those of surplus. Such movement is possible where secondary rights of access exist for herders to bring their animals into areas they do not usually use. However, mobility as a means of coping with drought runs into serious constraints where drought conditions are so widespread that herders must go far beyond those regions with which they are familiar. Extensive movement brings its own risks, in terms of animals finding the fodder unfamiliar and indigestible, greater exposure to disease and conflict with local peoples unaccustomed to harbouring pastoral herds. In many areas, also, there has been a tightening of rules controlling access to grazing, given changes in tenure, increased population growth, extension of farming and the establishment of irrigation and other projects. In addition, drought conditions are likely to increase competition for scarce fodder between local animals and herds from elsewhere, further constraining access in such periods for those with weak claims to exploit local pastures.

For the Sahel in the period following the 1973 drought, it was suggested that areas of irrigated agriculture, such as the Office du Niger rice- and sugar-growing scheme in central Mali should be used as a holding ground, providing fodder for the most valuable and vulnerable classes of stock in years of drought (SCET 1976). However, there is no evidence for such a plan having been put into effect during the subsequent drought of 1984, nor is it clear how it would have been done in practice. Herders already bring their animals to the harvested rice fields of the Office du Niger towards the end of the dry season, since it provides a fairly reliable source of water and forage at this time. One might expect an intensification of such linkages in times of drought. However, many irrigation schemes are often difficult for drought-stricken herds to reach and use. In many cases, livestock owner-ship and access to grazing have not been encouraged in the design and management of irrigation schemes. As drought conditions will also hit irrigated areas as well as rainfed production, irrigating farmers may be unwilling to see their few crops threatened by the arrival of other people's herds (Sørbo 1992).

Within rainfed areas of Sahelian West Africa, drought years witness a lengthening of the normal pattern of movement practised by transhumant herders. However, such movement is constrained increasingly by pressures on available grazing resources, changing rules of resource tenure and a tightening of national boundaries. Much movement by herds in drought years may become more permanent as pastoralists recognize the need for access to more assured grazing. For example, it is estimated that the national cattle herd of Côte d'Ivoire grew very substantially in the years following the droughts of 1973 and 1984, with many Sahelian Fulani entering and settling permanently in the northern part of the country (Herman and Makinen 1980).

In the case of Zimbabwe, during the very severe drought of 1991–2, some communal area herds have been able to exploit the grazing resources of commercial farms nearby, which had been far less affected by drought due to their lower stocking levels. While such grazing was illicit, and constituted 'poaching', in many cases commercial farmers turned a blind eye in the interests of maintaining good relations with neighbouring communities (Scoones 1992b).

Within commercialized systems, farmers often hire grazing elsewhere, to provide for certain animals and transport their stock by truck or rail. Whether or not the farmer does this will depend on the cost and avail-ability of such grazing, in relation to both expected returns from the transported stock and the costs of pursuing some other option. In Zimbabwe, a government proposal was developed in 1984 to examine such a strategy in the event of future droughts (Zimbabwe 1984). This would have involved intervention to take certain classes of cattle from communal areas to graze in the national parks. The conclusion reached was that such a policy would only pay for itself if the animals were transported one way. However, no suggestions were made regarding how those animals saved from drought would subsequently be used, nor whether their original owners would be able to claim them.

Transport of fodder
While the purchase of fodder from elsewhere is a regular activity for many commercial ranchers, it is relatively rare for small-scale herders. When drought strikes, it must be decided whether to support purchase and distribution of fodder to the small-scale sector and, if so, on what terms. There are various options, including:

○ Provision of credit to allow herders to buy their own fodder;
○ Subsidized transport and distribution of fodder; and
○ Establishment of animal feeding centres to which fodder can be brought.

Information about such schemes comes from Zimbabwe, where the costs and returns from the distribution of fodder in the form of briquettes was examined (Zimbabwe 1984); from the Sudan, where groundnut cake was distributed in the Kordofan region (FAO 1992); and from the Sahel, where groundnut and cottonseed cake and agro-industrial by-products for feedstuffs (such as molasses, rice bran, etc.) were provided during the drought.

In all cases, provision of feed only makes sense to a selected group of animals of high value, who would probably otherwise die (Bayer and Waters-Bayer this book). Animal feed is usually bulky and expensive to transport. In some cases, agro-industrial by-products already find a ready market within the country, or as exports. Where draught oxen are used for ploughing, fodder supplies must also be available, since loss of oxen would damage substantially the country's capacity to grow food grains. Re-allocation of fodder to drought mitigation amongst pastoral herds will then have a significant opportunity cost. Emergency feeding is unlikely to be an economic strategy for keeping alive a large number of animals. Although the transport and administration of such animal feeding schemes are minimized when animals to be fed are kept in an enclosure, such methods then raise another series of questions about who will care for the selected animals, and on what terms owners will be able to claim their animals following the drought.

Provision of credit
Credit can be provided to enable herders to buy fodder or to pay for transport of their herds to better grazing areas. Little evidence has been found on this form of intervention as a means of mitigating the impact of drought. Pastoral credit schemes are infrequent, and have mainly concerned restocking, the purchase of grain and money for investment in trade (Oxby 1989; Martin *et al.* 1992; Shanmugaratnam *et al.* 1992). While credit can play a very useful role in generating further economic activity, it is vital to clarify and agree the terms under which credit is being supplied and to whom (Swift this book). Evaluation of project work among pastoral associations in Chad has demonstrated the much greater effectiveness of loans given to individuals, rather than those given to the group as a whole (Martin *et al.* 1992).

Drought-proofing
There are means by which small-scale pastoral systems can be made less vulnerable to drought, through improving productivity levels (Bayer and

103

Waters-Bayer this book). To date, the evidence is patchy, but experiments with hay collection and cultivation of grain plots within rainwater harvesting structures provide some basis for hope. Similarly, indigenous breeds, able physiologically to adapt as drought conditions worsen, offer greater potential than the conventional reliance on exotic breeds. The greatest potential for improving pasture productivity lies in the development of high value, rainfall run-on areas—such as *bas-fonds, dambos, vleis, fadama* (Scoones 1991). However, it is precisely these high value resources which are under greatest threat from rival users. Clarification and enforcement of resource tenure rules remain therefore central elements in all pastoral development strategies.

Questions raised by destocking programmes
A number of important questions are raised by destocking experience to date, to which no clear answers can be given.

○ Will support of livestock prices encourage destocking by small-scale pastoralists? And at what level should this support be given?
○ In what form should money be held from sales, to enable subsequent restocking? How could herders be assured of the transfer of livestock entitlements' from the pre- to post-drought period? For example, would destocking best be achieved through the promise of x animals in the post-drought period in return for having destocked y animals early in the drought (with $x < y$)?
○ What happens to prices, and systems of transport and marketing, if everyone destocks at once?
○ What other useful inputs can be supplied to support destocking measures, such as mobile abattoirs, radio programmes giving information about livestock prices, or radio interviews with herders reflecting on their strategies, past and present?
○ What role can usefully be played by high-technology monitoring systems, to alert and inform pastoralists about grazing conditions in different areas? There is very little experience or evaluation of such programmes. However, the little evidence available would suggest that such formal systems play only a very minor role in the provision of information to herders (Touré 1990).

Phase two: the bottom of the drought cycle

During this period, animal numbers have already fallen below fodder availability and yet, herd numbers continue to fall, due to a continued squeeze on herders' incomes and their need for cash. Possibilities for intervention in this period include:

○ Provision of food aid to relieve pressure on food prices and supply grain directly to pastoral populations;
○ Credit to fund purchases of cereals, and avoid unnecessary sales of livestock; and
○ Support to livestock prices.

104

Following the drought of 1984–5 in the Red Sea Hills of eastern Sudan, provision of large amounts of food aid led to a 50 per cent drop in cereal prices, greatly relieving the pressure on herders' incomes (Coles 1989). Such a major impact on food prices was probably due to the large quantity of food imported in the post-1984 period, and the advantageous position of the Red Sea Hills close to the main port of entry, Port Sudan. Elsewhere, evidence is less clear for food aid having had a major effect on improving people's ability to cope, either through direct provision or as a result of falling grain prices. For example, in the case of Darfur in 1984–5 it is argued that food aid had a negligible direct effect on survival rates (de Waal 1989).

Phase three: the begininnings of recovery

In this phase, rainfall, grain harvests and pasture conditions have recovered from the previous drought conditions. By contrast, animal numbers are much lower than in the pre-drought period and, in some cases, herd size is still falling, due to the difficulties faced by many impoverished households, who must continue to sell animals to purchase their cereal requirements. Some pastoral households have become totally destitute and must receive food relief. Others may leave some of their members, while taking off their few remaining animals to distant pastures, in the hope of reconstituting herd numbers.

Traditional mechanisms for restocking after drought

Pastoral households have a variety of mechanisms to restock their herds and flocks following drought. In some cases, the household may be able to rebuild assets through a variety of means, and thereby re-enter the pastoral economy. However, as noted earlier, it is probably more difficult than formerly to reconstitute herds by spending a few years farming, and re-investing harvests in livestock, due to increased pressures on available farm-land.

Many pastoral societies have a tradition whereby animals are loaned between households and friends. For example, the *habbanae* system of cattle loans amongst the Fulani of West Africa has been widely documented, as have stock friendships among many east African pastoral groups (NOPA 1992). However, where drought conditions have been widespread and all households badly hit, there will be few surplus animals available for such arrangements. At the same time, some observers have argued that there has been a decline in the incidence of such mechanisms of solidarity, given increased individualism and market orientation amongst producers. Such loans were never a means by which all could have access to sufficient animals to enable their survival, but rather a means by which relations between households could be consolidated. The most marginal social groups (such as the poorest, those with weak kinship links to better-off households, widows and divorcees) would be unlikely to have access to these animal loans even in normal times.

Illegal methods of acquiring livestock may be important for certain

105

groups, where government authority is weak. Currently, cattle raiding appears to be far more prevalent in east, than in West Africa. It is difficult to judge, in the absence of any data, how important such mechanisms are for individual families. However, since access to armed men is likely to be associated with wealth, raiding tends to result in a redistribution of livestock from weaker to stronger members of society.

Post-drought rehabilitation

Options for intervention in the third phase of the drought cycle range from those aimed at rehabilitating the livestock sector, by enabling the destitute to re-enter pastoral production, and reducing pressures on herders' incomes, to those encouraging a major shift to other forms of livelihood. They include:

○ Restocking of pastoralists;
○ Food aid;
○ Support to diversification of incomes;
○ Credit;
○ Irrigation scheme development;
○ Other forms of crop production;
○ Doing nothing.

Here, attention will be given to restocking since, as was noted earlier, there are strong arguments in favour of both retaining a small-scale pastoral sector in dryland Africa, and making use of excess pasture resources in the post-drought period. Of all interventions to moderate the impact of drought on pastoral communities, restocking has received the greatest attention. Several studies have already been undertaken to examine the options available within restocking programmes, such as the number and species of animals to be distributed per household, choice of recipients and terms on which animals are distributed (Toulmin 1986; Fry 1988; Oxby 1989, 1994; Moris 1988; Kelly 1993). The objectives put forward by restocking programmes include the following three.

Making use of available grazing. With pasture conditions returning to normal, but animal numbers greatly diminished, there exists a large gap between the supply of and demand for fodder. This gap represents a waste of grazing resources, which could be transformed into valuable livestock products. In the absence of grazing animals, such fodder will rot or be consumed by wild animals, termites or bush fires. It may be necessary for some grazing ecosystems to have a period of time to recover from drought, permitting the re-establishment of plant cover, germination and growth of bushes and reconstitution of seed reserves in the soil. Low grazing intensity for a couple of years post-drought should encourage such a recovery. However, a prolonged absence of grazing from an area may have serious long-term adverse consequences. For example, in areas where grazing pressure is very light, former areas of grassland may become invaded by shrubs and trees that have low fodder value. Low grazing pressure also brings increased risks of damage by hot bush fires.

Assuring rights to grazing lands. Land that is not clearly being occupied and exploited will risk encroachment from other people—for grazing or farming—as they may argue that it is not being put to good use.

Remobilizing the destitute. It is a waste for destitute pastoralists to be stuck in food relief camps. First, their specific knowledge and skills are not being put to good use, nor do they necessarily have interests or skills of particular value for alternative production systems, such as irrigated farming. Second, it is expensive to provide food aid to such populations. Third, there are costs in terms of social justice and cultural cohesion, since the destitute have usually lost, not only their means of making a living, but also their ability to take part in the broader society of which they have been part. Enabling them to become self-sufficient producers provides them with the capacity to meet not only their food needs, but also their social obligations.

Experience with restocking pastoralists

Almost all restocking programmes have been carried out by NGOs, on a fairly small scale, usually dealing with a few hundred households at most. This localized, small-scale focus reflects the overall constraints of establishing a restocking programme, in terms of the availability of large numbers of stock for distribution and the underlying concern, felt by some agencies, that restocking will only lead to overgrazing in the near future. Emphasis on the small scale is also a reflection of most NGO approaches to development, whether agricultural, pastoral or more generally. Close contact with particular villages or camps tends to encourage greater levels of responsiveness by NGOs to local needs than is true of large donor or government programmes. However, the impact of such small-scale activities is, inevitably, limited. In addition, NGOs have often developed projects without considering the broader national and regional context within which they must operate, and the longer-term trends that will ultimately affect the viability of their interventions at the local level (Hogg 1992).

The approach taken by restocking programmes has varied greatly, according to circumstances and the experience of the implementing agency. Terms have varied from the loan of a couple of heifers per family, to the gift of 80 small stock, accompanied by a year's supply of grain, a donkey and household equipment. The cost of interventions consequently varies greatly. A comparison of this sort is shown below in Table 1, which compares alternative restocking packages pursued in the period following the drought of 1984 (Toulmin 1986). As can be seen, there is a wide range of costs per household, depending on the number of animals involved and other items included within the distribution. The programme with the highest cost per household provided animals worth between three and four years' supply of food grains.

An assessment of restocking as a method of mitigating the impact of drought also needs to set costs of restocking against those of other forms of intervention, or of doing nothing. A common alternative strategy has been the attempt to settle impoverished pastoralists in irrigated agriculture. Costs per household of such an option are usually very high, with

Table 1. Projects giving credit for herd reconstitution (Toulmin 1986)

Scheme and place	Number animals allocated per household and species	Index of cost per household*	Number households restocked	Framework of scheme
Tin Aicha, NE Mali	1–3 cows, 1–3 sheep, depending on size of household	220	200	Part of settlement scheme for desti- tute nomads
Relance du Mouvement Cooperatif, NE Mali	5–10 small stock, largely goats	100	5 000	Part of pro- gramme to re-establish herder co-op- eratives, including setting up grain reserves, irrigation, etc.
Oxfam, Gourma Mali	20–30 small stock	600	45	Part of wider programme to establish her- der associa- tions, grain stores, credit fund
Government of Niger	Average of 1 cow, 1 sheep, 2 goats	186	no data	Herd reconsti- tution scheme funded through the *Caisse Nationale de Credit Agricole*
Oxfam/habba- nae, Niger	2–3 cattle plus some small stock and transport animals	200–215	300	Project for des- titute herders
USAID, Niger	1-2 cattle	100–200	200	Part of Niger Range and Li- vestock Project setting up co- ops, credit fund, etc.
UNHCR, SE Ethiopia	1 cow, 1 donkey, 2–3 sheep & goats	no data	no data	Resettle refu- gee Somalis
LMB, NE Ethiopia	2 cows, 2 camels, 12 sheep and 15 goats proposed	400	5000	Redistribute post-drought livestock popu- lation, aid destitute
Oxfam, Kenya	50–80 small stock, pack animals, domestic equipment and grain	1 600–1 700	70	Pilot for more extensive pro- ject in 1985–6

* Index based on 100=US$75 in 1984

108

estimates ranging from US$17 000 to $60 000 per hectare in northern Kenya (Hogg 1985), and annual running costs frequently exceeding the expected annual output. 'Doing nothing' may be the easiest course for governments to follow post-drought since the cost of providing food aid is usually borne by outside agencies. In addition, it has been common to assert that pastoralists are largely to blame for their own impoverishment (due to overgrazing and their irrational attachment to their herds), and that a substantial shake-out of households is necessary to achieve a better balance between livestock numbers and the environment.

Restocking in Kenya
Much of the recent work on restocking has been carried out in Kenya, by Oxfam, and this body of experience provides a valuable source of information regarding the problems encountered and issues which must be considered before embarking on such a programme (Fry 1988; Moris 1988; Kelly 1993). Restocking projects have been undertaken amongst the Boran of Isiolo district, the Somali of Wajir, the Turkana of Turkana district and the Samburu of Samburu district. In addition, over recent years, restocking projects have been run by several Christian missions in north-east Kenya to help rehabilitate drought victims. There are many issues which need to be considered in establishing a restocking scheme (Fry 1988; Oxby 1989; Kelly 1993). The main issues are listed in Box 1 and discussed further below.

Restocking schemes have tended to distribute animals drawn from a relatively local area, to avoid problems of disease, and animals being unfamiliar with local grazing conditions. Thus, the main effect of restocking has been to redistribute animals within an area, rather than to increase substantially overall livestock numbers. Such redistribution has allowed impoverished families to become mobile again, spreading out over a much

---

Box 1. Restocking schemes: issues to be considered

○ Number and kind of species to be distributed

○ Number of households to be restocked

○ Choice of recipient households

○ Terms of the distribution—loan or gift?

○ Timing

○ Selection and purchase of animals

○ Associated equipment

○ Other supporting inputs, such as animal health

○ Monitoring

○ Broader policy research and networking activities to improve the resilience of pastoralists to future droughts.

109

wider area and, thereby, reducing problems of localized grazing pressure. The agency involved in restocking provides a ready market for those fortunate livestock owners who have been able to retain sufficient numbers of their own animals, or those who were able to buy up stock and care for them during the drought crisis. In an evaluation of Oxfam's work in northern Kenya, concern is expressed regarding the large sums of money being paid out to Somali livestock traders for purchase of goats to enable restocking to be undertaken (Fry 1988). Given the large number of animals being sought for distribution, it is hard to know what alternatives would have been possible.

Most restocking schemes have relied on small stock, especially goats, due to their resilience in adverse conditions, and relative speed of reproduction in comparison with cattle or camels. Their divisibility also permits occasional sales without diminishing greatly the viability of the herd.

In terms of herd numbers, Oxfam's experience supports a policy of giving enough animals for pastoral households to become self-sufficient. While the distribution of, say, five goats to 1000 families would clearly have wider impact than of 100 goats to 50 families, in the former case, there would be little impact on the overall viability of those 1000 households. It would be better to give them cash. Oxfam has also made available to restocked households a variety of other goods, such as a year's supply of grain, an animal for transport, and several items of household equipment, such as a cooking pot, jerrycan for water, rope and bucket. The justification is that saving money, by keeping costs to a minimum, will not achieve the overall objective of re-establishing the small-scale pastoral sector.

Choosing which households to restock has been determined by the desire to reconstitute viable production units. Hence, chosen households have usually needed to contain enough labour to care for animals and a willingness to become mobile again. It is clear that restocking cannot be seen as a way of rehabilitating the most vulnerable and impoverished of households, who lack the labour needed to become independent again. For them, other options may need to be considered, which involve a shift away from a mobile pastoral economy.

The terms offered to restocked households have varied from loans to be repaid within a certain number of years, to the outright gift of animals. Arguments can be drawn up in favour of either policy. Some households note the advantage to them of it being known that animals are on loan, rather than a gift, since this makes them less the target of envy, and of importuning relatives. Animals repaid through loans provide an important source of animals for restocking further households, thus spreading the benefit of the programme. However, loans are complex and expensive to administer. Repayments have frequently been designed on assumptions which turn out to be over-optimistic (for example, taking goat reproduction rates of 25–30 per cent per year, when actual rates are often closer to half of these). Hence, in some cases, households have been made to repay animal loans before they have attained any degree of independence, thus impoverishing them again, in order for these animals to be loaned on to other households being restocked. Conclusions from Oxfam's work suggest that it may often be better to give animals outright, rather than establish systems of repayment (Fry 1988). In such cases, choice of households for restocking becomes particularly important as recipients are being provided with very substantial windfall assets. An alternative approach to a formal system of livestock loans might be to encourage restocked households to consider other ways in which they might repay their debt to the funding agency, or to the broader community (Kerven, pers. comm.). This broader reciprocity would fit better with traditional norms, than the return of a precise number of animals on a given date.

Following any crisis, there will be some people better able than others to survive and reconstitute their holdings (such as those with access to other sources of income, good luck and contacts). The timing of restocking initiatives needs to recognize people's own capacity for rehabilitation and allow sufficient time for such processes to get under way. Otherwise, there is the risk that project interventions substitute for such mechanisms.

Arrangements must be made for the selection and purchase of animals for restocking. Project staff are often not the best judge of good stock, and may end up choosing animals which no one really wants. One alternative is to provide people with cash to buy their own animals. The risk here is that some part of the cash may be used for other purposes.

Other inputs may also be necessary to support restocked herds, in particular provision of veterinary services, to ensure greater survival rates. In several of the Oxfam projects, veterinary services were an integral part of the overall programme. Support to pastoral organization and institution building at the local level are also important auxiliary activities that may greatly strengthen the capacity of pastoral communities to withstand drought in future (Sylla this book).

While it is very useful to have detailed information on the performance of restocked households, monitoring of restocked households can be very costly to carry out well, and may impose constraints on the easy movement of restocked families away from project headquarters.

Local level work is clearly vital to support the particular households covered by a restocking exercise, but important work also needs to be done at higher levels, to inform and influence decisions made regarding national policy which affects the pastoral sector. Hogg (1992) argues that NGOs tend to be particularly weak in this respect. The establishment of an alliance between pastoral organizations, NGOs and the policy research sector is probably a prerequisite for engendering effective debate and lobbying to take place within government and among the relevant agencies within a given country (NOPA 1992).

Consequences of regular restocking interventions
Thought must be given to the possible consequences of having regular restocking programmes in a given pastoral area, in terms of the likely changes in strategy pursued by herders, who expect such programmes to be implemented. On the positive side, it has been argued that if herders have greater assurance of access to animals through a restocking programme, they will be more willing to destock early in a drought, thus

minimizing herd losses and reducing the need for large-scale destocking and restocking programmes. On the other hand, the assurance of future restocking might discourage households from making their own efforts to rehabilitate themselves, since they might contrast their own hard work to become viable again with the windfall gains of a fellow household which receives a large number of animals and other goods, having failed to rehabilitate themselves. Although there is insufficient evidence as yet to judge the strength of these differing effects, given the very limited number of households benefitting from restocking programmes, the latter effect is likely to be minor.

Contingency plans and early warning systems

Early warning systems provide a means by which to monitor changing conditions during a cycle of drought and to respond appropriately. But do administrators and politicians take any notice of early warning systems? Does the science of prediction and anticipation have an impact on the ground? The evidence from Africa is mixed. While the ability of early warning systems to increase their predictive power has undoubtedly improved over the past decade, the ability to respond to and mitigate the impact of drought in pastoral areas of Africa has not.

In most cases there appears to be a 'missing link' between early warning and response (Walker 1989; Buchanan-Smith *et al.* 1992; Davies 1992). There are many reasons for this. In many cases it is unclear what the early warning system is trying to measure. Most are geared to identifying crises—famine or major food deficits—but are not well attuned to highlighting other forms of risk, stress or vulnerability. National governments or international donors often respond slowly and the benefits of any anticipatory information are lost. Early warning tends to be linked to food delivery alone, rather than triggering support to vulnerable populations in other ways. Different messages provoke different responses from the different agencies involved, while different information sources have different levels of credibility.

The social and political context within which responses take place must also be understood. If governments or donors are unwilling to respond, excuses for inaction can always be found. Inadequate details, suspected inaccuracies or untimely data delivery can be used to discredit early warning information or delay response. The link between information delivery and response is also plagued by the practical, logistical difficulties of transportation, finance and administrative capacity.

Experience from Ethiopia, Sudan, Chad, Mali and Turkana District in Kenya points to a number of characteristics of successful early warning systems (Buchanan-Smith *et al.* 1992). Such systems are most effective if based on a decentralized network, where decision-makers are close to the problem and the people affected. They are most credible if they are transparent, accountable and jointly 'owned' by both donors and governments. These systems have the greatest impact if emergency and development aid can be merged and provide more than food aid alone. Flexibility

Box 2. Turkana District drought contingency plan and early warning system (Buchanan-Smith *et al.* 1992)

In 1987 an Early Warning System (EWS) was established in Turkana district, Kenya. The system relies on the monitoring every month of information on the rural economy (particularly livestock), environment and human welfare by mobile agents. The system appears effective at picking up changes in the pastoral economy, especially the slow onset of drought and its effects. The rapid impact of raiding (often combined with drought) is more poorly predicted by the EWS. The early warning system has four levels: normal, alert, alarm and emergency. Each level is linked with a pre-programmed response as part of the district contingency plan. Potential responses include: emergency veterinary campaigns, livestock purchase schemes, food-for-work, restocking, relief feeding and cereal supply, nutrition and health support.

The EWS thus provides clear messages to decision-makers. The EWS and contingency plan are managed at the district level by a drought management committee (DMC). In 1990–1, the EWS signalled an 'alert' warning and the DMC approved a livestock purchase scheme and food-for-work in the area. Both were initiated before serious stress levels were observed. However, some problems were faced. For instance, due to the absence of a district-level drought contingency fund, there were delays in getting donor financing. The lack of transport, holding facilities and veterinary care also meant that many of the livestock purchased subsequently died. Also, the lack of targeting in the livestock purchase scheme meant that the particular needs of poorer herders were not addressed, while the ability to purchase animals far exceeded the supply.

Despite the evident successes of the Turkana EWS and contingency plan approach, questions about its sustainability arise. Monitoring, feedback and response in pastoral areas are complex and expensive, especially if interventions persist after the cessation of an 'alert'. At the moment, the system is funded by donor agencies, and such reliance is likely to continue.

is enhanced when a response system has been worked out in advance, enabling the most appropriate response from a range of options to be chosen in relation to a particular crisis (see Box 2).

Achieving effective early warning and contingency plans is clearly not easy. It must combine ongoing donor commitment to sustaining early warning systems and a thorough political commitment by national and local governments to responding to signals. Neither of these conditions is usually met in full. Thus the 'missing link' between warning and response remains a serious problem in much of Africa (Buchanan-Smith *et al.* 1992).

Conclusions

Policies to cope with the impact of drought need to be based on certain key principles which include: flexibility to respond to changing circumstances; diversity to relate to the specific conditions of a particular place; and subsidiarity, to ensure that decision-making is devolved to the lowest level consistent with assuring accountability and efficiency (Swift this book).

Drought is only one among a number of risks faced by herders. Other important sources include uncertain access to grazing and water, disease, raids and conflict and the price of livestock in relation to other commodities. A range of interventions exist to help moderate the impact of drought upon pastoral communities. The interventions which can be pursued depend on their timing within the drought cycle and the specific circumstances of people and place. However, the overall ambition of such interventions should be the support of small-scale herders within a mobile pastoral sector. There will be other important measures which need to be taken, in the institutional, tenure and economic spheres, to support such ambitions (see Sylla; Lane and Moorehead; Holtzman and Kulibaba this book). Restocking alone, without tackling these other areas of policy, while addressing the needs of particular households in the short term, does nothing to assure them, or the social and economic system of which they are a part, a longer-term future.

There is probably an inevitable 'shake-out' of people from the pastoral sector during each drought crisis, due to population growth, and to the failure of certain households to make a living. However, it cannot be assumed that destitution is the result of poor management (Mace 1989). Instead, it may simply be due to bad luck.

Interventions within the drought cycle are faced by a number of uncertainties regarding the likely intensity and duration of drought conditions. For example, it is difficult to know where one is within the drought cycle, and whether conditions are likely to worsen further. There are risks associated, on the one hand, with reacting too early by destocking and then finding that it was not necessary, as rainfall and pastures improve and, on the other hand, not reacting rapidly enough, and then finding that pasture conditions have deteriorated further and animal prices have collapsed.

Diversification of incomes remains a very important strategy to supplement incomes from livestock, as well as a substitute when herds have been decimated. Pastoralists have always had such auxiliary incomes, from woodcutting and charcoal making, to trade, sale of labour, craft work and so on. Formal interventions to encourage alternative incomes have tended to be unsuccessful, whether irrigated agriculture, fishing or craft work. There are clearly limits to how far outsiders can identify promising areas for supporting alternative forms of income generation. As a result, it may be better to provide access to credit, by which means pastoralists can themselves identify and choose what best to do.

The range of options available for drought mitigation depends greatly on the structure of the livestock sector, and the availability of some 'slack' within the system. For example, the existence of a large-scale commercial livestock sector in southern Africa provides some room for accommodating drought within the communal areas. Elsewhere, as in the Sahel, extensive movement may provide the degree of mobility needed to cope with very great variation in grazing availability. The intensity of drought impact will be much greater where this 'slack' has been taken up, such as through cultivation of former grazing reserves and barriers to long-distance movement of stock.

Since livestock represent not only a source of food, but also a future asset, herders will place great weight on trying to get them to survive through drought. Ideally, a mechanism is required to enable herders to destock early with an assurance of gaining access to livestock capital in the post-drought period. The practical details of such a mechanism must be worked out with herders on the ground.

7. New directions in rangeland resource tenure and policy

CHARLES LANE AND RICHARD MOOREHEAD

Analyses from all over Africa at both micro- and macro-levels show that development interventions in rangeland areas have so far failed to generate expected higher levels of productivity, improve the welfare of local communities or protect rangelands from degradation (Sandford 1983). Indigenous pastoral land tenure systems are often identified as the obstacle to progress. Pastoral common property resource management has been judged as unable to produce higher levels of commercial off-take, to limit stock numbers within the carrying capacity of land or to protect land from overuse. This 'evidence' has provided the basis for reform of indigenous land tenure systems through the application of new administrative requirements and revisions to national legal frameworks.

The 'old orthodoxy' (Lane and Swift 1989) or 'mainstream view' (Sandford 1983), portraying pastoralists as economically irrational and operating with inherently destructive communal land tenure systems, has been challenged and is now recognized as a flawed basis on which to design future rangeland development strategies. However, these mainstream views, and the policies they spawn, continue to encourage the withdrawal of pasture land from pastoral production, for the benefit of encroaching farmers and commercial production and for acquisition by individuals and the state.

The viability of opportunistic grazing systems within dynamic environments, together with the need for mobility as an essential component of African rangeland resource management, has now been demonstrated (e.g. Sandford 1983; Behnke and Scoones 1993). However, it remains to be seen how this thinking can be adopted by policymakers and put into practice through the design of new administrative provisions and tenure arrangements.

Indigenous land tenure

Land tenure is defined as the 'terms and conditions on which natural resources are held and used' (Bruce 1986:xxvii). It can be described as the manner in which pastoral resources are owned: that is, the relations of *property* advocated by policymakers and practised by herders. Property has been defined as:

> ... a claim to a benefit (or income) stream, and a property right is a claim to a benefit stream that some higher body—usually the state—will agree to protect. ... Property is *not* an object, but is rather a social relation that defines the property holder with respect to something of value against all others. Property is a triadic social relation involving benefit streams, right holders and duty bearers (Bromley 1992:4).

In this context it is important to make a distinction between 'property' and 'non-property', particularly with regard to pastoral resource tenure. This is because of the widespread and continuing confusion both in literature and policy over 'open access' resources—which are, by definition, not owned by anyone, are not subject to tenure rules and are therefore not property at all—and 'controlled access' resources which may be owned by several overlapping bodies. 'Controlled access' resources are generally managed by either the state (national property), communities (communal property), or individuals (private property, sometimes known as 'closed access resources'), or by some combination of these.

All pastoral resources are held in Africa under 'controlled access' systems, often communal in form. 'Communal' land tenure relates to that system of tenure in which access to land is based upon membership of a group (Bruce 1986). Tenure is thus a social institution; a relationship between individuals and groups consisting of a series of rights and duties with respect to the use of land (Birgegard 1993). Tenure touches all aspects of life through its role in people's survival, the distribution of wealth, political power, cultural expression and so on. This means that enforced changes in tenure are likely not only to alter the way people relate to land as a resource, but also to have a profound effect on the entire social fabric of society. As we will see in the case material reviewed below, such effects are unpredictable and have a destabilizing influence on national and local affairs.

Tenure systems can be envisaged as a matrix in which rights to different resource categories are partitioned within a hierarchy of different ownership groups, ranging from the individual producer up to the largest tribal or ethnic group (Behnke 1991, 1994). Mobility is possible because these ownership groups are not territorially distinct, but possess overlapping and potentially conflicting rights to different categories of resources in one area. Such tenure systems differ from those which have more uniform individual title with prescribed rights of disposition. But this does not mean that African communal land users have a less strong sense of property, or lack security of tenure with respect to their land (Bruce 1986).

Conventional approaches to African pastoral resource tenure

Broadly speaking there are three prevailing economic models of African rangeland use and tenure (see Box 1).

Box 1. Major theories of land tenure

The tragedy of the commons (Hardin 1968, 1988)

○ Most influential theory held by policy-makers in Africa today;

○ Animals are held individually, while the range is owned by 'everyone' or 'no one';

○ Herders will always invest in more animals because benefit accrues to individuals;

○ Privatization of the resource is necessary.

The property rights school (Demsetz 1967; Behnke 1991, 1994)

○ As resources become increasingly scarce they will become progressively more controlled;

○ Increased population pressure will convert opportunistic grazing strategies to continuous use;

○ Costs of policing resources become less than benefits;

○ Herders can develop management institutions of their own.

The assurance problem approach (Runge 1981, 1984; Bromley and Cernea 1989)

○ Where communities have low and uncertain incomes and are critically dependent on natural resources, communal forms of property are more efficient;

○ Institutions act to co-ordinate actions to promote voluntary support;

○ Mobility is enhanced through reciprocity.

All three models are based on simple and persuasive theories about the relationship between land/natural resources and the means by which they are used by rural land users. However, none of them is free from ideology, and they are presented as truths despite inadequate empirical testing and rigorous evaluation.

The tragedy of the commons

It has become a dogma of the development community in Africa that pastoralists will degrade the resources they use if they are left to their own devices, because, while herders own their animals individually, the range they exploit is 'open access'. Herders will seek to intensify the exploitation of a resource without competing for restrictive title to it because the benefit of increasing production (adding another animal to their herd) will accrue to individuals, while the cost of degrading the resource will be borne by everyone. Since each herder follows the same strategy, there is a 'tragic' movement towards over-exploiting the resource, as herders are aware of the decline of pasture, but self-interest will prevent them doing anything about it.

The hypothesis that comes from the tragedy of the commons directly links resource degradation to a 'common' system and suggests that a sustainable environmental policy will only come about through the promotion of private property and/or through coercive measures. According to this argument, the costs of exploiting the pasture are 'externalities'—costs everyone using the resource has to bear—and the logic that follows is that the resource will never be rationally used unless those who benefit individually have also to pay the costs of their actions. Private property achieves just such an end by 'internalizing' the 'externalities' of non-exclusive resource exploitation. It is inherent in this theory that there is a fixed 'carrying capacity' for any particular piece of range. Herders left to their own will not bring this change in tenure about; thus it needs to be done by an outside agency, most often by the state.

Responding to what he regards as misinterpretation of his theory, Hardin has tried to make clearer the type of commons to which he was referring in his original statement (Hardin 1988). In response to criticism Hardin concedes that his theory only applies to 'open access' commons, and thus the 'tragedy' is confined to *unmanaged* commons. However, it is clear that pastoral commons are not included in the three categories of commons he describes ('privatism', 'socialism', 'commonism'). It is also evident that in talking of 'open access' systems he is *not* referring to property systems.

In his new classification, 'socialism' is closest to pastoral communal land tenure. However, by reiterating the primacy of the motivation for individual maximization, he is adopting an economic model to explain behaviour, and failing to acknowledge the existence of the benefits (mutual support, security) that come to individuals from collective behaviour in the public interest, as is displayed by traditional pastoral societies.

Property rights

In property rights theory the evolution of individual rights to land and the mechanisms to enforce such rights are related to levels of resource productivity, effects of population pressure, and the application of rural technologies. Under increased population pressure intensification of land use is reflected in a shift from opportunistic grazing—where pastures are exploited in periods of maximum production and then left to recover—to more continuous resource utilization. Intensification of land-use will occur first in more productive resources, such as fertile dry season grazing areas.

The theory of property rights is deeply rooted in economics. In this theory the value of property determines the nature of the rights that pertain to it. According to an early proponent of the theory, common property regimes exist where resources have low value and the cost of control over their use is relatively high (Demsetz 1967). As a resource acquires greater value or scarcity, the prevalence of individual maximizing behaviour provides an incentive to over-exploit it. Only then do institutional innovations occur to conserve it. These generally take the form of a shift from non-exclusive to more exclusive forms of access.

However, providing greater control over resource use incurs costs. Shifts to private property rights only occur where the transaction costs, or what Demsetz called the costs of 'policing', are exceeded by the benefits afforded by control of a resource. Demsetz suggests that the persistence of Native American communal hunting grounds on the North American Great Plains was due to the fact that the costs of containing roaming herds of bison were too high. He believes that enclosure of the plains by cattlemen only occurred once relatively low cost barbed wire became freely available.

If this process is left to develop to its logical conclusion then land either becomes degraded through over-use, or land users invest in the capacity of pastures to sustain continuous grazing. This investment can be made as capital, or as time and effort. The incentive for investment comes from the right to exclusive use. If this is not found in customary tenure arrangements then it must be provided by state legislation. The profound effect land titling can have on rural economies is recognized by economists and development practitioners alike. The perceived benefits have justified its formulation throughout the African rangelands.

These examples suggest that the privatization of common property is most likely where resources attain high value, or where there is growing scarcity. The recurrent theme in this analysis is the inter-relationship between an increase in grazing pressure and the relative costs of protecting land. Where there is grazing pressure and the costs of protection are exceeded by the value of production then land will be enclosed. Were this not to happen, common property rights would be unable to limit 'free-rider' behaviour and destruction of resources would inevitably follow.

Implicit in this is the notion that there is some kind of linear progression and historical continuum in the privatization of rangelands. It suggests that commons date from the time when there was a surfeit of resources in relation to population density. As populations increase and resources become more scarce, property will become privatized. In other words, common property regimes only work where resources are not scarce and it does not matter that maximizing individuals operate as 'free riders'. However, while this provides an explanation of changes in property rights in some locations, it does not explain why some scarce and highly productive resources, like Swiss Alpine meadows, have persisted as commons for thousands of years (Netting 1978).

The assurance problem
Much of the debate on common property has refuted the basis of the tragedy of the commons and concentrated on the study of the conditions under which communal property systems have, or might, come into being. The tragedy of the commons theory assumes that all rural producers in a community practise the same livelihood, have the same interest in a resource and can act entirely independently of their fellow producers.

This is manifestly untrue for most inhabitants, including pastoralists, living in rural communities in the developing world.

Runge (1984) argues that if expectations, assurance and actions can be co-ordinated to predict behaviour, there is less necessity for herd owners to pursue 'free-rider' strategies: indeed, co-operative behaviour might be encouraged as a utility maximizing strategy. For Runge, the institutions of society exist to co-ordinate and predict behaviour so that there may be significant incentives for a group to develop institutions which promote voluntary co-operation; he suggests an 'assurance problem' as a key to understanding how public goods are used and might be managed in the future.

In later work Runge (1986) adds to this by suggesting that where communities have low incomes, are critically dependent on a local agricultural and natural resource base and face a high degree of uncertainty with respect to income streams, communal forms of tenure are cost effective and efficient. He argues that relative poverty imposes a strict budget constraint on rural communities with regard to transaction costs (costs of policing, registering and adjudicating titles), making the management of a private property regime too costly for a subsistence economy to bear. Where the distribution of basic natural resources—in particular rainfall—is variable and where income streams are uncertain, communal property systems, by allowing access to other areas, act as a hedge against environmental risk.

At the village level, Runge argues, production decisions by individuals are based on the expected decisions of others, and this places a premium on the importance of customs, rules and conventions that co-ordinate decisions in a community. He suggests that in differentiated rural communities a certain number of producers will have an interest in free-riding on customary institutions, but that if a critical mass within a community coalesces around co-operative norms, communal property can come into being. He further argues that the more homogeneous a community, the more likely optimal outcomes are, and the more heterogeneous, the more difficult co-operation becomes.

It is a major implication of this analysis that outcomes, such as over-grazing, do not necessarily arise from the strict dominance of a free-rider strategy (although resource misuse may still occur), but from the inability of interdependent individuals to co-ordinate and enforce actions in situations of strategic interdependence (Runge 1986).

A wealth of evidence is now becoming available to show how customary tenure systems in Africa have been undermined by the inability of rural producers to co-ordinate their actions, and that this inability is often due to the imposition of unsuitable land tenure legislation and pastoral policy by both donors and the post-colonial state. At the same time, field experience and theory are converging to show that, where local producers are given the opportunity and the resources to develop their own management institutions and tenure systems, they are well able to do so. The following section of this chapter briefly examines case material from herder societies in Africa, in the light of the discussion so far.

Theory in practice

There are three major processes of political and economic change presently under way in Africa which profoundly affect pastoralists' tenure systems: the nationalization of their resources; the sedentarization of the herders themselves (often involving land-use planning and land titling); and the privatization of the range.

Nationalization

The tragedy of the commons argument has legitimized the takeover by government of the ownership and management of pastoral resources in many parts of Africa. It is viewed as legitimate, even necessary, to intervene because herders will degrade their resources if left to their own devices. In fact, current research reveals that the nationalization of herders' resources has very different results to those intended. It is being increas-

---

Box 2. The inland delta of the river Niger (Moorehead 1991)

In the West African country of Mali, the nationalization of pastoral resources followed the French colonial policy of considering all land that was 'unused' (i.e. not tilled for agriculture) as being unowned, and therefore legitimate state property. In one particular area—the inland delta of the river Niger, one of the most important pastoral resources in the whole Sahel—this policy ignored one of the more sophisticated pastoral tenure systems found in Africa. Under the customary system, dry season flood pastures, which form the hub around which some two million cattle transhume each year, were divided into some 30 pasturing territories allocated to sub-clans of Fulani transhumant pastoralists. Each of these territories had reciprocal grazing rights with each other to allow all Fulani groups access to the flood pastures as the flood waters fell each year. Outsiders were only allowed access on payment of a fee. Herd movements were controlled in great detail, each herd belonging to clan members with an appointed place within a hierarchy which controlled the order in which animals entered the flood pastures as the waters fell. According to the conditions pertaining each year, resource managers responsible for each territory set the dates on which crossings into the pastures took place.

With the nationalization of pastoral resources, the livestock service began to set the dates at which livestock was allowed into the area, without reference to pasture conditions pertaining in the drylands each year. An inflexible, untracked policy endeavoured to keep animals in the upstream areas of the delta for as long as possible during the dry season, with the result that animals moved on to flood pastures when they were dry, so preventing the regeneration of the pasture resource itself. Whereas before a clear hierarchy allowed owners of pasture preferential and flexible access to the flood pastures each year, and clear rules applied to strangers wishing to use the area, the colonial and post-colonial governments considered all herders as citizens of Mali and, at least in theory, provided them with equal use rights.

---

ingly shown that nationalization of the range is undermining customary tenure regimes without replacing them with effective systems (Box 2).

The perforation of the Sahel through the provision of thousands of 'public' wells and boreholes in dryland areas is breaking down water point tenure systems in a similar manner. Former tribal and clan-based ownership of customary wells, built by the herders themselves, effectively controlled access to pastures. This is being broken down by the provision of these 'public' facilities. Access to these wells is often uncontrolled, and sometimes heavily armed herders (from a different country) are able to monopolize use of these water points and exclude the traditional managers of the area (Thébaud 1993). In Mauritania, religion has played an important part in dissolving customary management systems, as Koranic law provides much broader access to water and grazing resources than the customary system. Conflict between herding groups often arises because of this issue (Zeidane 1993).

Ironically the take over by the state of pastoral resources may well be creating the conditions for the tragedy of the commons to take place. Where the state is unable to provide adequate management and yet at the same time insists that 'everyone' has a right of access through citizenship, the stage is effectively set for herders to have an interest in investing in more animals individually, while ignoring the public cost of such action, for the simple reason that if they do not make use of the pasture, someone else will. Crucially, they no longer have any say in who the 'someone else' is, and can take no action to prevent their entry onto the range. There also exist significant interests in maintaining an ambiguous tenure system, because it often provides the post-colonial state with formal and informal revenue from the arbitration of conflict, while allowing élite interests in state structures access to pastoral resources they never had before (Diakité 1993).

Sedentarization, land-use planning and land titling
It is a short step, using the tragedy of the commons perspective, from believing in the incompetence of herders to believing their mobile pastoral strategies are evidence of their disorganized lives, and from there to imposing policies aimed at settling herders down, often in unsuitable places. Governments often see herders as escaping their administration (especially where they move across national frontiers), as potential threats to security and as evaders of their fiscal dues. All these concerns inform the prevalent wish by African governments today to sedentarize nomadic and transhumant populations.

Settlement of nomadic pastoralists is the greatest single transformation of pastoralism as both a production system and way of life. Despite the inherent contradiction of settling people who rely on varying degrees of mobility to exploit natural resources, settlement has been pursued as either an overt policy objective (e.g. villagization in Tanzania; Box 3), the product of administrative action (e.g. famine response in the Sahel), or as the inevitable consequence of land tenure reform and the push for privatization sponsored by Western aid donors.

Box 3. Villagization in Tanzania

Tanzania offers perhaps the most concerted attempt in Africa to settle its rural population. The scale and uniformity of Tanzania's 'villagization' programme highlights the problems of this policy for pastoralists. Ujamaa villages were to become 'islands of socialism in a capitalist sea' (Coulson 1979:3). Yet, ironically villagization was to pose the greatest threat to communal land use.

The demarcation of communal rangelands into villages has the potential for disruption of customary pastoral land-use patterns. Village boundaries not only divide communal rangeland areas into discrete administrative units, they also provide the potential for exclusion from access to resources. This is because village land areas are unlikely to cover the whole area that makes up an ecological land-use unit, particularly in those times when migration is extended to include distant forage and water resources in times of drought. Villagization has had less effect on pastoral land-use patterns than might have been expected. This is due less to the few concessions made to pastoral communities—like 'Operation Imparnati' in which Maasai communities in Monduli were allowed to orient to a central location, rather than build their homes in a village centre (Ndagala 1982)—than to the fact that many villages have yet to be officially demarcated, and mobile pastoral land use has persisted.

The new tenure arrangements operate to facilitate 'arbitrary encroachment, invasion and alienation in favour of outside individuals and institutions (including government) against the interests and wishes of villages' (URT 1992:61). This is particularly prevalent in rangeland areas where there is thought to be a surfeit of fertile land. In the process around a quarter of a million pastoralists (mainly Maa and Tatoga speakers like the Barabaig) who rely on communal lands for livestock production, now find the best of their lands taken and their movements restricted. This is perhaps best illustrated by the Barabaig case, in which more than 100000 acres of prime grazing land was acquired by government for a parastatal wheat scheme. Indications are that the scheme has completely undermined the Barabaig grazing system (Lane 1991), adversely affecting the environment (Lane and Scoones 1993), and Barabaig welfare (Borgerhoff-Mulder 1990; Lane 1991; Blystad 1993).

Throughout the rangelands of Africa, governments are investing in land titling programmes in the belief that only through registered titles can a sufficient level of tenure security be provided for the achievement of higher levels of production and the protection of resources from destruction. Such land tenure reform policies are based on the premise that indigenous land tenure systems are an obstruction to development, and only through more formal registered title will rural land users be encouraged to make land improving investments or induce lenders to finance such investments through the provision of credit.

Village titling presents a double-edged sword to pastoralists. There are obvious advantages from having registered title to land as protection from land grabbing, but this also poses the problem of how to maintain opportunistic grazing systems when confined to a permanent location. A

Box 4. Village planning: Dirma village, Tanzania

Barabaig herders traditionally migrate out of the Dirma village in the dry season to gain access to permanent water in neighbouring villages in return for letting herders from other areas come to Dirma in the wet season to make use of the rich pasture resources found there. The basic assumption on which the village plan was based regarded the traditional grazing pattern as haphazard (*kiholela*) and inconsistent with development objectives.

[The] planners have arbitrarily assumed that current land-use is inadequate and destructive to the environment and the plan prescribes replacement of existing agricultural and pastoral practices with 'modern' and 'scientific' methods (*ya kisasa* and *ya kitaalamu*), without elaborating on what these concepts mean (Johansson 1991:1).

Maps of 'planning areas' designating fixed 'land-use zones' failed to take account of the diversity of natural resources within the village boundary. They also failed to provide for the complexity of the traditional land-use pattern or to accommodate the inter-relationship between resources in and beyond the village. The plans treated all villagers as a homogeneous group and gave no recognition to the different interest groups found within the village. Some villagers and some of their leadership saw the plans as a means to protect land from encroachment. Others wanted to be able to take up the more fertile land for themselves by acquiring individual title and sublease it to commercial farmers. What none of them realized was that this same process could also restrict the traditional migratory pattern and ultimately deny them access to water in the dry season.

study of villages in Hanang district, Tanzania shows that those Barabaig who settled in villages on the semi-arid Hanang plains were forced to compromise their herding strategies by limiting the extent of their migration to the distance their herds can travel to and from the homestead in one day. The concentration of animals within the village has had an adverse ecological impact, encouraged a trend towards agropastoralism and resulted in a decline in levels of production (Kjaerby 1979).

Village land-use planning has also been proposed as an adjunct to the titling programme. However, it has been implemented by procedures developed for urban planning which have proved inappropriate for the diverse tenure systems found in rural environments. Another example from Tanzania (Box 4) illustrates just how inappropriate conventional land-use planning procedures can be in the context of pastoral areas.

In West Africa there is growing support, particularly among donors, for land-use planning based around the concept of 'village territories'. The approach aims to clarify issues of tenure, redefine the responsibilities and rights of local communities to manage their resources and to pursue a participatory diagnosis with local people of the many environmental, economic, institutional and social problems they face (Toulmin 1993). On the surface, this approach appears promising for re-establishing the ability of local groups to manage the resources they depend upon. The approach lays down a series of steps involving the participation of rural producers including: discussion and diagnosis of problems; the election of local resource management committees; the establishment of legal boundaries to settlements' resources; the elaboration of a management plan and the subsequent implementation of the programme. The fundamental shift in the nature of relations between local people, the state and extension agents entailed by this approach, makes this initiative, without doubt, a great improvement on the 'top-down' approach practised before.

One particular aspect of the 'village territory' approach however gives rise to concern in its implications for pastoralist tenure and access rights. The 'territory' concept is derived from settled farming villages with a defined set of resources surrounding them. Herders, particularly in more marginal areas, rarely use a contiguous set of resources within a comparatively manageable area to make their livelihoods; indeed, one of their principal strategies is to move continuously between and within agroecological zones. This means they rarely possess defined 'territories' and often use resources exploited by other production systems at other times of the year (i.e. fields belonging to farmers), and may only have secondary or tertiary rights of access to these resources. There is a danger that the 'territory' approach may empower sedentary farmers to exclude transhumant and nomadic pastoralists from grazing areas they previously had access to, and this may particularly be the case where the farmers themselves are beginning to own and herd their own livestock, or where population growth is leading to the cultivation of former areas of pasture that were strategic in allowing herders to use other marginal resources in different seasons of the year.

Privatization
The privatization of pastoral resources is the logical policy extreme of the tragedy of the commons hypothesis, and has been rewarded by some of its most tangible failures.

In Botswana, for instance, the introduction of borehole drilling technology and the emergence of an increasingly rigid social order has allowed a new élite of wealthy land owners to monopolize new water sources, obtain an increasing share of the national herd and control the best grazing areas. The Tribal Grazing Land Policy ranches that were set up in the late 1970s to improve the productivity of rangelands dramatically failed either to reduce numbers of livestock to a notional 'carrying capacity' or improve rates of return to investment. In fact they were actually less efficient than cattle posts in communal areas. Under the new national policy for agricultural development, it is now being proposed that the communal lands, presently part of Tribal Grazing Lands Policy areas, should be fenced. There are good reasons for believing this will effectively allocate grazing land as *de facto* private property to wealthier borehole owners, reduce the capacity of the land for supporting livestock, and, most important of all, deprive anything up to 60 000 people of their livelihoods on the cattle posts, in particular the poorest sector of the population made up of the Remote Area Dwellers (White 1992). By contrast, a tracking strategy would allow higher numbers of animals to be kept on the range and utilize surplus feed in wetter years (Abel 1993).

The case of Botswana raises the important issue of the co-existence of private and common property rights within the pastoral system. Both in Botswana (White 1992) and in Kenya (Galaty 1993a,b), the privatization of some ranges has had disastrous consequences on herders using the communal areas, as private owners dual graze their stock on the communal lands when the grazing on their private pastures is exhausted, or when they want to regenerate their private land. In Kenya group ranches have failed because assurance was undermined. There was no integrity of the membership group; others could come in and gain land for collateral for loans or for speculation; there was no political power to exclude others and there was a lack of clarity regarding the rights of inheritance (Galaty 1993a,b).

In contrast to this an example of how resources become (informally) privatized when they become more valuable comes from Senegal (Guèye 1993). Conflict between the Fulani herders and Sérère cultivators surrounds land that was abandoned by the Sérère 40 years ago and has been used by the Fulani for herding since then. The plan to build the Cayor canal to supply water to Dakar has meant this land now has a high potential for irrigation and is consequently very valuable. In the first instance this provoked conflict between the Sérère and the Fulani over customary rights to the land, but when powerful outside interests began to try to get access to the irrigable land beside the canal, the Fulani and Sérère communities came together to prevent these outsiders from intruding. These two communities have now agreed to exploit the area—on a household basis, and mainly for agriculture—and to manage allocation on an inter-community basis. In this process land that was customarily farmed as household property became communal pasture, and is now in the process of becoming more tightly controlled at the household level once again.

The fundamental premise of the arrest of degradation and improvement of pastoral productivity upon which the privatization argument is based has been shown to be flawed. While research in Thailand lends support to orthodox property rights theory by concluding that 'security of land ownership in Thailand has a substantial [positive] effect on the agricultural performance of farmers' (particularly in terms of improved access to credit for investment in improvements for greater productivity) (Feder et al. 1988:148), research in Africa suggests that a direct correlation between individual title and higher levels of production is more elusive. In a comprehensive study of household survey data from Ghana, Kenya, and Rwanda, Place and Hazell (1993:10) found, with few exceptions, that 'land rights are not found to be a significant factor in determining levels of investment in land improvements, use of input access to credit, or the productivity of land', and thus provide little support for ambitious land registration and titling programmes under way throughout Africa.

Privatization, land titling and land-use policies in the dryland pastoral areas of Africa have clearly failed to meet the targets set for them, and in doing so, have illustrated the weakness of the tragedy of the commons approach to the problems of pastoral development. The examples given above show that the tenure regimes advocated by supporters of the tragedy of the commons argument provide little protection from alienation of pastoral resources to outsiders. They also lead to the double allocation of pastoral resources; limit strategies of movement in the face of environmental risk; take little account either of the diversity of resources pastoralists use, or the herders who use them; often marginalize the poor and diminish the access of herders to key resources they need to sustain their livelihoods. Further, the costs of implementing private property systems are huge in terms of the time and resources that must be committed to survey work and conflict arbitration.

This overview of land tenure policy and its relationship to the major theories of land tenure allows us to make three observations:

o The privatization model neither provides equity nor efficiency for pastoralists in uncertain environments, either in terms of livelihoods, or the sustainable management of resources. Policies of nationalization and of privatization can have debilitating effects on communal tenure systems, without providing effective or equitable alternative regimes.
o There is a need to move away from technical solutions towards social and economic issues; away from improving productivity on private ranges towards improving the manner in which reciprocal tenure agreements can build management consensus between resource users as stakeholders in the ranges on which they depend.
o Increased attention needs to be paid to the physical characteristics of resources and their relationship to tenure systems, and on the relationship between tenure systems and institution building. It is being increasingly appreciated that the brokerage of interests between different interest groups in range resources (between and within production systems) is a strategic issue in creating equitable and efficient tenure systems.

The implications for land tenure of the new directions in African range management and policy

Thinking on non-equilibrium land-use places the natural characteristics of pastoral resources at the centre of the debate. In arguing that pastoral resources are often subject to high variability within and between seasons and across large areas, it suggests that tenure systems for herders should support their tried and tested strategies of mobility in order for them to maintain an economically optimal stocking rate (Behnke and Scoones 1993).

This review of theory, policy and practice has shown that the tragedy of the commons school has clearly not provided a satisfactory solution to pastoral land tenure, and indeed has done much to debilitate and destroy tenure systems evolved by herders themselves. The major theories of resource tenure, while providing powerful tools for understanding the decline of pastoral tenure systems, have as yet not been able to generate appropriate policy options for pastoral tenure systems in Africa.

Rapid population growth in pastoral areas of Africa, and its spill-over on to rangelands, often with ever larger areas being put under agricultural land, makes it increasingly difficult for herders to maintain their strategy of mobility as a hedge against environmental risk. Of particular importance is the take over of key dry season pastures by farmers as private agricultural property (both *de facto* and *de jure*), often removing from herders' control resources they need to sustain production from more marginal resources at other times of the year (Bayer and Waters-Bayer this book). Herders are making efficient use of these more marginal dryland resources at the moment only because they have access to wetlands, and the loss of key pastures ensuring survival in the dry season may mean that these areas will cease to become productive in the future. There is an urgent need for tenure systems that allow herders to maintain their livelihoods through access to these key resources in the future.

The political and economic processes currently under way in many African countries—decentralization, liberalization of political activity, structural adjustment and aid conditionality—present both opportunities and threats to herders. Opportunities come in the form of a growing commitment to participatory approaches to development, with local producers choosing their own priorities and having some of the power to manage their own resources. Threats are represented by the possible usurping of these processes by sedentary farmers who are better represented in current political and economic power structures. If this happens, herders' interests in new land-use planning and titling initiatives will continue to be marginalized.

There is a growing knowledge of how pastoral land tenure and management systems worked in the past and how pastoralists' livelihood strategies have been undermined. In particular, there is a growing awareness of the effectiveness of their tenure systems and range management practices, of which thinking on non-equilibrium land-use is an example. This knowledge, combined with the new climate of political liberalism, decentralization of power and participatory approaches should be used by planners and development workers in the pastoral sector to lobby for tenure and management systems that are specifically adapted to herders' needs, and which support their tenure rights (Perrier this book).

There are three key hypotheses that characterize new directions in African range management policy (Scoones this book), each of which have tenure implications (Box 5). Tenure systems that embody the attributes described in Box 5 are necessarily communal; resources belong to a cohesive group of herders often linked by ties of kinship and consanguinity. Because of the variability of the resource base, both in space and time, such tenure systems are complex, often with overlapping or differentiated property rights. A pastoral group may share reciprocal access agreements with similar neighbouring groups, who have the same interests in, and dependency on, a defined set of resources. Within these larger groups, preferential access and resource management powers may be devolved

129

Box 5. Tenure implications of the key hypotheses which form the new approach to range management

Hypothesis	Tenure implications
○ Carrying capacity has to take account of management objectives of herder	○ Devolution of authority to local groups
○ Unpredictable productivity	○ Ability to respond quickly
	○ Simple rules
○ Heterogeneous nature of range resources	○ Need for access to or incorporation of a range of agro-ecological areas

on 'founding' sub-clans or lineages with lesser rights accorded to more recent arrivals, while outsiders may have to pay fees to enter the range. The legitimization of such an order is often historical; tribes or clans may be indigenous to the area or may have acquired the right to use the area by force. Where herders increasingly impinge on areas customarily used by farmers a set of shared interests may bring the two producing groups together. Often farmers provide access to grazing in return for milk and other livestock products and give the animals they own to pastoralists to herd for them (Bayer and Waters-Bayer this book).

Many previous pastoral tenure systems were appropriate to the management system practised by herders and the physical characteristics of the resources. They responded quickly to unpredictable environmental events, in order to maximize access to available pasture, while providing more regular access to a set of heterogeneous range resources over seasons. They achieved this by vesting the ownership of resources in larger social groupings, which could provide the policing necessary to retain ownership of the range, while at the same time providing a simple and quick decision-making process through kinship links, legitimized by widely held beliefs and providing a set of clear rules, understood and accepted by everyone.

It may be utopian, however, to believe that it is still possible to re-animate customary communal management systems to perform these functions. It is increasingly argued that many of the kinship and other linkages that existed in the past to hold pastoral communal tenure systems together have either been destroyed or severely undermined. The diversity of interests, including those of wider economic and political structures, non-herding owners of animals and the increasing divergencies between rich and poor herders themselves also undermine traditional systems. Any land tenure policy for pastoralists living in uncertain environments that ignores these divisions is unlikely to succeed.

There are also legitimate doubts over whether such a system would address increasingly severe issues of equity within the pastoral sector. There are many examples of key resources being taken over by wealthier and more powerful groups within societies in Africa, and support given to traditional pastoral structures might only help these elements to achieve greater control over valuable resources. Within agropastoral areas, herding groups using disconnected pastures between farming areas (such as the Wodaabe in Niger) might be marginalized in this process. Finally, it is by no means clear that many pastoral societies have the capacity to organize in parts of Africa: the most telling example of this is perhaps Somalia, where the breakdown of central government has led to internecine warfare between herding peoples.

To sum up, the major constraints to establishing communal systems are:

o A potential lack of support from wider socio-economic structures that have an interest in the *status quo*;
o The capture of key resources by sedentary populations that might have better access to the political structure;
o The heterogeneity of interests within herder groups;
o Barriers across transhumant routes (international frontiers, fenced, private property); and
o Insecurity.

Options for the future

The issue of appropriate tenure rights for herders needs a many-stranded approach, which will allow promising ideas to be tested on the ground, supported by the wider social and economic framework in each area and incorporated eventually into national policy. This implies that the identification and adoption of new approaches to pastoral tenure rights will need to be carried out in two linked areas: applied approaches based on research and policy formulation and adoption.

Applied approaches based on research
Any new approach must be firmly based on sound empirical research. Research priorities include:

o Focus on the economic aspects of comparative tenure regimes in order to complement work already carried out in drylands on productivity by hectare and livestock unit basis.
o Increased understanding of the dynamics of tenure systems and the manner in which they evolve in response to increasing returns, and to fixed factors of production for pastoralists and agropastoralists in areas receiving different levels of rainfall.
o Particular attention must be paid to key resource areas, including: water sources, salt-licks, transhumance routes, low-lying areas of higher productivity, strategic fodder reserves (such as trees) and access to farm land. Access of herders to other important inputs such as agro-industrial by-products must also be considered.
o Historical analysis of overlapping interests and rights in a given resource which have developed over recent decades. Examination of the issues of secondary and tertiary rights of access for pastoralists to ranges in different areas is also important.

○ Understanding of differentiation within these groups to ensure issues of equity which will underlie the legitimization of the system.

○ Research to identify the positive role the state can play in supporting local tenure systems, perhaps through a process of 'procedural law' (Vedeld 1993). At present there is much ambiguity between different systems of conflict with alternative structures open to different people (Swift this book).

The research described above will allow a number of 'best chance' areas and groups of herders to be identified in different countries. Tenure agreements might then be drawn up and initiatives tested in the field in line with approaches in other sub-sectors (marketing, range improvement, and so on; see other chapters in this book). Initiatives tested in different countries must be co-ordinated, especially where they are taking place among herders following similar production strategies and using similar agro-ecological areas. This co-ordination, which might be provided by an information network for pastoralists, should bring together the herders themselves, as well as planners and policymakers.

Policy formulation and adoption

Of fundamental importance for the future will be the clear support of government and technical agencies for initiatives carried out on the ground, and provision of recourse for herding groups whose tenure rules have been broken by outsiders. Equally, it will be important to find means by which new tenure arrangements can be brought speedily into effect, so that herders can be reassured of the security of tenure they hold over the resources to be managed. Sustainable pastoral land-use should be recognized formally as constituting a development initiative (or *mise en valeur*), to enable it to be considered on a par with cultivation. In practical terms this must be preceded by a dialogue between the different actors. This could be facilitated by fora that include representation from land users, researchers and policymakers and will need to be convened and conducted in a collaborative atmosphere.

As a counter to the high levels of land tenure insecurity in rangeland areas, it may be necessary, if only in the short term, to provide protection through zoning of pastoral lands. This prescribed protection of rangelands from further alienation and encroachment gives local land users time to come to terms with political contexts and judicial provisions. They can then explore the means by which they might reassert communal land rights, help design new tenure systems that make use of those existing indigenous tenure arrangements that promote sustained land use in uncertain environments, and link these with wider administrative frameworks.

Pastoralists are unlikely to be able to assert rights to communal lands in the context of the push for privatization that is well under way throughout Africa today. Unless there is a shift in power relations between local land users and the state, between recipients and donors, between wealthy and poor members of pastoral society, then the *status quo* can be expected to persist. Devolution of power to the periphery is unlikely to occur without concerted pressure from below. Rangeland users have to be empowered if they are to compete on equal terms with other land users, provide a challenge to the top-down approach and begin influencing land policies in their favour (Perrier this book).

Responsibility for which type of tenure system should be used in a given area should be left to local user groups. There can be no prescribed, rigid model of land tenure. In different areas, different tenure arrangements will be developed by local users, who will learn at their own pace what is most suitable. The role of outside investors and development agencies should be facilitatory, and should adopt an incremental approach to project planning which allows adaptive management to changes in tenure systems. An appropriate role for government and other actors in the pastoral sector is to strengthen institutions for conflict management and the provision of information and legal support to weaker groups (Sylla and Swift this book).

8. Pastoral organizations for uncertain environments

DJEIDI SYLLA

This chapter examines the experience of African pastoral organizations and asks: what are the most appropriate organizational forms in uncertain environments? The discussion is based on three assumptions: that opportunistic behaviour and mobility remain the best ways of managing natural resources for pastoralists in uncertain environments; that authority must be devolved, with a hierarchy of management institutions capable of resolving conflicting claims to key resources at local, regional and national levels; and that reference must be made to the socio-economic framework within which pastoral organizations operate. Like any production zone, the pastoral zone, and the rules and practices affecting it, are a projection of social, economic, cultural and political relationships, which themselves vary according to circumstance and from place to place.

The chapter starts with a brief discussion of institution building, setting the debate about institutional development in pastoral areas within a broader context. Next, a series of case studies of pastoral organizations from different parts of Africa are examined. These are used to develop a comparative analysis of institution building experience. Drawing on these lessons, the chapter concludes with a summary of key principles for institutional and organizational development in the pastoral zone.

Institutional development

Recent development theory has been much concerned with institution building, a process which has developed in three stages (Fowler *et al.* 1992). The first stage occurred immediately after independence and was characterized by the creation or strengthening of state institutions. Institution building then began to focus more on the potential offered by the non-governmental sector and community development. The third stage began in the 1980s, when institution building focused on the establishment of a favourable institutional environment for the development of citizens' associations, strengthening wider civil society. Other factors, such as the move towards a more participatory approach in development, the crisis of the state in Africa and the advance of economic liberalism and political pluralism all have a bearing on the change of orientation in favour of institution building.

There are many arguments in favour of supporting pastoral organisations. According to Marty (1990): 'The vast investment poured into the livestock sector has failed to achieve anything, because of the exclusively technical definition of the activities and the indifferent participation of the producers.' Swift and Bonfiglioli (1984) see the advent of pastoral organizations as unavoidable as people become aware that channels of communication between the state and pastoralists are needed. According to Sihm (1989), the establishment of pastoral associations is the result of economic considerations, since setting them up should reduce the cost of successive crises and emergency interventions in pastoral areas.

In fact, there have always been traditional pastoral organizations in Africa (Sylla 1989). Rediscovery of this organizational model is due to a combination of factors: a new and more positive perception of pastoral societies on the part of decision-makers; the need to stabilize pastoral areas in the face of recurrent climatic crises; the redefinition of the concept of pastoral development; and the search for better technical results and more sustainable programmes.

Pastoral organizations: experiences from Africa

The following section offers six brief profiles of different types of pastoral organization from nine countries in Africa. The case studies highlight a range of institutional and organizational issues that have contributed to their successes and failures.

Case 1: Group ranches in Kenya (Sources: Oxby 1982; Little and Brokensha 1987; Graham 1988; Lane and Swift 1988; Pratt 1990; Galaty 1992, 1993a).

The group ranch policy was introduced in Kenya during the 1960s with three main objectives. The first was to prevent the invasion of land traditionally occupied by pastoralists by guaranteeing the land rights of pastoral communities. The second was to provide an institutional and economic framework for local investment, by granting land titles to be used as security when applying for credit. The third was to modify pastoral practices with a view to greater integration in the market economy through increased production and better resource management.

The group ranches have provided a degree of land tenure security for pastoralists through land registration. For those pastoralists who were able to invest in land the policy has resulted in increased income. In addition, the policy has encouraged pastoralists to consider the implications of finite land resources and tackle landholding issues.

There have, however, been a number of problems. Many herders do not have enough animals to provide for their families and are therefore neither interested nor prepared to reduce the size of their herds, whereas technicians have always considered ranches as structures to improve livestock productivity and rangeland management through controlled stocking. The herders much appreciated title to pasture land and access to funding to invest in water points and anti-parasite dips, whereas the promoters were looking for an increase in the rate of livestock marketing.

Group ranches created a vacuum of authority. Traditional rules of reciprocal use of range were undermined by a new structure that did not take into account the need for co-operation in using variable resources. Due to the variability of rainfall, ranches are not large enough to support all the livestock in dry years. Informal movements of livestock, as used to happen traditionally, have resumed. The consequence has been increased pressure on collective lands.

Although the ranches increased herders' participation in decision-making, it did not put them beyond the reach of other influences. Some members of the group ranches have become impoverished, leading to the dismantling of land titles and the takeover of land by non-herders.

Case 2: Grazing reserves in Nigeria (Sources: Ingawa *et al.* 1989; Salih 1992).
Grazing reserves were introduced in Nigeria in 1964 to sedentarize Fulani pastoralists, protect grazing lands against encroachment by agriculture and encourage pastoralists to invest, by providing some security of tenure.

The grazing reserve policy has brought a number of benefits. For instance, the installation of infrastructure, such as water supplies and roads, has stimulated local development. Equally, the recognition of the need to allow some private exploitation rights has encouraged herders themselves to make investments to improve the quality of rangeland. Also moving from diffuse usufruct to more specific rights through the issuing of Certificates of Occupancy to Fulani herders has increased the level of tenure security for this pastoral population.

The major problem arising from the establishment of the reserves has been the failure to integrate the agricultural and pastoral production systems. For grazing reserves to develop effectively they must be integrated with the broader social and economic environment, particularly as livestock producers depend on co-operation with cultivators. Settled pastoralists need markets for sale of their products and for the purchase of household and farm goods. Almost all sedentary pastoralists grow subsistence crops and they often hire labour for crop production. Unfortunately, reserves have all too often been planned as exclusion zones to separate communities, in part because of the belief that the primary need was to preserve land from arable encroachment. The consequence has often been to exacerbate, rather than alleviate, inter-community tensions.

Case 3: Dam groups in Botswana (Source: Fortmann and Roe 1981).
Between 1974 and the early 1980s, the government of Botswana launched a dam programme which was designed to provide water for livestock. It was intended that the reservoirs should be handed over to the district councils in one of two ways: total control by the authorities or hand-over to user groups. The management system was accompanied by agreements signed

between the beneficiaries and the authorities, dealing with maintenance and distribution, payment of dues and limiting watering capacity.

User groups kept the dams in satisfactory condition because the infrastructure was simple and cheap to maintain. Management rules (e.g. number of users, types, forms and times of use) were devised and applied flexibly; users were able to adapt the regulations to their own situation. The dams have shown that the pre-condition for effective management of these water points was collective management. The dam groups thus provide a good example of *ad hoc* group formation around water supply in the dry season.

However, there have been a number of problems noted. The dams were enclosed to protect them against direct access by livestock, so the users were encouraged to use the water for other purposes. In local culture, surface water does not belong to anyone, hence the difficulty of preventing people from gaining access to it. Most herders were older people or employees, as young people were away at work in town. They would have preferred direct access without the need for pumps, because of labour constraints. Because the water points were built by the government and given to the people with no contribution on their part, they were seen as belonging to the government, but very rarely to the user groups.

In applying the management rules, some groups encountered a lack of support from the rest of the community. Such groups were weak, with little social legitimacy. Groups with strong leaders or substantial social cohesion, enjoying the support of the broader community, achieved the best results.

Case 4: Grazing associations in Lesotho (Sources: Swallow and Brokken 1987; Lawry 1987).

Recent range policy in Lesotho has emphasized a dual strategy. On the one hand, the aim is to vest greater control over local management decisions in grazing associations, and on the other, to develop the institutional capacity for better administrative regulation of grazing, principally by reinforcing the role of the chief in range management matters.

The associations have been able to attract more than 50 per cent of herders and to collect their membership dues. Grazing patterns are established to take account of grazing needs over a full annual production cycle, thus reducing livestock pressure on the rangelands. The use of penalties (fines paid by offenders) is of great assistance in ensuring respect for the rules governing pasture use. Most of the investments needed are low-cost and affordable.

The grazing associations, however, are not traditional environmental management structures and their success is greatly dependent on external support. The operation of the associations (regulations, fines, environmental management) is currently not viable without the support of the project technicians. The role played by village chiefs in the past in setting aside winter grazing areas has declined due to political and social changes affecting their authority. The associations sometimes do not seem to have the necessary social authority or legitimacy to enforce regulations.

By abolishing certain traditional rights, the new rules governing rangeland use favour association members over non-members and neighbouring communities. Although members may come from the same valley, a number of factors weaken the social and economic cohesion of the associations. These include the demographic composition of households, age differences, gendered interests, place of residence, number of head of livestock, alternative income sources, factional quarrels and differences in production strategies.

Case 5: Pastoral associations in the Sahel (Sources: Shanmugaratnam *et al.* 1992; Vedeld 1992, 1993; Zeidane 1993).
The formation of pastoral associations (PAs) has been supported by the World Bank in a number of Sahelian countries, including Mali, Mauritania, Niger and Senegal. Institutional support to associations has been seen as a route towards improving range management and increasing herd productivity. Service support, including literacy training, credit provision and para-veterinary facilities, has been a component of all projects.

In each case organizations have been formed at various levels. For instance, in Mali voluntary organizations are formed with groups of around ten families. Pastoral committees bring these groups together and pastoral units are made up of several committees. In Mauritania a federation of PAs has begun to articulate herders' needs and rights at regional and national levels.

The size of PAs differs between countries. In Senegal the size of pastoral units is small enough to make management feasible. However, in Mauritania the territory covered by some PAs is too large to stimulate involvement by the members. Lack of clarity over boundaries has proved problematic in Mali where continued disputes with farming communities hampers PA development. The unwillingness by governments to recognize pastoral land rights and territorial boundaries makes such conflicts inevitable and decentralized natural resource management difficult.

The legal status of the PAs varies between countries. The associations are legally recognized in Mauritania, Niger and Senegal, making it possible to confirm rights over resources. However, in Mali the lack of legal status means that it has been impossible to obtain government authority to settle land tenure and administrative problems at a local level.

Membership of PAs is variable. For instance, in Niger only 30 per cent of herders are members of the PAs and non-members continue to have equal access to range and water resources. In Mauritania Koranic law sometimes makes it difficult to exclude non-members. This has made effective resource management initiatives difficult to implement. In Mali the owners of the majority of livestock do not live in the PA area, making PA establishment and the enforcement of regulations problematic. In Mauritania, the pattern of existing social stratification has limited access to PA activities, with richer, male herders taking leadership positions. In all cases women play a very limited role in PA activities, with the result that their particular needs are not catered for.

In most cases the PAs are not yet self-sustaining. They continue to be dependent on external funding and technical support. Systems for generating local revenues through taxation or income-generating activities have proved difficult to realize.

Case 6: Grazing schemes in Zimbabwe (Sources: Froude 1974; Danckwerts 1974; Sandford 1982; Cousins 1987, 1992; Scoones 1989b).
Communal area (CA) grazing schemes were first implemented in Zimbabwe in the late 1940s. By 1973 there were over 300 in Masvingo Province alone. These broke down during the liberation war, but many have been revived and new ones started since independence in 1980. Grazing schemes are aimed at improving natural resource management of CA grazing areas through the introduction of rotational grazing and controlled stocking. This is intended to result in increased beef production through the improvement of range condition. Grazing schemes are also seen as routes by which other animal husbandry measures can be introduced, such as controlled breeding.

Schemes require the establishment of a grazing scheme committee, as part of the Village Development Committee local government structure. Committee membership tends to be dominated by larger cattle owners. Depending on local politics, 'traditional' leaders may play a role. Conflict between established patterns of organization and new structures are often central to disputes in the establishment of grazing schemes. The committee draws up a set of by-laws for the operation of the scheme, usually with the assistance of the national agricultural extension agency. These include the management of local contributions, the involvement of local labour, the rotation of grazing and the regulation of livestock numbers. The committee is vested with powers to enforce the regulations, but these are rarely used.

The scale of existing and proposed schemes is enormously variable. Ward-level schemes mean that a larger area, including a greater diversity of natural resources, are available and the likelihood of local boundary disputes is reduced. However, ward-level institutions for management present problems. Village-level schemes may result in the emergence of more effective institutions, allowing management of a localized grazing resource, but greater boundary problems exist and seasonal or drought movement of stock may cause problems.

Grazing schemes are characterized by a clash between official and local objectives. Official objectives focus on beef production and environmental protection against presumed 'overstocking' and 'poor range management practice'. By contrast, local interest is focused on the capturing of exclusive rights to grazing land, the maintenance of cattle numbers and the reduction of herding labour. Environmental changes are locally perceived to be the result primarily of rainfall fluctuations, rather than 'overgrazing'. There is consequently much local suspicion that grazing schemes will be a means of introducing destocking 'through the back door'.

Many boundary disputes plague grazing schemes. These result from competition for exclusive rights to particular key grazing resources. Effective operation usually requires fencing. This results in a very high cost, far exceeding expected returns in improved production. Technical questions about the merits of rotational versus continuous grazing remain unresolved, as the assumed benefits to be realized from rotational schemes is unproven. The levels of proposed 'carrying capacities' for grazing schemes assumes a beef production system. A more realistic assessment of potential stock-holding, appropriate to the local production system, is needed. The planning of paddocking and scheme boundaries sometimes does not include explicit consideration of existing patterns of livestock use. External support has been largely technical, with planning often done at a distance and with limited consultation.

Grazing schemes have had variable success. Successes appear to be centred on schemes that have an appropriate scale for management (in terms of ecology and institutional capability), that have resolved conflicts over overlapping rights (feasible only when land availability is not very constrained) and have unified local institutions involving both rich and poor. The opportunities for this combination of factors is rare. Where problems remain unresolved, schemes may collapse (following the withdrawal of donor support) or may be hijacked by influential cattle owners.

Comparative analysis of institutional development in pastoral Africa

As the previous section has illustrated, pastoral organizations have a number of common aspects which influence the process of institution building. This section will examine four of these—level of organization; size; regulatory mechanisms; and top-down versus bottom-up mechanisms—and attempt to develop a comparative analysis of experience across cases.

Level of organization
There are many permanent organizations found in all African pastoral societies, whose structure and operation are not disrupted by the temporary departure of some of their members, nor by the occasional inclusion of members from outside. These organizations may be at the grassroots or at a higher level. There are abundant examples of traditional institutions, past and present, which have been effective in managing natural resources at small group level.[1]

More recently, the new pastoral associations in the western Sahel are based on grassroots organizations which may correspond either to village structures in agropastoral areas (Senegal), or to water points and the rangelands they serve in pastoral areas (Senegal, Mali, Niger; Case 5). At the same time, traditional natural resource exploitation and management practices draw on forms of organization, such as lineages, clans, segments or factions.[2]

---

[1] Amongst these are the Afar in Ethiopia (Noronha and Lethem 1983); Turkana (Barrow 1991) and Boran (Hogg 1983; Swift 1991) family groups; and the *kgotla* structure in Botswana (Niamir 1990).
[2] For instance, clan and lineage organization amongst the Somali and Samburu peoples (Little and Brokensha 1987), and segments or factions amongst the Tuareg (Gallis 1967).

The experience of group ranches in Kenya (Case 1) reflects an attempt to bring several families into an organization broader than that of direct producers. In Zimbabwe, intermediate structures comprise councils at ward level and development committees in villages (Case 6). In countries such as the Central African Republic, there are various levels moving from the National Livestock Producers Federation, the Federations of Pastoral Interest Groups and the individual groups to the agropastoral action zones in charge of land-use management (Marty 1990).

In addition to these varying forms of permanent organizations, there are many *ad hoc* ones. These can be integrative or grassroots, and are set up outside the permanent organizational base. They may become operational around a particular technical activity, or in response to particular constraints or interests. They are therefore characterized by extreme flexibility. This type of organization covers structures at higher levels, such as the conference dealing with *bourgou* pastures in the central delta of the Niger river in Mali (Gallais 1973), or grassroots structures, such as the dam groups in Botswana, which are designed specifically to provide seasonal water management (Case 3). Further examples are given in Box 1.

Some pastoral organizations, such as the grazing associations in southern Africa (Cases 4 and 6) or the group ranches in Kenya (Case 1), are trying to restrict mobility by encouraging sedentarization and the use of semi-intensive systems. As these pastoral organizations mainly stress permanent resource management structures and adopt an exclusive and relatively

---

Box 1. *Ad hoc* pastoral organizations: some examples

○ The camel herders in the Kidal and Menaka areas of Mali, who co-operate during the cold season transhumance to the Tamesna region. This form of co-operation in natural resource exploitation refers to a single type of animal, at a given time of year and to a precise social category of the herders. During the rest of the year, these herders are members of other social groups, tribes, factions and families.

○ On returning from transhumance certain Peuhl from the western Sahel establish contracts with sedentary farmers to graze their animals on agricultural residues following the cereal harvest. During this period, the *ad hoc* group comprises both the transhumant herders and the host farmers. As soon as the crop residues are exhausted, the herders return to their respective territories to take up their position again within their permanent resource management structures.

○ Among the Arabs of central Chad, the basis for co-operation between herders is the herding group, known as a *ferik*, comprising about 20 families. Resources are managed by these herding groups, whose composition changes from year to year as a result of marriage and new alliances (Niamir 1990).

○ Social organization for the use of natural resources amongst the Turkana in Kenya changes with the season and even from week to week according to particular local needs (Watson and Lobuin 1991).

---

fixed type of membership, they do not exploit the benefits of *ad hoc* groups. Hence they are less able to handle mobility and do not provide much institutional flexibility.

Most pastoral organizations tend to make a rigid distinction from the outset between members and non-members, referring back to Western legal concepts. This is more obviously true for grazing associations and group ranches than for pastoral associations in the Sahel, where the coexistence of exclusive and residual rights governing access to water means membership is less rigid.

The strength of pastoral organizations derives from the link between permanent and *ad hoc* organizations; this makes it possible to reduce risks and use resources most effectively. This is achieved through physical and social mobility, organizational flexibility and organizational complementarity.

Size of pastoral organizations
Small organizations undoubtedly have the advantage of social cohesion and are often the result of grassroots initiatives. If the area to be managed is small, it is easier to develop resources and establish mechanisms to regulate the use of such resources and settle disputes. Monitoring is also simplified. It is generally in small organizations that exclusive pastoral rights are most vigorously defended; managing a small area helps to make herders feel responsible for and identify with areas of land. This is certainly true for organizations in the western Sahel, which have developed around traditional pastoral wells (Thébaud 1990), as well as modern wells built by the herders (Nieuwkerk *et al.* 1983).

However, in cases where landholding issues arise on a regional scale, as in the central Niger delta in Mali, small organizations are unable to influence events, because they are dispersed and isolated and lack legitimacy and authority. When the space to be managed is too small to allow the full cycle of pastoral production to take place, small organizations can only deal with a portion of the resource to be managed. It may therefore be necessary to resort to a larger structure comprising several pastoral groups (Sylla 1985).

Clearly, large organizations are able to cover larger areas, resulting in greater fodder availability, species variety, access to key resource areas and so on. Large areas are also vital in view of the climate in dryland zones, where scarce rainfall necessitates greater flexibility and the use of a broad range of pastoral resources. Coverage of large areas may also help, in some cases, to develop greater solidarity between different groups and to broaden social organization. Large organizations may enable herders' needs to be expressed at regional or national level, for example the Peuhl Association of north-west Niger and the Fulani Association in Nigeria (Niamir 1990).

Disadvantages of large organizations centre on problems of control and monitoring. Pastoral associations in Mauritania have encountered this difficulty (Zeidane 1993), and the same goes for environmental management programmes in northern Mali (Sylla 1985). Management regulations tend to be defined in a rather general way. Large areas may include places where tenure is uncertain and which do not lend themselves to the reconciliation of conflicting interests, as in the delta or the valley of the Niger river in Mali, thus complicating the search for solutions (Cissé 1982; Lane and Moorehead this book). Sometimes, it is necessary to seek political solutions at the national level, such as the decree limiting agriculture in pastoral areas in Niger.

Regulatory and enforcement mechanisms

Regulatory and enforcement mechanisms are currently a subtle mixture of traditional and modern. In traditional regulatory mechanisms, the social structure defines the source of power needed for enforcing rules. The means of enforcing rules vary among different groups. Some have an informal 'police force', such as a warrior caste, or official supervisors who monitor the activities of their people or of outsiders. But most groups rely on the observations of each individual member to report transgressions and trespass. Some groups impose fees and penalties for transgression of rules. But the ultimate means, often used when all else fails, is confrontation; in the case of inter-tribal disputes, this may lead to warfare.

Consultation mechanisms are used in order to determine both the rough delimitation of grazing areas and specific rights associated with them and to reach agreement about resource management approaches. Consultation may take place at a local level in order to resolve disputes. For instance, in Senegal relations of *cousinage* enabled the settling of long-running and bitter conflicts between agriculturalists and pastoralists (Guèye 1993). There are also cases where consultation takes place at the supra-national level, such as between Niger and Mali, whose authorities meet at regular intervals to discuss cross-border transhumance.

Various decrees have been promulgated, along with measures for their implementation, in order to reinforce the legal powers of pastoral organizations over grazing areas, as in Senegal, Niger or Mauritania (Case 5). In addition, the presence of state agents helps to ensure respect for the regulations in many cases, as in Lesotho (Case 4).

Other mechanisms of authority include contracts established between pastoral organizations and local authorities, as in Senegal (Shanmugaratnam *et al.* 1992); the integration of pastoral organizations in local politico-administrative structures, as has occurred in Botswana and Zimbabwe (Cases 3 and 6); or the super-imposition of pastoral organizations and local administrative structures, as in the case of the Afar in Ethiopia (Hogg 1990).

Institution building from the top-down and from the bottom-up

Top-down and bottom-up approaches to institution building may appear contradictory. However, closer analysis shows they may complement each other.

The pastoral organizations reviewed so far in this chapter (see Cases 1–6) have been generated from outside pastoral society by both national

143

authorities and donors. This instigation of institutions from the top should not be rejected out of hand, as some devotees of grassroots intervention might be tempted to do. The main thing is to ensure that such initiatives establish mechanisms to ensure participation and to strengthen the organizational and decision-making capacity of pastoral organizations. To put it another way, they should allow solutions to evolve, rather than impose them from outside. In an ideal world, pastoral organizations would emerge at the grassroots on the basis of raised awareness and a recognition of the need for collective action by the herders themselves. However, there are some important reasons why judgement of the top-down approach should not be too severe. Although organizations established by the state or external agencies have sometimes become instruments of control rather than participation, it is none-the-less true that advantage should be taken of such opportunities. If the role of external initiatives in pastoral situations is to kick-start the autonomous development of pastoral organizations, institution building instigated by the state or other external actors may be justified and acceptable.

Initiatives, such as the Nigerian Herders' Association or the Pastoral Network Committee in Kenya, are pastoral organizations promoting the interests of herders at national levels. Equally in Mauritania, some pastoral leaders have begun to speak in terms of a herder movement at regional and national levels. Such groups are responsible for negotiation and consultation in connection with the place of herders in society, including issues relating to the management of pastoral resources (Zeidane 1993).

Strengthening the institutional capacity of grassroots pastoral organizations must be linked to the macro-level, to broaden their perspective. Working solely at the grassroots may lead only to minor alterations in the pastoralists' situation, whereas many problems faced by pastoralists relate to broader policy issues (Hogg 1992). Pastoral organizations should be set up at various levels in order to incorporate both the most decentralized levels and the highest decision-making levels. For instance, it would be naïve to think that land tenure systems in pastoral areas could be redefined without government approval. It would be just as naïve to think that governments will do this on their own. Ways of achieving change could include political pressure exerted by intermediate (regional or national) pastoral organizations, and using the grassroots organizations' practical knowledge to implement such a policy in the field.

The need for an institutional division of the functions of pastoral organizations thus argues in favour of complementarity between top-down and bottom-up approaches. However, much broader issues are raised by such a division of functions, which must be part of a gradual and continuous process of institution building.

Pastoral organizations and natural resource management: key issues

The experience considered here raises broader issues of a conceptual, legal, sociological and political nature. The institutional strength and effectiveness of pastoral organizations in natural resource management depends on the way these issues are viewed and resolved.

In many areas there appears to be a conflict of objectives between herders and development programmes. For example, some projects are designed on the basis of meat production and environmental protection, despite the fact that these objectives do not necessarily correspond to the primary concerns of the local population (e.g. Cousins 1992 for Zimbabwe; White 1992 for Botswana). Very often, the standard approach does not reflect the way herders see things, and is based on the false assumption that they will change their behaviour as a result of an increase in their income and the maintenance of a controlled number of animals on the rangelands. Herders consider pastoral organizations of this type to be useful mainly in respect of obtaining and safeguarding certain land rights, as overgrazing is rarely seen by the herders to be a major problem (Perrier this book). Secondly, the concept of natural resource management is often either too broad or too limited. In Mauritania, pastoral organizations have readjusted to smaller management areas which are easier for local communities to control, following the example of Senegal (Case 5). By contrast, in Kenya, Botswana, Lesotho and Zimbabwe (Cases 1, 3, 4, 6), the extensive, rather than intensive, nature of land use and differences in the seasonality and variability of grazing areas, have not been recognized. This has led herders to seek pasture in areas outside the land allocated to the pastoral organizations, thus demonstrating the faulty conception of the recommended management model.

Another shortcoming is the way land is divided up without sufficient regard for existing social organization. This has led to numerous difficulties in ensuring herder participation in group ranches in Kenya (Case 1). In the case of the grazing reserves in Nigeria (Case 2), no account was taken of the integration between farmers and herders and an artificial separation was set up. In Mali, the fact that the associations have not established institutional links with farmers remains a major constraint to the co-ordinated management of resources. Also in Mali, as well as in Niger and Mauritania, the lack of a clear boundary to the territory to be managed leads to misunderstandings and difficulties for the pastoral organizations when applying regulatory measures (Case 5).

Inadequacies within organizations have resulted in a variety of common difficulties:
o The institutional weakness of the associations due to the absence or disappearance of local structures;
o Inability to master complex planning and management systems in the absence of adequate training and participation;
o Uneven ability of grazing committees to mobilize labour and local funds and to monitor project implementation.

All these elements have been either ignored or inadequately perceived by the various projects. It is important to remember that resource management in itself is not always enough. It should be seen as a complement to other activities such as animal health, drug procurement, credit, restocking, extension work and so on. This integration is reflected in the aims of the World Bank projects in Mali and Niger (Case 5).

Legal recognition of pastoral organizations

Legalizing pastoral organizations means increasing their legal capacity to design and enforce natural resource protection and management measures. There are some cases where herders have individual rights, as well as formal recognition of their associations, as in the case of the group ranches (Case 1). Elsewhere, as in Senegal or Mauritania, because of an imprecise framework, pastoral organizations are not in a position to impose legal management regulations (Case 5). However, in Senegal, placing the relationship between pastoral associations and the local administration on a contractual basis is a way of consolidating the legal procedures. In cases such as Mali, the lack of recognition of pastoral organizations makes them institutionally weak and unable to manage their territory.

Traditional pastoral organizations enjoy an unwritten consensus on the part of the herders themselves that the management rules and practices they recognize deserve wider recognition. In the case of the Afar in Ethiopia, traditional organization of resource management is not only recognized, but also forms the basis of the government's administrative structure (Hogg 1990). In Sudan, on the other hand, the government's decision to abolish the traditional chieftaincies and tenure systems led to great confusion and innumerable conflicts between pastoralists with regard to natural resource use (Adams 1982). However, the principle of legalizing traditional management structures where they can still be effective must be weighed against the existence of structures which are no longer operational. In Botswana, for example, former collective resource management systems have largely disappeared as a result of changes within local society (White 1992). In Mali too, the *dina* code is losing its original coherence and has been profoundly modified by the combined effect of its own internal contradictions and external factors (Cissé 1982).

Legalization of pastoral organizations should go hand in hand with the search for solutions to land tenure problems (Lane and Moorehead this book). Pastoral organizations in the Sahel have been trying to incorporate exclusive rights and residual rights within tenure systems with varying degrees of success. Although the exclusive users of water points and certain pastures are the members of pastoral associations, arrangements are nevertheless made to enable others to have access to these resources, with rules limiting the number of days on which such access may be granted. Despite these efforts, which reflect the spirit of local natural resource management practice in the Sahel, there is still another step to be taken: adapting the general arrangements defined by governments to individual circumstances, so that the principle of differential rights may genuinely reflect realities on the ground.

146

Pastoral societies are not homogeneous
In Kenya, grazing blocks reflect neither local territorial arrangements nor traditional social organization (Pratt 1990; Barton 1993). The design of group ranches is also based on Western models of commercial agriculture, which have little in common with indigenous organizational systems (Jacobs 1975; Boutrais 1990). An alternative approach is to try to integrate traditional elements as far as possible, as shown by the experience of pastoral organizations in Senegal and Mauritania (Case 5). In fact, in these cases, the division of resource management units is based on territory and social organization; the traditional organizations selected are villages in the agropastoral context of Senegal and clans in Mauritania.

Pastoral societies are not homogeneous. Sometimes, they are founded on unequal social stratification (nobles, freemen, castes and slaves) which discourages democratic processes. New social classes have also recently emerged in the towns, whose interests do not necessarily coincide with those of pastoralists, even if some of these city dwellers are of pastoral origin. Differentiation within associations themselves is a major constraint encountered by grazing associations in Lesotho (Case 4). Although the members belong to the same geographical area, a range of factors weaken social and economic cohesion. This contributed to the 'dilemma of achieving coordinated common behaviour in an environment characterized by producer heterogeneity' (Lawry 1987).

In Mali, since the latest droughts, there has been a radical change in livestock ownership; government officials and city traders have gained control of the majority of herds. As these 'new herders' do not live in the pastoral area, a serious problem arises in terms of decision-making, the establishment of pastoral organizations and collective management procedures. The new livestock owners tend to favour completely free access to rangeland (Shanmugaratnam et al. 1992) and sometimes use their political influence to slow down the process of empowering herders. In the case of Somalia, an originally fairly homogeneous pastoral society has gradually set up new élites whose production strategies are often contrary to those of pastoralists. This is highlighted by the acquisition of the best land for individual purposes and by the enclosure of formerly collective rangeland (Doornbos et al. 1992; Graham 1988).

The role of women in pastoral organizations is generally approached in two ways: through the development of specific women's activities or by the integration of women in a broader production process (Sylla 1989). In almost all pastoral societies, women's social and economic status remains low. According to Horowitz and Jowkar (1992), 'discrimination against women is related not only to legal measures favouring men, but is also rooted in androcentric indigenous interpretations of customary rights to land and its products.'

There are several reasons for encouraging women's participation in pastoral organizations and natural resource management activities. Women are direct users of natural resources: collecting and working wood, fetching water, gathering wild cereals and straw for the camps and so on. Ecological changes can have a particularly harsh impact on

147

women. War, drought and migration have meant that many women have taken up new responsibilities in herd and resource management. They have therefore become decision-makers who should not be ignored either in institution building or in natural resource management.

In most pastoral areas, women lack access to land rights. On the group ranches in Kenya, only 1 per cent of women have been able to acquire land title, meaning that land privatization has helped to make women even more vulnerable (Pointing and Joekes 1991). Another problem concerns the very concept of ranches in which meat production, requiring mainly male animals, comes into competition with milk production. This may mean that women no longer have enough milk available to meet their own and their children's nutritional and economic needs (Horowitz and Jowkar 1992). Finally, literacy training, which is an important tool in institution building, involves very few women in Sahelian pastoral organizations (Shanmugaratnam et al. 1992).

Political aspects and the role of the state

In setting up pastoral organizations there is often a conflict between the state's macro-economic need to increase revenue and the herders' livelihood needs. Pastoral land tenure is basically collective, with adjustments in certain circumstances to take account of individual ownership. As land has little commercial value, a policy of liberalizing access as in Kenya, can lead to the disintegration of traditional, local natural resource management practices. This trend is beyond herders' control, and so it is incumbent on the state to at least adopt a careful approach, if not to revise its development objectives.

There is a question as to who has final responsibility for selecting the criteria and general orientations defining 'good' natural resource management. In this regard, it may be that donors themselves have too big an influence on the state. As Anders Hjort points out, the questions we should ask are: 'Who decides? Who has the right to decide in the place of local people? And how can we get away from preconceived ideas originating in a different cultural context to that of pastoralists?' (Hjort 1991).

Experience shows that although solutions must be local, state support is also important. For example, the experience of grazing associations in Lesotho and dam groups in Botswana (Cases 3 and 4) has shown that the technical support of state agents has been a determining factor in the gains achieved.

In administrative and legal terms, the legalization of pastoral organizations can only occur within a standard legislative and political framework defined at national level. Although some states, for instance in the western Sahel, have committed themselves to official recognition of pastoral organizations, there is a clear need to go much further (Case 5). This is why in Senegal, Mauritania and Niger, despite the fact that the state has defined the overall legal and institutional framework for pastoral organizations, more localized enforcement measures and regulations must still be put in place; otherwise the pastoral associations will not really be in a position to manage natural resources locally. To ensure effective management, the

148

state must support the establishment of decentralized institutions and make a sincere commitment to share responsibility with grassroots communities (Thomson *et al.* 1991).

Comparative lessons from dryland Africa: ten conclusions

Use ad hoc *organizations.* Ad hoc organizations blur the lines of institutions involved in natural resource management. Institution building should focus more closely on the potential they offer in terms of spatial, temporal and social mobility. This means that apart from seeking to set up permanent organizations, it is wise to seek ways to integrate herders in *ad hoc* natural resource management organizations. In this way, current monolithic concepts can be replaced with a more dispersed approach, with several flexible levels of organization linked together in various ways. However, this approach will be far from easy and will present even greater challenges to pastoral institution building.

Membership must be flexible. Herders in dryland Africa generally respect two basic principles, which demonstrate their acceptance of a common set of ethics. First, all herders understand and condone the need of other herders to drive livestock wherever water and pasture can be found. Second, no herder would think of preventing the access of another to water and pasture when there is enough to go round. It is this reciprocity and solidarity which has enabled herders to develop strategies to cope with the extremely difficult conditions in their environment. Pastoral organizations might therefore place long-term solidarity before short-term benefits in natural resource management. It is therefore vital to develop institutions where membership is an extremely flexible concept.

Support bottom-up and *top-down approaches.* Bottom-up and top-down organizational approaches are complementary as they can be part of an effective distribution of management functions. For instance, external shocks, like severe drought or disease outbreak, which are beyond the capacity of small pastoral organizations, need wider assistance in order to buffer risks. Although priority should be given to the bottom-up approach, the tasks of defining and strengthening the place of pastoralists within overall civil society, as well as macro-political issues, may be better resolved at a higher level. When providing assistance to pastoralists, support should therefore also be given to organizations at the top, if they show the potential to become genuine consultative structures defending herders' interests. In conditions where local natural resource management structures have been weakened for one reason or another, there may be no alternative to the establishment of local pastoral organizations through external intervention.

Support small organizations. Experience shows it is important to begin by working with small organizations which are more coherent and more able to produce immediate results from collective action. Smaller size also enables herders to make economic investments, define and enforce precise management rules and set the boundaries of the area to be managed. In order to take account of herder mobility and the unpredictability of natural resources, both enclosed and more open spaces should be included in the management of small land areas reflecting exclusive and residual rights. Land access is also a tool in strengthening power and responsibility for resource management.

Although pragmatic considerations suggest that it may be necessary to try to manage natural resources on a very broad scale, attention should be paid to fostering small-scale management within this. However, small-scale management should not be an end in itself. The day will come when it will be necessary to take a broader view. Management on a wider scale may then draw lessons from the experiences of small groups and take advantage of the collective dynamics already set in train.

Support weaker groups. Contests over access to resources in uncertain environments are, at the same time, opportunities for the rich, but also sources of vulnerability for the poor. In addressing these issues, management and policy responses need to address ways of strengthening institution building for conflict management, and the provision of information and legal support to marginalized groups.

Take into account traditional systems. Natural resource management by pastoral organizations should be based on traditional systems. Where these have failed or are no longer appropriate, account should still be taken of the traditional territory within which herders move, which may well have been defined coherently in terms of historical overlapping interests and rights. Where traditional systems are applied, this should go hand-in-hand with enhancement of traditional decision-making procedures, in order to root natural resource management in the socio-cultural perceptions of the herders. In this regard, it should not be assumed that traditional systems are egalitarian or democratic in all cases. While they should be taken as they are to begin with, with their qualities and their defects, the questions of monopolization or exclusion can gradually be settled, or at least tackled, as part of the institution building process.

Do not focus on one strategy or group in isolation. In view of the complexity of natural resource management and the fact that herders often do not see overgrazing as a high-priority problem, it is unwise to choose this theme as a starting point in setting up pastoral organizations. Natural resource management needs to be part of a cluster of strategies that reflect varying conditions and concerns. All such strategies must have a participatory approach. The more groups involved, the more complex is the structure to set up and the more it is necessary to understand the heterogeneity of interest groups, including hidden groups like absentee herd owners. Emphasis should be put on identifying conflicting interests. Equal chance should be provided to each group by providing them with the same level of information and awareness. This

150

is of special importance when legal texts are already being used in order to change or fix tenure.

Planning must be flexible. The setting up of pastoral organizations must be an iterative and adaptive process. This is very demanding. It requires a lot of time and appropriate methodologies must be found to implement the process. It would be wiser to tackle this in terms of flexible programming, rather than a rigid project framework (Perrier this book).

The geographical, ecological and social resources of a given group must be defined. These must be on a broad enough scale to include a variety of grazing areas, but still on a small enough scale to be managed effectively. This becomes more difficult when dealing with particularly prized range-lands and key resources. There must be flexibility in drawing up technical natural resource management plans, in order to take account of the need for mobility associated with disruptions such as drought and also with traditional pastoral solidarity. Planning thus cannot be prescriptive; it must be adaptive and flexible (Scoones; Perrier this book).

Treat both privatization and collectivization with caution. Experience shows that land-holdings should be seen neither as a completely private nor a completely collective affair. In cases where systematic privatization is being pursued, the state is not always in a position to prevent this happening nor to control all land transactions. Privatization in pastoral areas is always a very sensitive matter where land tenure is fundamentally collective in character. While privatization may sometimes lead to or result from investment and growing interest by herders in a given territory, it may, in other cases, be accepted by herders only because it enables them to guarantee land rights, although it changes nothing in their natural resource use strategy.

Poorly applied collective rights also have well known drawbacks, such as manipulation and covert expropriation by powerful individuals. Moreover, in situations where collective ownership does not safeguard private interests, herders will tend to adapt land tenure to their needs and constraints, taking advantage of existing legal contradictions or confusion. It may therefore be possible to envisage a system in which private rights are protected on a small scale, through local resource development, as in the case of individual pastoral wells in the Sahel. Collective rights would be handled at community level, rather than exercised by the state. This could be done by supporting traditional collective tenure systems where these are still operational (Lane and Moorehead this book).

Support decentralized authority. Pastoral organizations operate within a context which is both modern and traditional. There is much ambiguity between different systems for resolution of conflict; the choice of structure will be determined by the kind of judgement being sought. It is essential that this ambiguity be clarified. It is appropriate to strengthen decentralized institutions which can respond to the particularities of local environments. This means that the state must speed up the process of administrative

151

decentralization and codification of enforcement mechanisms. This decentralization process should follow the principle of subsidiarity, in which power and responsibility are devolved to the lowest institutional level consistent with provision of services and maintenance of accountability (Swift this book). However, when beginning to set up pastoral organizations, state presence in the field is still necessary for technical reasons. In a long-term perspective, the state should always be prepared to deal with conflicts that pastoral organizations are unable to resolve. There is a need to define both a general framework for legal process and a specific set of agreements on a case-by-case basis, to ensure that these measures are appropriate to field reality.

9. Dynamic ecological systems and the administration of pastoral development

JEREMY SWIFT

This chapter speculates about some potential consequences of new ideas about dynamic ecological systems for the administration of development in pastoral areas. Pastoral areas have been subject to very interventionist forms of administration based on several powerful premises, such as that scientists and administrators know better than pastoralists what needs to be done and how to do it, and that there are important interests of the state involved in pastoral areas which are amenable to state intervention.

These ideas about the rationale, style and purpose of pastoral administration are now under threat from dynamic ecosystems theory (Ellis this book). This comes at the same time as other threats to pastoral development bureaucracies. It is widely recognized that the administration of pastoral development has been unsuccessful, even by the low standards of rural development in general. The declining legitimacy of the state and the failure of many African economies have triggered programmes of structural adjustment which question previous habits of bureaucratic spending and previous ways of doing things; pastoral administrations are likely to be prime targets for retrenchment. Many donors have now largely withdrawn from projects in the dry pastoral areas. There is a general, although possibly exaggerated, perception that population is increasing and the environment is declining rapidly in the pastoral areas, making changes inevitable. Food insecurity is widespread, perhaps increasing, and this is seen as unacceptable. Civil security has declined catastrophically in many pastoral areas, with harsh consequences for pastoralists themselves and also, which is more politically important, for the security of the state.

So the forces for change in pastoral administration come not only from dynamic ecosystems theory, but also from a much broader range of economic and political pressures. In looking at the potential consequences of the new ecological ideas, we must also take into account these broader processes if we are to have any hope of success.

In this chapter the term 'administration' is used in a very general sense, to mean the processes by which everyday economic life—especially the management of natural resources—is organized and carried out. This

153

chapter is more an attempt to provide a framework for analysis, and to identify an agenda and order of business, than to provide solutions.

Pastoral organizations and institutions: a framework

Organizations and institutions are the two crucial structural components of pastoral administration. Each of these may be either formal or informal. Within organizations and institutions, individuals or small groups may follow divergent strategies. Pastoral administration is the complex outcome of this mix of individual strategies, and formal and informal institutions and organizations.

Institutions are the rules of the game in which individual strategies compete. Institutions are 'the humanly devised constraints that shape human interaction . . . they structure incentives in human exchange, whether political, social or economic. . . . Institutions reduce uncertainty by providing a structure to everyday life. . . . Institutions include any form of constraint that human beings devise to shape interaction' (North 1990: 3–4). Institutions are such things as land tenure rules or the structures and rules regulating trade. Although the two words are often used interchangeably, strictly speaking organizations are not the same as institutions. Organizations are 'groups of individuals bound by some common purpose to achieve objectives' (North 1990:5). Organizations thus include government departments or herder associations. Organizations operate within the framework—the rules and constraints—provided by institutions.

Pastoral organizations and institutions may be either formal or informal; the latter are often also called customary. Formal in this connection means established in written law, created by conscious, recorded decision with established precedents. Formal institutions important for pastoral development include, for example, those elements of national constitutions and legislation dealing with land ownership and use, property rights in animals or trade. Formal organizations include the judiciary, government bureaucracies such as the veterinary service, political parties, aid agencies such as the World Bank or Oxfam, schools or churches.

Informal or customary organizations and institutions are those which exist without comprehensive formal recognition by the modern state; they are the habitual ways—not established in written law—a pastoral society manages its everyday affairs. Informal institutions important in pastoral development include customary land tenure rules, rules and conventions about marriage, inheritance or trade and customary procedures to resolve conflicts over access to resources or animal theft. Informal organizations involved in pastoral development include all those by which pastoral society itself is customarily structured, based on kinship, descent, traditional politics or geographic proximity.

Table 1 summarizes this simple distinction, with one example in each box of the matrix. In practice, the extremes of one category merge with those of the other, so the four boxes of the matrix are not completely watertight.

When herders accept institutional rules and constraints or participate in

154

Table 1. The organizational basis for pastoral administration

	Formal	Informal or customary
Institutions	The land law	Customary land tenure
Organizations	The range department	A customary neighbourhood association

organizations, they give up some of the benefits of individual action in return for the benefits of co-operation. The benefits of co-operation are both direct (for example, the capture of economies of scale in production or trade) and indirect. The most important indirect benefit is in the reduction of uncertainty about the activities of other individuals. Institutions reduce uncertainty for economic actors by reducing the transaction costs, especially the costs of acquiring information about other actors' intentions and activities, reaching and policing agreements and enforcing sanctions. Co-operation also has costs, however, both in terms of economic options forgone (for example, the option to free-ride on a resource) and in terms of the transaction costs of co-operation itself.

Institutions and organizations are the result of trade-offs between the benefits and the costs of co-operating. Organizing has a transaction cost, and more constraining forms of organization and institution have higher transaction costs; they are unlikely to evolve, or to be successfully introduced, unless the benefits from co-operation substantially exceed the costs. Benefits and costs are not evenly distributed, especially in the heterogeneous and hierarchical societies characteristic of many pastoral areas.

Institutions form part of the set of constraints, which also includes environmental risk and resource availability, determining the economic potential of particular land uses. Institutions are dynamic: they evolve and change in response to changes in the costs and benefits of organizing, as these are perceived by participants, depending also on who are the winners and losers from changes in the distribution of benefits and costs. The task of institutional and organizational analysis and design in pastoral areas is to encourage this evolution by proposing new types of institution and organization which reduce transaction costs and enhance the benefits of particular types of action in the pursuit of pastoral development objectives.

The main thrust of this chapter is that for effective pastoral administration there must be an appropriate mix, which will vary according to particular circumstances, of formal and informal institutions and organizations; that this mix should shift in the direction of strengthened informal institutions and organizations; and that the mix will be different in non-equilibrium and equilibrium ecosystems.

Arguing for a strengthening of informal institutions and organizations in development is not the same as arguing for decentralization. Decentralization normally concerns devolution to formal institutions. Although decentralization may often work in the same general direction as that being

155

proposed here, an argument in favour of giving increased power to informal institutions goes beyond decentralization; indeed it may well be easier for a strong central government to devolve power to customary institutions.

A single administrative type or several?

It is unlikely that a single set of administrative solutions will be suitable for all pastoral areas, even if other factors (e.g. ethnicity, administrative tradition, external economic and political environment) are held constant. The degree to which dynamic ecosystem theory explains events in the drylands appears to vary substantially according to, among other things, the degree of aridity itself. Other characteristics of pastoral administration also vary with the degree of aridity, and this covariance is important, since it suggests that several administrative models, or a very variable model, will be necessary. The starting points, in the sense of the actual situation of different pastoral groups, are also very variable, and this is also an important influence on likely administrative reform outcomes.

Table 2 shows some of these variables, arranged on a scale from very dry to wetter pastoral environments. In Africa, these extremes range from below 100mm to as much as 1000mm annual rainfall. In the pastoral environments of the Middle East and central Asia, the precipitation range is much less, although the characteristics of drier and wetter environments are similar. At the dry end of the range, environmental variability is high and, if dynamic equilibrium theory is correct, non-equilibrium dynamics dominate. Not only is risk to producers high, but also that risk is much more likely to be covariate, affecting large numbers of producers simultaneously and reducing their ability to devise local risk reduction or insurance institutions (Platteau 1991; Dasgupta 1993). In such circumstances, management units should be large to take account of the need for large-scale mobility, the likely small size of production units (households or camps) and the need to pool risks within a large unit.

Table 2. Some differences between dry and wet pastoral environments

| | Pastoral environments | |
	Dry	Wet
Ecological variability	High	Low
Level of risk	High	Low
Covariance of risk	High	Low
Need for mobility	High	Low
Size and permanence of basic production units	Small	Large
Size of resource management units	Large	Small
Transaction costs of organization	High	Low
Necessary benefits for organization to be successful	High	Low
Availability of technical innovations	Low	High
Marginal productivity gains from innovation	Low	High
Need for government/donor support	High	Low

In the dry areas, the transaction costs of any form of organization or institution are high, meaning that there must be substantial benefits for people to organize willingly, or for government to organize people with any chance of success. There are few proven technical innovations available off the shelf, and the benefits from them are small and variable. There is also probably a high and continuing need for government and donor support.

One lesson of Table 2 is that there is unlikely to be a single model of pastoral administration adapted to the needs of all pastoral ecosystems. The distinction between drier, largely non-equilibrium, ecosystems, and wetter, more equilibrial, ones, is critical: the characteristics of pastoral environments listed in Table 2 suggest that administrative frameworks for dryland areas will be very different from those useful in wetter areas.

Three general principles

The basic premises of non-equilibrium ecological systems theory suggest three general principles to be followed in the design of new forms of pastoral administration. First, a need for great *flexibility and diversity* in institutional and organizational design to enable administration to track appropriately the dynamic changes which will occur in ecosystem properties. Second, the importance of *subsidiarity*, i.e. administrative tasks should be carried out as near to the level of actual users of resources or beneficiaries of administration as is compatible with efficiency and accountability. Third, the need to reduce the *transaction costs* of organizing as far as possible in order to obtain a viable transaction benefit-cost relationship. Put another way, we should be seeking a modified Occam's razor in administrative design: we should seek not to multiply administrative levels unnecessarily, try to have powers and responsibilities devolved and authority delegated to the lowest level compatible with the results we are trying to achieve and try to reduce transaction costs as far as possible. In many cases, this will mean customary pastoral institutions themselves carrying out administrative tasks now done by government agencies. Our recent improved understanding of how pastoral societies function suggests that subsidiarity, flexibility and transaction cost reduction are mutually reinforcing, not antagonistic.

A further general principle would be, where possible, to move some tasks now performed by a formal administrative organization to the market (see Holtzman and Kulibaba (this book) for a more complete discussion).

Flexibility in pastoral administration
There is a great variety of informal types of pastoral institution and organization now found in rangeland areas (Sylla this book). It is sometimes tempting to speak of customary or 'traditional' pastoral institutions (kinship or political system) operating in parallel with, or in contrast to, the formal administrative apparatus of the state. However, pastoral administration usually consists of at least four intertwined strands:

157

○ A largely customary set of rules and institutions, based on the kinship system (who is descended from whom, who marries whom), regulating use of and access to some sets of resources (labour, and in many cases animals); I shall call these 'kin institutions'
○ A largely customary set of rules and institutions, based on geographic considerations (who lives where), regulating use of and access to most land-based resources (grazing, browse, supplementary fodder, fuel, water, salt, agricultural land); I shall call these 'geographic institutions'
○ A set of formal institutions and organizations set up by government to regulate land-based resources, technical matters, pastoral development and administration generally; I shall call these 'formal institutions'
○ A set of hybrid or mixed institutions and organizations, combining formal elements and customary elements, sometimes explicitly, sometimes only implicitly and in practice; I shall call these 'mixed institutions'.

In this chapter I will refer to kinship and geographic institutions (the first two categories in the list above), together as customary institutions.

The strength and relative effectiveness of these four types of institution vary widely, but in almost all cases all four types are present. In northern Kenya and southern Ethiopia, for example, among Boran pastoralists, kinship and geographic institutions are strong and regulate many aspects of pastoral life and livelihood. Formal institutions are correspondingly weak (Swift and Abdi 1992). In other places, customary institutions (kinship and geographic) are apparently weak and formal institutions strong. This was argued to be the case in Mongolia after full collectivization in the 1950s, and is thought to be the case in the central Asian states of the former Soviet Union. In Africa, it is believed by many administrators that formal institutions have overtaken customary institutions in many places, for example, in Kenyan group ranches.

Two points may be made here. The first is that however strong the formal institutions are, we are beginning to realize that customary institutions are tenacious and tend to persist, despite the apparently overwhelming hold of formal institutions. In Mongolia, rapid decollectivization in the early 1990s might have led to an institutional vacuum. In fact, customary institutions, mainly of geographic rather than kinship type, persisted through severe repression early in the socialist transformation, followed by 40 years of heavy central planning and administration, and re-emerged rapidly after the dissolution of the pastoral collectives in 1991 and 1992 to regulate and co-ordinate pasture and natural resource allocation and use (Mearns 1993; Potkanski and Szynkiewicz 1993).

Similarly in Africa, the collapse of even the pretence of formal range management institutions, such as grazing blocks and grazing schemes in many parts of Kenya and Tanzania, revealed the persistence of customary forms of pasture land tenure and resource allocation. In many areas (for example, among Kenyan Boran, some Tanzanian Maasai and no doubt many others), kinship institutions continue to provide the only even partly reliable safety nets for destitute pastoralists through clan-based livestock redistribution (Swift 1991; Potkanski 1994), despite several decades of persistent government and donor attempts to deny them legitimacy. In all African pastoral economies such kinship institutions (including pre-inheritance of livestock within restricted families, and clan- or lineage-based redistribution) continue to provide the means by which new households are equipped with a viable household herd for independent pastoral production.

The second point concerns mixed institutions. These have had little attention in the literature, perhaps because they are not the obvious responsibility of any one field (anthropologists focus on customary institutions, political scientists on formal institutions), but it is likely that they are widespread and effective. School committees in pastoral areas of Kenya are a good example. They are formal committees, set up with local government backing and support, but operating at least partly according to customary procedures and making decisions on natural resource use (for example, reserve pastures around the school) in line with customary rules. These mixed institutions may offer an important way forward when we come to think about the design of new forms of pastoral administration.

Subsidiarity in pastoral administration

Once it is recognized that a variety of customary institutions and organizations continue to perform valuable roles in administering pastoral areas, it makes sense to ask whether some administrative powers currently held by government, and which duplicate those exercised by pastoral society itself, can be delegated to pastoral society, thus lightening the burden on government and perhaps leading to more efficient administration and substantial cost savings. Such delegation of responsibility is also likely to lead to a more flexible response to the management needs of a dynamic ecosystem. The task is to identify what administrative roles are indeed performed effectively by what customary organizations and institutions, what are the shortcomings of this, how the shortcomings can be overcome and what would be the advantages and disadvantages if government were to withdraw partly or completely from such roles.

Transaction costs

The subsidiarity argument can be made in a more formal way. Because of the great variability and unpredictability of dryland environments, the transaction costs of organization are high. It is therefore important to try to reduce them as much as possible. One way to do this is to shift greater responsibility for pastoral administration onto customary institutions and organizations, and internalize transaction costs within the overall decision-making process of the local pastoral economy. Since pastoralists in the drylands are already transacting through customary institutions and organizations over a wide range of issues, the marginal transaction cost of additional activities may be low. For example, members of neighbourhood groups meet regularly to co-ordinate their movements; if these meetings are given greater decision-making powers, backed up by the sanctions of the formal legal system where necessary, the additional cost is low and the benefit high. The main transaction costs are also shifted from the bureaucracy on to those who have most interest in an efficient outcome.

There is also a strong self-policing element in such a course of action. Because people are transacting over such a wide range of issues essential to their continuing membership of the community, the cost to them of ignoring rules and flouting conventions is very high and will have repercussions for the whole of their community membership and the benefits they get from it. Where, say, land tenure is removed from customary rules and made subject only to formal law, herders can ignore the rules without jeopardizing the benefits of their membership of local communities: the costs of doing so are low (e.g. the risk of a fine in court), the benefits of free-riding may be high (e.g. access to reserved pasture), and the chance of being detected is low. On the other hand, where land tenure is part and parcel of a comprehensive set of customary institutions regulating many aspects of everyday economic life, the benefits of free-riding may be the same, but the costs are very high (e.g. exclusion from local economic and social networks and from the ritual community) and the likelihood of detection is also high. The overall transaction cost calculus is very different in the second case from the first.

The following section considers these questions in greater detail in relation to specific administrative topics. In summary, I argue that the guiding principle should be that the boundaries between local community action and action by the bureaucracy can potentially be rolled back—that is, subsidiarity can be achieved and the transaction benefit-cost calculus improved—in many cases by allowing customary or mixed institutions to carry out tasks at present managed by government.

Key tasks of pastoral administration

This section looks at some of the key tasks of pastoral administration. In each case I ask whether and how the task is performed by customary organizations and institutions, how this relates to the role of the bureaucracy and what the prospects are either for reducing the role of formal administration or for making it more efficient. Because of its paramount importance, I give most attention to natural resource tenure. The principles set out apply also to other areas.

Natural resource tenure

One of the most basic sets of administrative tasks to be carried out in pastoral economies concern natural resource tenure and allocation. Dynamic ecological systems require tenure systems to be flexible, to allow reciprocal access in bad years, to allow mobility on varying scales according to the conditions of the year, to allow for highly variable scales of exploitation and to include detailed provisions for access to and management of key resources (Lane and Moorehead this book).

Almost all African pastoral societies have had, in recent memory, customary institutions to manage access to natural resources which include many of these characteristics. The strength of such institutions can be classified on a continuum from weak to strong. If we ignore for a moment recent influences on these institutions, we can identify reference points at either end and in the middle of the continuum.

○ A classic example of a case where resource tenure institutions have probably always been weak is the Wodaabe Fulani of West Africa. Their land-use system is based on rapid movement and the use of interstitial pastures between powerful and long-established villages or other pastoral societies. The Wodaabe do have rules regarding access to water and dry season grazing, but these are flexible and adapted to changing conditions as the Wodaabe move their territory (Swift 1984).

○ In systems where natural resource tenure institutions have historically regulated mainly boundary conditions (who is allowed access to the resource), there are generally much fewer detailed rules about resource allocation among members of the controlling group itself. However even here rules exist and are administered. This is probably the most common case in Africa, including for example most West African Tuareg and Fulani (Bernus 1974; Gallais 1975), and major east African pastoral groups such as the Turkana, Barabaig and Maasai (Homewood and Rodgers 1991; Lane 1991).

○ Cases where both external and internal rules of access are clearly articulated and administered, conflicts are rapidly adjudicated and parties to disputes accept that adjudication, used to include the Niger inner delta Fulani in West Africa (Gallais 1967; Moorehead 1991), several Sudanese and Somali pastoral groups (Howell 1954; Said 1994), and still include the Boran in Kenya and Ethiopia (Swift and Abdi 1992), and herders in Lesotho (Swallow 1991).

Most of these types of customary resource tenure institutions have undergone considerable transformation in the twentieth century, generally in the direction of a weakening of customary controls as a result of increased state control, an increase in market relations and an increase in population pressure on resources. In some cases, customary institutions themselves have been captured by élites within the society and benefits redirected towards private economic activity. There is almost everywhere a great deal of competition between customary and state institutions for natural resource tenure. The surprise is, however, the extent to which customary tenure institutions continue to play a role in many cases.

Dynamic ecosystem theory, together with the principles of subsidiarity and reduced transaction cost, suggest that administrative reform in the field of pastoral land tenure should concentrate on restoring and supporting customary control of resources, and rolling back attempts by the state to manage such resources in detail. This would restore flexibility and local accountability, would bring social and private costs into line, would ensure that users were in a position to make effective decisions about resource use with full knowledge about the likely consequences and would improve the benefit-cost calculus. This latter point is especially important. Non-equilibrium environments require flexibility and opportunism in movement. Appropriate tenure rules and incentives would provide a framework

Box 1. Administration of pastoral resource tenure

Case 1: Somalia (Source: Said 1994)

In Somalia, pastoralists have a tradition of co-operation in the management of rangelands. Successful co-operation takes place where there are groups of users without wide differences in wealth or in economic objectives, where customary contract law (*xeer*) is well developed and where functioning customary kin and clan structures facilitate co-operation on a wide range of issues. Co-operation is undermined where the government claims management sovereignty over the rangelands, where individual rich herders or merchants introduce different management objectives or where donor-assisted projects undermine customary decision-making and enforcement processes. The lessons drawn for a more successful rangeland development strategy include: strengthening the force of customary *xeer* contracts by putting them in written form and using them as a basis for formal laws, a closer and more symbiotic relationship in pastoral areas between customary authorities and locally elected officials and the bureaucracy, and the alignment of development plans for range and water with customary common property resource boundaries and management rules.

Case 2: Lesotho (Source: Swallow 1991)

In Lesotho, a strong central government has based an evolutionary pasture land tenure regime in part on customary institutions and organizations. There are important differences in grazing regime between village pastures and cattle posts in the mountain rangelands, especially in determining conditions of access and times when grazing is permitted. The *maboella* regime governing access to village pastures is a customary system developed in the early nineteenth century by the paramount ruler Moshoeshoe and administered by local chiefs and headmen. It is designed to protect village common grazing for particular uses during certain times of the year and regulate access to particular categories of pasture and wood resource. Although declining traditional authority and financial incentives, and increasing population, have put *maboella* regimes under stress to the point where they have virtually collapsed in some areas, in others the scarcity of alternative resources has strengthened the *maboella* regime. This is particularly the case where the village chief is a major livestock owner and so has a personal incentive to make the system succeed, but where nevertheless he does not abuse the system; where the chief and the village development committee participate in leadership of the grazing system, and where the regime is firmly based on the customary system. The policy recommendations in this case were that *maboella* regimes were appropriate to current conditions, but that they needed to be strengthened by better institutional mechanisms governing access and enforcement.

within which pastoral groups could negotiate the use of each other's territories according to very variable local conditions. The transaction cost of a government department doing this would be very high, and there would be substantial scarcity rents to be captured in the process, encouraging corruption. On the other hand, where it can be done by herder representatives themselves, as an extension of normal local interaction, the cost would be low. In this case, the role of formal state institutions could be restricted to providing legal redress and adjudication in case of dispute. Some cases of actual pastoral institutions illustrate these issues (Box 1).

These two cases, taken from a large literature, show that customary arrangements can provide the basis for modern development and that formal institutions and organizations can be redesigned to provide a more effective and symbiotic relationship with them. But it would be wrong to assume that this is a simple task everywhere. The processes of modern state formation, the extension of market relations of production, growing population pressure and many other forces have had a powerful impact on customary institutions, and in some cases have altered them beyond recognition, or beyond the possibility of useful reform. Customary tenure institutions have, in most cases, been profoundly modified by their subordination to formal institutions. Pastoral natural resources are also in many cases the source of considerable economic benefits, access to which is jealously guarded and will not be given up lightly by those in the bureaucracy or modern economic sector who have appropriated those benefits.

A good example is the customary land tenure regime of the inner Niger river delta in central Mali (Moorehead 1991). A comprehensive and very effective integrated tenure and management system for all the resources of the area—water, arable land, fisheries, pasture, woods—was designed in the early nineteenth century by the paramount ruler Sheku Amadu on the basis of earlier rules. This system survived the imposition of French colonial authority almost intact, and the main outlines of it also survived the transition to Malian independence in the early 1960s. However, the rich resources of the delta were too attractive to remain unappropriated by outsiders and rich insiders. The Malian state imposed an increasingly extractive fiscal policy, helped by the monetization of the delta economy, and also nationalized the delta resources, creating the conditions for a 'tragedy of the commons' in an area previously characterized by strict customary rules on natural resource use. As a result, the state opened up former communally managed resources to those with preferential links to the various structures of the state, especially civil servants and wealthy traders. Nevertheless, there are policies which could be adopted to give local communities more power to allocate and control the use of local resources. A new land tenure system should be based on the outline of the old, but with appropriate modifications (Moorehead 1991; Lane and Moorehead this book).

It can be concluded that customary institutions remain critical in pastoral administration and that the relationship between the formal and customary systems is the key area for reform. Two types of reform can be identified which would move pastoral administrations towards a more satisfactory division of tasks between customary and formal institutions. In the first place, the relationship between formal natural resource tenure legislation and administrative rules on the one hand, and customary tenure laws and

163

rules on the other, needs to be clarified, and the formal legal system revised to delegate relevant powers to customary institutions where feasible. The formal system needs to support the customary system rather than, as at present, ignoring or undermining it.

There is also a need for attention to new types of mixed institution, combining elements of formal and customary institutions in a way that enables formal institutions to support the decision-making capability of customary institutions.

Figure 1 depicts some of these relationships and processes in the context of the present administration of natural resource tenure and management. Land-based natural resources are arrayed from the pastoral point of view in an ascending hierarchy of size of territory, together with some typical management decisions taken at each level in the hierarchy. The 'legal regime or institutions' column shows schematically how formal and customary regimes coexist in parallel, but with changing relative authority. The final column—'key organizational actors'—is difficult to complete in general for all African pastoral situations, although it would be easy to do so for any particular pastoral society. In general, management tasks are carried out at the different levels by an ascending hierarchy of customary organizations, ranging from the household to inter-clan or territorial councils, where the latter exist. At present, local government and technical services intervene at several territorial levels in the schema.

Our understanding of dynamic ecological systems suggests two main changes in the current pattern shown in Figure 1. The need for flexibility and subsidiarity suggests that the role of formal administrative organizations should be reduced and replaced by strengthened customary or mixed organizations; probably in most cases the change requires the creation and strengthening of an enabling institutional framework including legislation and training, major infrastructure investments and a mechanism for conflict resolution.

A reduction in the formal administrative and technical services of the state, accompanied by a strengthening and expansion of customary and mixed organizations, needs to be accompanied by a redefinition of the respective roles of formal and customary law relating to natural resources. The main changes would be a retreat of the provisions of formal law governing access to key pastoral resources and refocusing of formal law on strengthening the provisions of customary law which regulate access to natural resources. This sort of legal devolution would be accompanied by the definition of a clearer set of tasks for formal law, especially defining the boundaries within which customary law takes precedence, providing guarantees to minorities and the less powerful and providing formal reconciliation and conflict resolution mechanisms when customary law fails. The effects of these proposed changes are shown in Figure 2.

Services
Dynamic equilibrium theory suggests important changes in the way services (including veterinary and human health and extension) are provided

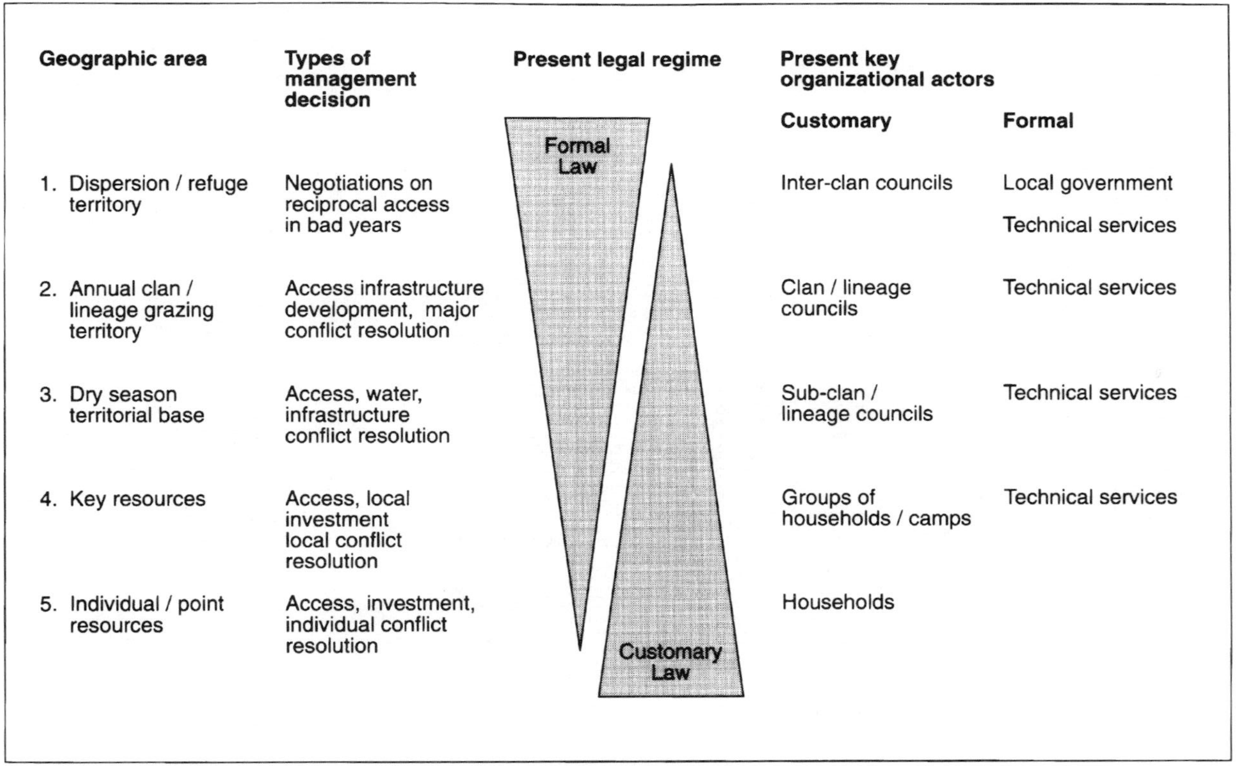

Geographic area	Types of management decision	Present legal regime	Present key organizational actors	
			Customary	Formal
1. Dispersion / refuge territory	Negotiations on reciprocal access in bad years		Inter-clan councils	Local government
				Technical services
2. Annual clan / lineage grazing territory	Access infrastructure development, major conflict resolution		Clan / lineage councils	Technical services
3. Dry season territorial base	Access, water, infrastructure conflict resolution		Sub-clan / lineage councils	Technical services
4. Key resources	Access, local investment local conflict resolution		Groups of households / camps	Technical services
5. Individual / point resources	Access, investment, individual conflict resolution		Households	

Formal Law

Customary Law

Figure 1: *Present institutional and organizational relationships in the administration of pastural tenure*

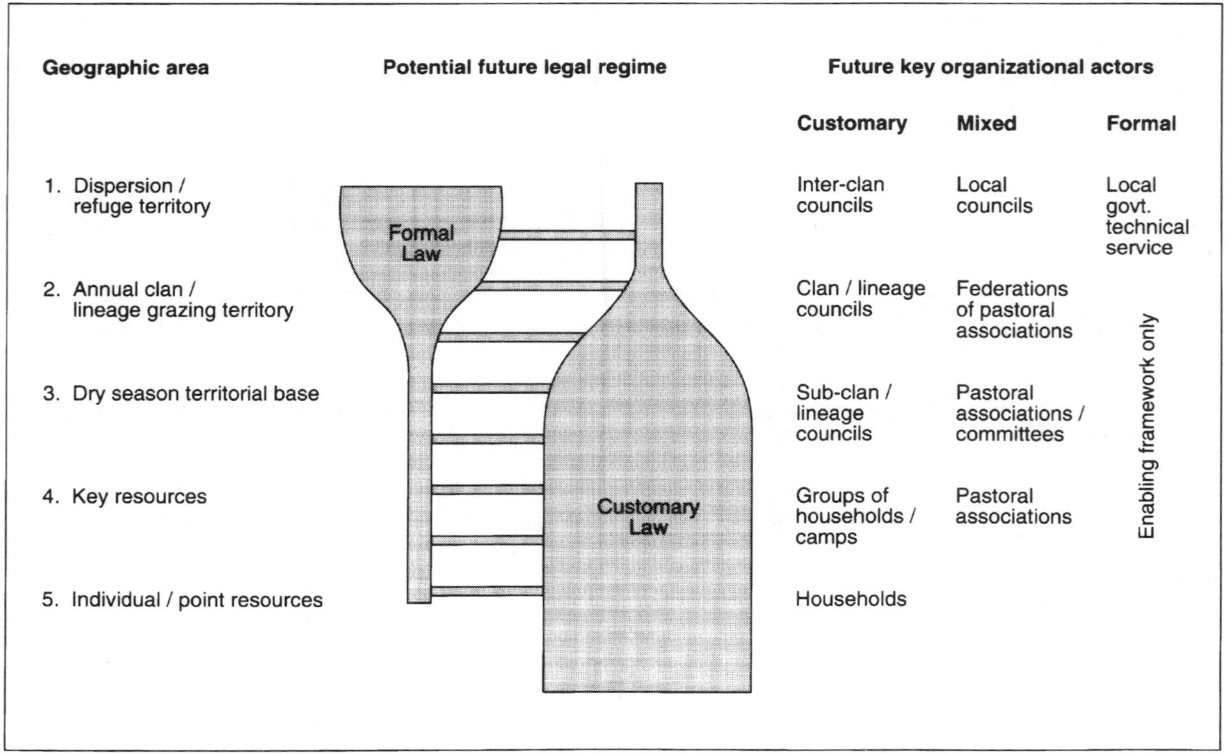

Geographic area

Potential future legal regime

Future key organizational actors

Geographic area	Customary	Mixed	Formal
1. Dispersion / refuge territory	Inter-clan councils	Local councils	Local govt. technical service
2. Annual clan / lineage grazing territory	Clan / lineage councils	Federations of pastoral associations	
3. Dry season territorial base	Sub-clan / lineage councils	Pastoral associations / committees	
4. Key resources	Groups of households / camps	Pastoral associations	
5. Individual / point resources	Households		

Formal Law

Customary Law

Enabling framework only

Figure 2: *Potential future institutional and organizational relationships in the administration of pastoral tenure*

to pastoralists; pressure for some of these changes also comes from the broader macro-economic and political trends mentioned earlier.

It is generally accepted that pastoralists in many cases have well developed, accurate and appropriate technical knowledge about pastoralism, including animal and human health. Such knowledge is not necessarily spread equally throughout the society (there may, for example, be important class, occupational or gender differences), but is often available and is embodied in the best practice of recognized local herding experts. Such knowledge provides an important, but underutilized, resource for development. However this often is not enough. Additional technical knowledge and inputs are likely to be required which are sensitive to local knowledge, but which introduce concepts and resources not locally available. The problem is how to achieve this.

The first need is to clarify the real costs and benefits of service delivery. One key element is the cost of not coping adequately with major external adjustments to the pastoral livelihood system. Droughts, an essential force driving non-equilibrium systems, incur major costs (through lost production, death of animals, destruction of capital and the opportunity costs of relief, among others) to both pastoralists and the state. Pastoralists whose herds are lost or sold, cannot follow their preferred tracking strategies and substantial production losses are incurred. Inefficient veterinary and public health services result in similar losses.

There are perhaps three main lines to be followed if new and more effective administrative procedures are to be adopted in the provision of services. First, there needs to be a clear definition of a minimum set of public interest interventions, where services that can only with the greatest difficulty or inefficiency be provided through the market, are provided free by the state. Control of major human and animal epidemic diseases fall into this category, as does primary education. Second, other services need to be provided through more imaginative mixes of decentralized barefoot and cost-recovery approaches. Third, and perhaps most important from the non-equilibrium dynamics point of view, is the need to construct some services, especially veterinary and human health, around a capability for rapid expansion and contraction according to circumstances. If major human and animal mortality is to be avoided during rapid ecological changes triggered by, for example, drought, services must have the means to mount rapid intervention campaigns against diseases known to be particularly dangerous in those circumstances (e.g. measles and contagious caprine pleuro-pneumonia).

Financial institutions

Financial institutions—including taxation systems, insurance and credit—are an underused instrument for helping pastoral economies track the variations of dynamic ecosystems. In Africa such financial institutions have not been designed to play a role in helping pastoral economies respond to environmental variations; indeed they have rarely been adapted to the special circumstances of pastoral economies at all. But it is now more generally recognized that a major redesign of such institutions is necessary.

A very dynamic environment, generating variable levels and different types of outputs, should not be taxed as though it had a stable and regular output. Different types of pastoral taxation have different advantages and disadvantages. A head tax on animals, common in West Africa, would be efficient and fair if it increased progressively per animal on larger herd sizes, but it never does, and anyway this is difficult and costly to gather. Sales taxes on animals, levied in many African countries, may disproportionately affect small herders who usually sell a larger proportion of their animals, and would also be especially burdensome in drought years when all herders sell more animals. Grazing fees, if calculated per unit of land, discriminate against small herders. Cost recovery for services may be an effective way of raising revenue, but rarely generates more than the cost of the service itself.

Whatever taxation system is chosen, the important thing from the point of view of a dynamic ecosystem approach is that it is applied flexibly, and that a moratorium on taxation is declared in the event of a serious downturn in the economy. There are precedents for this, especially outside Africa. Such a system would be especially effective if part of the taxation revenue was put into a special drought intervention fund managed in part by local herder organizations.

This comes close to an insurance scheme. Insurance has little history in pastoral areas of Africa (although there have been successes in crop insurance and insurance of plough oxen in Ethiopia). Livestock insurance has been relatively successful in the Mongolian pastoral economy, where overall risk levels are lower than in a typical African pastoral case, although still substantial (Templer et al. 1994). Livestock insurance may need external financial assistance (perhaps from a drought-intervention fund replenished from pastoral taxation revenues) on the relatively rare occasions of major disaster, but could perhaps handle regular small-scale droughts and other upsets. The administration of such a scheme would necessarily involve, or even be largely in the hands of, pastoral associations, because otherwise fraud would probably become unmanageable.

Credit should have a similar role. Livestock, with high returns and capital growth, are a natural medium for credit, both to re-establish breeding herds and to invest in fattening or marketing operations. But schemes for pastoral credit have been timid and have often gone wrong. Part of the problem has been that most pastoral credit has been subsidized, and has been heavily administered by donor agencies for fear it would be misused. As a result, transaction costs have been very high. In the event, donors have not been able to stop misuse, and the subsidy has often finished up in the hands of the wrong people. There is extensive scope for imaginative new approaches to credit for pastoral groups, either for targeted restocking by the group itself, or for commercial operations. Such credit should be designed to fit into and complement existing credit and insurance schemes already operated by pastoral groups, rather than creating new formal schemes.

In a dynamic ecosystem, formal and informal livestock insurance and credit must play complementary roles. Some risks are generally insured against and some credit is provided by the informal institutions of pastoral society. A household which loses its animals in an accident where it is not at fault will usually have some replacement animals rapidly provided through networks of kin or friends. A well known example is the *habbanae* loans of reproductive cattle to poor households among the Wodaabe herders of Niger (Bonfiglioli 1988), but there are comparable examples from most pastoral societies. Indeed, in many pastoral societies the concept of private individual animal ownership is tempered by a set of general rules where ultimate ownership of livestock is held by the clan itself, which may redistribute animals from a rich household to a poorer one to ensure the economic viability of the latter (see Swift 1991 for a description of this process among Kenyan Boran pastoralists).

Such customary insurance and restocking credit mechanisms work well in cases of individual household animal loss, since need is small relative to resources available within local economic and social networks. However, where losses occur together, such customary mechanisms are usually ineffective, since they cannot cope with the scale of need. Such covariate risks are of course characteristic of non-equilibrium environments.

This distinction suggests a need to rethink the roles of customary and formal credit and insurance. In areas of low, randomly distributed risk, customary institutions should be able to provide viable insurance and credit for pastoral households. It may be possible for formal credit and insurance to be channelled through such customary mechanisms, but this should not be subsidized. On the other hand, in areas of high covariate risk, and thus generally in non-equilibrium systems, there is also a need for intervention by government to provide livestock insurance and credit for restocking. Because losses will generally be very widely shared through the affected community, subsidization of such financial services is likely to be required.

Food security and drought planning

The bottom line of a non-equilibrium ecosystem, as far as pastoralists are concerned, is that there are irregular crises which threaten livelihoods and, in extreme cases, lives. Such crises can be planned for, not only to provide a safety net against human destitution and death, but also to provide a springboard for rapid economic recovery or adaptation after a crisis, so that the economy can continue to track the environment.

There is a conceptual hurdle to be overcome in doing this. Opportunism, an essential economic and management response to the variability of dynamic ecosystems, may be profoundly inegalitarian: it tends to produce winners (those who respond rapidly) and losers (those who do not). For this reason it may not be readily reconcilable with equity and safety nets, which stress protecting the losers from the consequences of a lack of sufficient opportunism.

It is evident that droughts and other extreme events in dynamic ecosystems are occasions when some inefficient herding households are driven out of the pastoral economy. Pastoral planning needs to accept this, and provide alternative forms of rural or urban employment for them. Most pastoral societies have concepts of 'good' and 'bad' herders, or 'deserving' and 'undeserving' poor. The former may in extreme circumstances lose their animals, but it is through no fault of their own, and they can be relied upon to recover rapidly, given the right circumstances. The latter are judged inept, spendthrift, and not able to respond creatively to assistance.

Although it is important not to let this view degenerate into a sort of social Darwinism, it does suggest that safety nets should provide security for a return to pastoralism by those with the skills and commitment to do so (who will most often be normally successful small herders), and that alternative policies should be adopted for those who do not. In this sense, safety nets are not contrary to the idea of opportunism, but become a part of the mechanism making it more effective. Safety nets prevent the complete destitution and facilitate the rapid recovery of committed herding households, not the perpetuation of existing wealth inequalities.

There is now beginning to be some experience in pastoral areas of Africa of drought contingency planning. Several countries (including Botswana, Mali and Ethiopia) have elements of such a system, but the most evolved system, operational since 1987, is in Turkana district in northern Kenya (see also Toulmin this book). The main components include an early warning system based partly on empirical indicators such as rainfall, vegetation production and animal and cereal prices, and partly on perceptions and indicators gathered directly from pastoralists. The early warning system is used both to guide normal district planning and also to warn of developing crises in the pastoral economy of the sort which predictably occur in Turkana. Plans are made in advance to intervene in the pastoral economy, particularly to maintain pastoralists' purchasing power and food entitlements in the event of a crisis, often through livestock market support and food or cash-for-work schemes. Large-scale human and animal immunization campaigns are also mobilized in advance of epidemics when conditions are seen to be deteriorating (DCPU 1992). Such drought contingency planning could provide similar services in other pastoral areas. By guaranteeing ultimate food security, it enables pastoralists to plan their strategy through the drought with some assurance of an effective safety net.

An important component, partly present in the Turkana plan through the public works scheme, is to encourage policies which create employment, both temporary and permanent, outside the pastoral sector, allowing occupational mobility and a reduction of the population dependent on a declining pastoral livelihood system. This has been done on some occasions in the past, for example in Somalia during the 1970s droughts when pastoralists were retrained as sea fishermen and farmers. Although in the long-term few of these pastoralists remained in such occupations, the schemes may have had important short-term benefits, although at very high cost. More thinking is needed about the possibility of generating such alternative employment. The continued availability of large amounts of food aid, and the possibility of using food- or cash-for-work to create fixed assets and infrastructure offers important possibilities in this respect, despite the rather mixed experience of the use of food aid in pastoral areas so far.

Civil security
Extreme insecurity and civil war are now a common condition of pastoral areas in Africa, and add enormously to the risks generated by ecological variability. It is worth mentioning briefly that the sort of approach to strengthening customary pastoral organizations and creating new mixed ones could also make a contribution to solving some of these problems. Pastoral organizations can play a key role in bringing the activities of irregular armed forces, armed militias and bandits under control by opening channels of negotiation between opposing groups, and regulating and policing conflicts before they escalate (FAO 1992). Properly constituted pastoral organizations, given the necessary powers, could perform these roles in a cross-border context, since they represent the only real authority in many such areas. The possibility that pastoral organizations might be able to perform such a role should provide a powerful political incentive to governments to support their creation.

Conclusion

This agenda implies an important new set of administrative roles and processes for both pastoral organizations and for government. In this concluding section, I discuss some of the general implications.

New roles for pastoral organizations
The agenda laid out in this chapter assumes a retreat from formal state administrative organizations and institutions, and a substantially extended role for customary and mixed ones. The great variety of existing customary and potential mixed institutions makes it difficult to generalize about the precise forms such institutions and organizations will take in each case, but some general considerations are nevertheless possible.

The first concerns potential problems with this approach. It is important not to romanticize pastoral institutions. In many cases institutions are deficient for modern administrative purposes—that was never their objective. In some cases, institutions with appropriate powers and jurisdiction have simply never existed. In others, they do exist, but are of a form—for example, extremely hierarchical or undemocratic—which would be largely unacceptable for contemporary development, making them inappropriate as the basis for new administrative tasks. In some cases, the use of customary institutions for modern administrative tasks would simply empty them of any real purpose. In still other cases, customary institutions have been captured by élites or by outsiders, such as merchants, and so would not perform in the public interest if given new powers or resources.

Despite all this, it is clear that, in some cases, customary organizations and institutions can provide the basis for new types of pastoral administrative structure. In many other cases, mixed organizations (part customary, part formal) provide the way forward, and planning should help create such mixed institutions with clearly defined powers and resources.

The creation of mixed organizations and the strengthening of customary institutions offers a new agenda for governments and donors, one

171

concerned mainly with building institutional capability among pastoralists (Sylla this book). The main challenges include:

o Research targeted at the operation of customary and mixed pastoral organizations and institutions and their ability to carry out new administrative burdens.
o Experiments with institutional design and strengthening, a natural task for NGOs. Also evaluation of previous experience drawing on a great deal of unwritten-up material available in agency files.
o Legal reform to provide a legal identity to new types of pastoral organization and some institutions and to strengthen key features of existing ones.
o Training for new roles and responsibilities offers a targeted agenda concerned with functional literacy, bookkeeping and record taking; the skills needed to run organizations and administration. Given existing disparities, training of women may be especially important.
o Support for pastoral networking between organizations to reinforce institutional capability.
o Reinforcing the ability of pastoral institutions to undertake advocacy for pastoral interests. Advocacy organizations should be strengthened, support should be given for para-legal training and support made available to encourage pastoral organizations to engage in the national formal legal system to defend their interests, in the first place concerning land.

New roles for government
This agenda also implies a substantial rethinking of the role of government, involving two main types of activity. First, the creation of an enabling environment or, in most cases, removing the present disabling environment, for pastoral development. Second, the provision of a more effective set of safety functions and interventions of last resort. This implies a general retreat from the current interventionist and managerial role of government towards a much more restricted and basic set of roles, including:

o Providing a legal framework within which a devolved pastoral administration can operate effectively, especially in respect of natural resource tenure; acting as a mediator for conflict resolution and as arbiter of last resort; guaranteeing a level legal playing field and equality of advocacy in disputes.
o Guaranteeing minimum democratic processes in local administration, including the protection of minorities and disadvantaged groups.
o Providing the appropriate macro-economic framework (Holtzman and Kulibaba this book), including an equitable and consistent set of policies concerned with subsidies, transfers, prices and general trade-offs between the pastoral and other sectors; providing consistent major infrastructure investments, especially roads.
o Ensuring major public interest services, especially primary education and the control of serious human and animal communicable diseases.

○ Providing minimum technical inputs and support as a contribution to a more indigenously generated process of technical innovation.
○ Guaranteeing minimum civil and food security, including safety nets against disaster.

This is an ambitious agenda, requiring major changes in government bureaucracies which have for several decades attempted, largely unsuccessfully, much more far-reaching programmes of activity. Such a retrenchment is currently under way as a result of economic and political pressures. Non-equilibrium ecosystem theory offers a powerful additional reason for attempting to achieve this in Africa's pastoral areas.

10. Improving the efficiency of opportunism: new directions for pastoral development

STEPHEN SANDFORD

This chapter distills what seem to be the key new directions for pastoral development and their importance in Africa, comments on some of the implications discussed or neglected by contributions to this book and sets out some ideas on the issues involved in getting the implications adopted by the development community.

The new directions for pastoral development discussed in this book will mean different things to different people depending on their interests and background. For policymakers and managers of pastoral or range development programmes in Africa, the following propositions constitute the essence of the new thinking:

○ In estimating carrying capacity, the objective of the users is one of the key elements to be considered. The correct estimate is not unique, but will differ according to this objective.
○ Grazing systems in many parts of Africa are not in equilibrium, i.e. livestock and vegetation do not control each other. External shocks (e.g. drought or war) rather than endogenous processes (e.g. low calving rates caused by malnutrition) determine livestock numbers and the state of the vegetation.
○ In these non-equilibrium systems grazing by livestock has only a small effect on the productivity of grasslands.
○ Therefore an opportunistic or 'tracking' strategy in which livestock numbers (and so the demand for feed) closely matches, in time, the production of grass is the best way to avoid wasting feed supply which, for the most part, cannot be economically stored.
○ African rangelands are heterogeneous in space, producing different amounts and qualities of feed at different times and in different places. This feed cannot economically be transported over any significant distance, therefore herd mobility is desirable to exploit them best.

How important are the 'new directions'?

The 'new directions' apply only to range systems in disequilibrium and are only important if such systems are relatively large and are already being managed (or are likely to become managed) in ways which are different to that suggested by the 'new directions'. Otherwise they may be interesting, but are of little practical importance.

The contour line of the 30 per cent CV (coefficient of variation) of annual rainfall represents a practical dividing line between non-equilibrium and equilibrium systems (Ellis *et al.* 1993). That contour line probably lies somewhat to the drier side of the boundary between sub-humid and semi-arid zones (defined in terms of length of growing period), possibly closer to this boundary in the bi-modal rainfall areas of east Africa and further away (almost at the semi-arid/arid zones boundary) in the Sahel (de Leeuw and Tothill 1993).

The arid and semi-arid zones of Africa account for 30 per cent and 27 per cent, respectively, of sub-Saharan Africa's domestic ruminant livestock population, measured in terms of animal biomass, and for 37 per cent and 18 per cent of its land area (Jahnke 1982). These proportions are not constant over time, but it seems fairly probable that over half of sub-Saharan Africa's livestock population lives in non-equilibrium systems at least some of the time. By this criterion the findings reported in this book are of importance.

The other criterion, that non-equilibrium systems are not already being managed opportunistically, downgrades the importance of the 'new direc-tions'. While some pastoral societies may limit the size of their livestock populations to some extent, the majority do not and are already broadly following opportunistic and mobile strategies. They do not exactly track changes in feed supplies, partly because they tend to destock too late and partly because they cannot rebuild stock numbers fast enough after the end of a drought. This is because natural population growth is slow and they lack the capital to buy in from other areas at a time when livestock prices are high.

If we define *efficient* opportunism as exactly tracking feed supplies in time and space, then the actual practice of traditional pastoralism is, at best, only semi-efficient. Elsewhere (Sandford 1982), I have calculated for an area with a CV of annual rainfall of 40 per cent that, given *average* rates of herd growth (drawn from Dahl and Hjort 1976) and other rather tight assumptions, traditional pastoralists cannot, on average over time, achieve more than 62 per cent, in the case of cattle, and 85 per cent, in the case of goats, of the stocking rates that perfectly efficient opportunism would achieve. On the rough assumption that total livestock output is propor-tional to livestock numbers (an assumption which, as the results reported by both Tapson (1993) and Abel (1993) have reconfirmed, is not unrealis-tic), the semi-efficient opportunism practised by pastoralists leads to lower output than would be obtained under perfectly efficient opportunism.

On reflection, the use of *average* annual rates of herd growth probably somewhat underestimates the efficiency of pastoralists' opportunism, since typically at the end of a drought not only do breeding females constitute an unusually high proportion of the herd, but also their calving/kidding rates are high. Both these factors will increase the rate of herd growth, although for poor families there will be an offsetting factor in the form of distress

175

sales in order to buy food. On balance it seems unlikely that the gain in productivity achievable simply from narrowing the gap between semi-efficient and more perfectly efficient opportunism will exceed 40 per cent of present productivity levels. That is much less than the size of productivity gain normally to be expected from improving technology in crop production, and, if achieved, would keep per capita output at or above present levels for fewer than 15 years at present rates of human population growth.

The 'new directions' are only of practical importance in so far as they:

○ Encourage the pastoralists (including the few commercial ranchers) in non-equilibrium systems who are not already practising opportunism to do so;
○ Inhibit those governments who would otherwise successfully force pastoralists to abandon opportunism;
○ Find ways of increasing the efficiency of the opportunism already being practised or of preventing its present level of efficiency from declining.

A detached appraisal suggests that adoption by governments and other development agencies of the 'new directions' might prevent the enormous waste of resources and energy that has characterized range development programmes in Africa over the last half century, but is not likely to have much impact on the actual management of livestock herds and rangelands in non-equilibrium systems since, for the most part, these are already being managed in an opportunistic way.

Improving the productivity of non-equilibrium systems

What are the techniques and strategies for improving the primary productivity of rangelands above present levels? Important distinctions are made between areas where plant-nutrient deficiency and soil-moisture deficiency are the key constraints on range productivity (Behnke and Scoones 1993; de Ridder and Breman 1993). There is abundant evidence that it is possible to improve the primary productivity of rangelands by selected measures to tackle these or other constraints such as seed shortages, or more general decline in the regeneration capacity of the vegetation.

There are now a number of well-justified dismissals of attempts to improve productivity by paddocked rotational grazing and legume reseeding (Bayer and Waters-Bayer this book), some experiences of improving the efficiency of use of existing production through patch use (e.g. Coppock 1993; Stafford-Smith and Pickup 1993), but virtually no discussion of how range productivity might be positively improved above current levels. Instead the discussion concentrates on whether or not traditional practices lead to a decline in productivity.

Twenty years ago in Botswana the range and livestock experts involved in developing the Tribal Grazing Lands Policy (TGLP) claimed that properly managed ranches could achieve (by control of livestock numbers, by improved water supplies and by fencing) a doubling of net range productivity over the levels achieved in the communal system. In reality, ranches (either commercial ones or research ranches mimicking commercial ones) have lower land productivity (by some indexes less than half) than the communal system (White 1992; Abel 1993; Scoones this book). Has the result of this, and many similar disasters in professional judgement, been a general abandonment by range scientists of any interest in increasing productivity, rather than a re-evaluation of the particular techniques involved and a search for more successful ones?

We need to re-examine the prevailing pessimism about the possibility of improving range productivity. The logical economic response to the increasing shortage of available rangeland would be to improve its productivity by the developments of other methods. Recent emphasis on the importance of 'patches' in livestock use of rangelands highlights the potential for such developments which previously tended to be discounted because of their limited size (Scoones 1989a; Oba 1993; Barton 1993). Even the development of new water points, in order to reduce the amount of energy spent by livestock in trekking to water so that this energy can be used instead in producing economic outputs, may regain respectability if the fear of consequent ecological degradation has receded (but see Nicholson, 1987, for a contrary view that distance trekked to water is not a significant factor in livestock performance).

Detailed micro-economic analysis has been mainly absent from the debate about rangelands. It may be that, although we know how to intervene to increase the primary productivity of rangelands, such interventions are not economic. The implications for government policy, if this is the case, are almost certainly that scarce development resources should not be devoted to scrabbling for the meagre rewards to be gained from increasing the efficiency of opportunistic pastoralism. As already noted, even near-perfect efficiency of opportunism will only add, at best, about 40 per cent to present productivity levels.

Instead, maybe the resources should be spent on re-equipping (e.g. by education, by grants of land or capital assets) the expanding pastoral population for non-pastoral occupations. Such non-pastoral occupations may be as settled and independent agriculturalists or in the urban or rural wage economy. There is increasing evidence that pastoral populations themselves see their future as much more secure if pastoral activities are buttressed by non-farm sources of income. Many pastoralists use any extra resources they acquire to promote such diversification, placing different family members in different occupations, most of them non-pastoral, and increasingly non-cropping either (Dahl 1979; Webb and Reardon 1992).

Increasing and preserving the efficiency of opportunism

Several of the chapters in this book directly address the issues of increasing or preserving the efficiency of mobile opportunism; others do so less directly. My general reaction is one of rather pessimistic caution. Chapter 6 on destocking and restocking shows that traditional intra-society mechanisms are becoming less effective and that outside interventions to facilitate destocking and restocking are likely to be too costly except where pastoralism is a relatively small sector. Chapter 5 on marketing addresses the same issue less directly, but a similar conclusion is probably inevitable.

One potentially very important factor in adjusting grazing pressure and feed consumption during the booms and busts of feed supply caused by a fluctuating climate is the ability of some livestock to survive periods of very low feed intake. Zebu animals can significantly reduce, at any rate for some time, their daily feed requirements. It is not clear how well established or precisely defined this ability by some livestock to reduce their feed intake is. Does it represent a reduction in basal metabolic rate and maintenance needs or does it include the effects of reductions in other activity or reflect changes in weight loss or milk production? For how long can livestock reduce basal metabolic rate and what are the effects on subsequent production parameters, including calving rates, milk yields and live-weight changes?

It should be noted that a reduction in a demand for feed by a third per animal is comparable to the decline in total feed demand caused by a collapse in cattle numbers (at the scale of a production system including emergency escape areas) in many droughts. It is also important because switching appetite back on at the end of a drought to take advantage of increased feed supplies happens relatively quickly compared to the slow build up of livestock numbers after a crash. If this ability to reduce feed demand is a characteristic particularly of indigenous livestock breeds, then conserving the efficiency of opportunism is substantially linked to conserving such breeds (Bayer and Waters-Bayer this book).

The increasing interaction and integration of livestock and crop activities has major implications for the efficiency of opportunistic pastoralism (Bayer and Waters-Bayer this book). The clearance of land for cultivation in the sub-humid zones south of the Sahel in West Africa has opened up land previously too heavily infested by tsetse flies for dry season grazing. Initially this may have helped long distance transhumants from non-equilibrium systems further north and increased the livestock populations (and efficiency of opportunism) of these systems. But as human population densities increase and more integration of resident cattle into the farming system proceeds in the sub-humid zones these transhumants get excluded, thereby ending the complementarity between wet-season grazing in the Sahel and dry-season grazing further south.

Land taken from pastoral use into cropping often produces more livestock feed, usually in the form of crop residues, in its new use. Except where irrigation is introduced, probably most of such land-use transfers do not take place in areas of non-equilibrium systems. A key issue (not only for equity but also for productivity) is whether the crop residues are available at times of feed shortage to the users of non-equilibrium systems, and whether the average increase in annual feed supplies, in the form of crop residues, is offset by increased inter-annual variability, such that in drought years one gets less feed from the crop residues produced in that year than one would have got from the natural pasture displaced.

Previous attempts (Sandford 1988; 1989) to find good evidence for relative inter-annual variability were largely unsuccessful and I was left to theorize that, except in places where deep-rooting perennial grasses or browse are important, the inter-annual *yield* variability of natural grazing is unlikely to be less than that of crop residues. The inter-annual *area* variability of natural grazing is, however, likely to be less than that of crop residues. Better evidence is still not available.

Productivity, stability and equity

Some of the discussion on land tenure, organizations and administration in this book (Lane and Moorehead, Sylla, Swift this book) is oriented towards questions of output and efficiency, but most of it is concerned with equity, with the usual contradiction between a respect for pastoral societies' values and liberal notions of equality within society. My personal opinion is that we social scientists have not yet structured our views rigorously enough to have any clear message for policy makers and practitioners except that everything is very complex, that Hardin (1968) was wrong and that livestock mobility is to be encouraged.

Elsewhere (Sandford 1983) I have proposed an analytic structure for looking at management issues in pastoral development in which the appropriateness of different alternative *forms* of management and organization is interrelated with and influenced by the *characteristics* of the particular pastoral situation being considered, the development *objectives* and *strategies* being pursued and the technical *components* to be included in the development programme.

For example, a pastoral development programme with a strong equity objective is likely to require a different project management structure to one whose objective is focused simply on efficiency; a pastoral system in which households and herds are relatively dense and immobile is likely to need a different veterinary delivery service to one of frequent and opportunistic movement; a programme for the delivery of range water supplies that has to rely on deep boreholes will have to be staffed and organized in a different way to one relying simply on hand-dug but concrete-lined shallow wells.

The structure provides a way in which a mass of detailed evidence from particular case studies can be sorted, generalized and memorized. Without some clear framework that policy makers and practitioners of pastoral development can easily grasp and use, social scientists will continue to be largely ignored. In my view this remains a serious gap.

Pastoralists may prefer to trade off stability against productivity and income, a strategy which can be described as 'risk minimization' (Swallow 1994). The 'new directions' espouse opportunism, a very unstable way of earning a living. There are various methods by which pastoralists seek to cope with the consequences of this instability such as diversification of species and of sources of household income (Perrier this book). But to what extent is the practice of opportunism determined by the natural environment or by a conscious choice about the trade-off between income (including subsistence) and stability?

Are there examples of different communities occupying the same environment practising different degrees of opportunism? Where two groups occupy the same general region (although exploiting different niches in it at different times), with one group (e.g. the Sakuye section of Borana in north Kenya) specializing in more drought-tolerant camels, while the other group specialize in more drought-susceptible cattle, to what extent do the camel herders justify their choice in terms of stability? Dahl's (1979) account of camel specialist Borana-Sakuye and cattle specialist Borana-Gutu in north Kenya emphasizes a common interest in risk absorption, rather than different attitudes towards the acceptability of risk.

The implications for donors and investment

In the 1960s and 1970s very substantial sums were spent by donors and national governments in Africa on range-development programmes. For the most part these were expensive failures, and the 1980s and 1990s have witnessed a marked reluctance to embark on similar large-scale schemes.

The 'new directions' confirm that many aspects of those schemes in non-equilibrial systems were misguided. The expensive and authoritarian ways of regulating livestock numbers, the dividing up of ranges into self-sufficient blocks and the creation of private ranches to bring these about proved to be inappropriate.

Some of the marketing components that involved creating 'disease-free zones' in order to gain access to high price export markets, were incompatible with opportunism (and also under-estimated the forces of protectionism in those markets). Other marketing components (e.g. the Livestock Marketing Division in Kenya) were well focused to serve opportunism, but involved too heavy a financial burden for governments (Holtzman and Kulibaba this book).

The previously much criticized veterinary and water-development programmes in retrospect now seem less ill advised, except in so far as the former were sometimes inefficiently implemented and the latter had some adverse equity implications that allowed 'outsiders' to gain access to what up until then had exclusively been pastoralists' resources.

Previously it was thought that veterinary services and water supplies merely allowed livestock populations to grow to the point where they destroyed the environment and competed with each other for starvation rations. Recent thinking in range ecology suggests that in non-equilibrial systems the danger to the environment from overstocking is relatively small and that starvation comes more often from exogenous adverse fluctuations in the weather than from endogenous herd growth (Behnke et al. 1993). Veterinary and water development programmes then become aids to more efficient opportunism, through more spatially and temporarily complete use of the feed resources available.

Recommendations for other components in future programmes need to be tentative since there is still too small a record of success. Investments in stock routes, holding grounds and canning plants deserve careful attention in spite of the caution expressed above. They remove livestock that will otherwise probably die from the rangelands early on in a drought and at prices that encourage destocking rather than retention. They may incur financial losses to the enterprises that directly operate them, but this may be offset by savings to governments' and donors' relief and rehabilitation budgets later on if pastoralists have money to buy food and restock (Holtzman and Kulibaba; Toulmin; Swift this book).

There is an urgent need to find ways of increasing the primary productivity of non-equilibrium systems, both in general and at particular times of year when otherwise serious weight losses and mortality will occur. Scoones (1989a, 1993) has drawn attention to the importance of 'key resources' for cattle survival in accessible patches, at the end of the dry season and in the early rains. The most economic way of increasing primary production is probably to multiply such patches. To justify these investments we also need models of feed budgets for years of different drought intensities, month by month, probably using biomass disappearance rates (de Leeuw *et al.* 1993), and probably distinguishing nitrogen from other biomass (cf. de Ridder and Breman 1993). Using such feed budget models, in conjunction with estimates of the impact of short-term feed shortage on mortality and productivity, we could calculate how expensive the creation of high productivity patches of quality feed can afford to be.

In a rather equilibrium environment in northern Nigeria we already have an example of legume-enriched fodder banks being used by pastoralists in this way (Bayer 1986b; Bayer and Waters-Bayer this book). In drier environments the type of investment will be very locale-specific, taking advantage of particular sites where soils and moisture are favourable. Chapter 3 has a useful discussion of the possibilities and the circumstances in which it may make sense to buy feed from outside the range and transport it, rather than to grow it within. In either case some investment may be needed.

Disseminating the implications

It has taken 25 years, a working generation, for insights from findings about ecological systems analysis to be incorporated into government policy (Ellis this book). This long time-lag has been the time it took for the first postgraduate students to whom the new findings became available at university to work their way to the top of the tree where they could change policy.

This highlights the key role of the academic community and the conservatism of policy makers. Academic curricula easily get out of date. It is common to meet middle-level livestock policy makers who seem to be somewhat familiar with the implications of Herskovits' (1926) article on the east African cattle complex. It is often the only piece of anthropology with which they are familiar, and it is now nearly 70 years old. But its message is still being taught in universities.

A determined effort needs to be made to bring the 'new directions' to the attention of the academic community in Africa and elsewhere and to convince not only the range scientists, but also those in the livestock or social science fields with livestock interests, of the major importance of the findings presented in this book. Otherwise livestock development professionals and policy makers will continue to repeat as valid propositions they learnt from their range management colleagues a decade ago.

References

Abel, N.O.J. 1993. Reducing animal numbers on southern African communal range: is it worth it? In: Behnke, R.H., Scoones, I. and Kerven, C. (eds.) *Range Ecology at Disequilibrium: New Models of Natural Variability and Pastoral Adaptation in African Savannas.* Overseas Development Institute, London.

Adams, M. 1982. The Baggara problem; attempts at modern change in Southern Darfur and Southern Kordofan (Sudan). *Development and Change* 13:259–89.

Akabwai, D.M.O. 1992. Extension and livestock development: experience from among the Turkana pastoralists of Kenya. *Pastoral Development Network Paper* 33b. Overseas Development Institute, London.

Antenneh, A. 1985. Financing livestock services. *LPU Working Paper* 6. International Livestock Centre for Africa (ILCA), Addis Ababa.

Arnold, G.W. and Dudzinski, M.L. 1978. *Ethology of Free-Ranging Domestic Animals.* Elsevier, Amsterdam.

Aronson, D.R. 1980. Kinsmen and comrades: towards a class analysis of the Somali pastoral sector. *Nomadic Peoples* 7.

Baker, R. 1975. 'Development' and the pastoral people of Karamoja, north-eastern Uganda: an example of the treatment of symptoms. In: Monod, T. (ed.) *Pastoralism in Tropical Africa.* International African Institute, London.

Barrett, J. 1992. The economic role of cattle in communal farming systems in Zimbabwe. *Pastoral Development Network Paper* 32b. Overseas Development Institute, London.

Barrow, E. 1991. Evaluating the effectiveness of past agroforestry programmes in a pastoral area. A case study of the Turkana in Kenya. *Agroforestry Systems* 14:1–38.

Bartels, G.B., Perrier, G.K. and Norton, B.E. 1990. The applicability of the carrying capacity concept to Africa: comment on a paper by de Leeuw and Tothill. *Pastoral Development Network Paper* 29d. Overseas Development Institute, London.

Barton, D. 1993. Community participation in range rehabilitation in Kenya. Case study paper for the conference on *New Directions in African Range Management and Policy*, 31 May–4 June, Woburn, UK. IIED, ODI and Commonwealth Secretariat, London.

Bayer, W. 1986a. Agropastoral herding practices and grazing behaviour of cattle in the subhumid zone of Nigeria. *ILCA Bulletin* 24: 8–13. International Livestock Centre for Africa (ILCA), Addis Ababa.

Bayer, W. 1986b. Utilisation of fodder banks. In: von Kaufmann, R., Chater, S. and Blench, R. (eds.) *Livestock Systems Research in Nigeria's Subhumid Zone.* International Livestock Centre for Africa (ILCA), Addis Ababa.

Bayer, W. 1989. Low-demand animals for low-input systems. *ILEIA Newsletter*, December:14–15.

Bayer, W. and Waters-Bayer, A. 1991. Wandern und Weilen: Beweggründe und

Strategien zur pastoralen Landnutzung am Beispiel der Fulbe in Zentralnigeria. In: Scholz, F. (ed.) *Nomaden–mobile Tierhaltung: Zur gegenwärtigen Lage von Nomaden und den Problemen und Chancen mobiler Tierhaltung.* Das Arbische Buch, Berlin.

Bebbington, A. 1991. Farmer organisations in Ecuador: contributions to 'Farmer First' research and development. *Sustainable Agriculture Gatekeeper* SA26. International Institute for Environment and Development, London.

Behnke, R.H. 1985a. Measuring the benefits of subsistence versus commercial livestock production in Africa. *Agricultural Systems* 16:109–35.

Behnke, R.H. 1985b. Open-range management and property rights in pastoral Africa: a case of spontaneous range enclosure in south Darfur, Sudan. *Pastoral Development Network Paper* 20f. Overseas Development Institute, London.

Behnke, R.H. 1987. Cattle accumulation and the commercialization of the traditional livestock industry in Botswana. *Agricultural Systems* 24:1–29.

Behnke, R.H. 1991. Economic models of pastoral land tenure. In: Cincotta, R.P., Gay, C.W. and Perrier, G.K. (eds.) *New Concepts in International Rangeland Development: Theories and Applications.* Proceedings of the International Rangeland Development Symposium, 14 January, 1991, Washington, DC. Utah State University, Logan.

Behnke, R.H. 1992. New directions in African range management policy. *Pastoral Development Network Paper* 32c. Overseas Development Institute, London.

Behnke, R.H. 1994. Natural resource management in pastoral Africa. *Development Policy Review* 12:5–27.

Behnke, R.H. and Scoones, I. 1993. Rethinking range ecology: implications for rangeland management in Africa. In: Behnke, R.H., Scoones, I. and Kerven, C. (eds.) *Range Ecology at Disequilibrium: New Models of Natural Variability and Pastoral Adaptation in African Savannas.* Overseas Development Institute, London.

Behnke, R.H., Scoones, I. and Kerven, C. (eds.) 1993. *Range Ecology at Disequilibrium: New Models of Natural Variability and Pastoral Adaptation in African Savannas.* Overseas Development Institute, London.

Bekure, S., de Leeuw, P.N., Grandin, B.E. and Neate, P.J.H. 1991. *Maasai Herding: an Analysis of the Livestock Production System of Maasai Pastoralists in Eastern Kajiado District, Kenya.* International Livestock Centre for Africa (ILCA), Addis Ababa.

Bekure, S. and McDonald, I. 1985. Some policy issues of livestock marketing in Africa. *African Livestock Policy Analysis Network Paper* 2. International Livestock Centre for Africa (ILCA), Addis Ababa.

Bernus, E. 1974. *Les Illabakan (Niger): Une Tribu Touaregue Sahelienne et son Aire de Nomadisation.* ORSTOM, Paris.

Berryman, A.A. 1991. Population theory: an essential ingredient in pest prediction, management and policy making. *American Entomologist* 37:138-142.

Bille, J. 1982. The measurement of conditions and trends in the southern rangelands of Ethiopia. *Joint Ethiopian Pastoral Systems Study Research Report* 3. International Livestock Centre for Africa (ILCA), Addis Ababa.

Birgegard, L.-E. (1993) Natural resource tenure: a review of issues and experiences with emphasis on sub-Saharan Africa. *Rural Development Studies* 31 Swedish University of Agricultural Sciences/International Rural Development Centre, Uppsala.

Birley, M. 1982. Resource management in Sukumaland, Tanzania. *Africa* 52:1–30.

Blystad, A. 1993. An anthropological approach to the problem of infant mortality:

the case of the pastoral Barabaig of Tanzania. Mimeo, Department of Social Anthropology and Centre for International Health, University of Bergen.

Bonfiglioli, A. 1988. *Dudal: Histoire de Famille et Histoire de Troupeau Chez un Groupe de Wodaabe du Niger.* Cambridge University Press, Cambridge.

Bonfiglioli, A.M. 1992. *Pastoralists at a Crossroads: Survival and Development Issues in African Pastoralism.* Nomadic Pastoralists in Africa Project (NOPA), UNICEF,UNSO, Nairobi.

Borgerhoff-Mulder, M. 1990. *Egalitarianism and Women's Status in Datoga Pastoralists of Tanzania.* Final Report to the National Geographic Society, London.

Boserup, E. 1965. *The Conditions of Agricultural Growth: The Economics of Agrarian Change Under Population Pressure.* Allen and Unwin, London.

Boserup, E. 1981. *Population and Technological Change: A Study of Long-term Change.* University of Chicago Press, Chicago.

Boutrais, J. 1990. *Derrière les Clôtures: Essai d'Histoire Comparée de Ranches Africains.* Cahiers des Science Humaines. ORSTOM, Paris.

Breman, H., Diallo, A. and Traoré, G. 1982. Les systèmes d'élevage au Sahel. In: Penning de Vries, F.W.T. and Djitèye, M. (eds.). *La Productivité des Pâturages Saheliens: Une Etude des Sols, des Végetations et de l'Exploitation de cette Ressource Naturelle.* PUDOC Centre for Agricultural Publishing and Documentation, Wageningen.

Breman, H. and de Wit, C. 1983. Rangeland productivity and exploitation in the Sahel. *Science* 221:1341–7.

Bromley, D.W. (ed.) 1992. *Making the Commons Work. Theory, Practice and Policy.* Institute for Contemporary Studies, San Francisco.

Bromley, D.W. and Cernea, M. 1989. The management of common property natural resources: some conceptual and operational fallacies. *Discussion Paper* 57. The World Bank, Washington DC.

Bruce, J. 1986. Land tenure issues in project design and strategies for agricultural development in sub-Saharan Africa. *Land Tenure Center Paper* 128. Land Tenure Center, Wisconsin.

Buchanan-Smith, M. 1992. Famine early warning systems and response: the missing link? Case study: Turkana District, north-western Kenya, 1990–91. In: Buchanan-Smith, M., Davies, S. and Petty, C. 1992. *Famine Early Warning Systems and Response: The Missing Link?* Institute of Development Studies, Brighton.

Carl Bro International 1982. *An Evaluation of Livestock Management and Production in Botswana.* Ministry of Agriculture, Botswana and CEC, Glostrup.

Casimir, M.J., Winter, R.P. and Glatzer, B. 1980. Nomadism and remote sensing: animal husbandry and the sagebrush community in a nomad winter area in western Afghanistan. *Journal of Arid Environments* 3:231–54.

Caughley, G., Shepherd, N. and Short, J. 1987. *Kangaroos: Their Ecology and Management on the Sheep Rangelands of Australia.* Cambridge University Press, Cambridge.

Chambers, R. 1983. *Rural Development: Putting the Last First.* Longmans, London.

Chambers, R. 1992. Rural Appraisal: rapid, relaxed and participatory. *IDS Discussion Paper* 311. Institue of Development Studies, Brighton.

Chambers, R. 1993. *Challenging the Professions: Frontiers for Rural Development.* Intermediate Technology Publications Ltd., London.

Chambers, R., Pacey, A. and Thrupp, L.A. (eds.) 1989. *Farmer First: Farmer*

Innovation and Agricultural Research. Intermediate Technology Publications Ltd., London.

Cissé, S. 1982. Les unites pastorales: l'élevage transhumant en question ou des questions posées par l'élevage. *Nomadic Peoples* 11.

Clark, J. 1991. *Democratising Development: The Role of Voluntary Organisations.* Earthscan Publications Ltd., London.

Clatworthy, J.N. 1984. Global ventures in Stylosanthes, III, South-east Africa. In: Stayce, H.M. and Edye, L.A. (eds.). *The Biology and Agronomy of Stylosanthes.* Academic Press, Sydney.

Clements, F. 1916. Plant succession: an analysis of the development of vegetation. *Carnegie Institute Publications* 241:1–512.

Coles, R. 1989. *Measuring Drought and Drought Impacts in Red Sea Province.* Oxfam, Port Sudan.

Conrad, V. 1941. The variability of precipitation. *Monthly Weather Review* 69:5–11.

Coppens, Y. 1994. East Side Story: The origin of humankind. *Scientific American* 270(5):88–95.

Coppock, D.L. 1991. Haymaking and calf management in Ethiopia. *Journal for Farming Systems Research-Extension* 2(3):51–68.

Coppock, D.L. 1992. Bigger calves make better cows. Fact or fantasy in variable environments? *ILCA Newsletter* 8:1–3. International Livestock Centre for Africa (ILCA), Addis Ababa.

Coppock, D.L. 1993. Vegetation and pastoral dynamics in the Southern Ethiopian rangelands: implications for theory and management. In: Behnke, R.H., Scoones, I. and Kerven, C. (eds.) *Range Ecology at Disequilibrium: New Models of Natural Variability and Pastoral Adaptation in African Savannas.* Overseas Development Institute, London.

Coppock, D.L. (1994) *The Borana Plateau of Southern Ethiopia: Synthesis of Pastoral Research, Development and Change 1980-91.* International Livestock Centre for Africa, Addis Ababa.

Coppock, D.L., Ellis, J.E. and Swift, D.M. 1986. Livestock feeding ecology and resource utilization in a nomadic pastoral ecosystem. *Journal of Applied Ecology* 23(2):585–3.

Coppock, D.L. and Reed, J. 1992. Cultivated and native browse legumes as calf supplements in Ethiopia. *Journal of Range Management* 45:231–8.

Cornwall, A., Guijt, I. and Welbourn, A. 1993. Acknowledging process: challenges for agricultural research and extension methodology. *IDS Discussion Paper* 333. Institute of Development Studies, Brighton and International Institute of Environment and Development, London.

Cossins, N. 1985. The productivity and potential of pastoral systems. *ILCA Bulletin* 21:10–15. International Livestock Centre for Africa (ILCA), Addis Ababa.

Cossins, N. and Upton, M. 1988. The impact of climatic variation on the Borana pastoral system. *Agricultural Systems* 27:117–35.

Coughenour, M.B., Ellis, J.E., Swift, J.E., Coppock, D.L., Galvin, K., McCabe, J.T. and Hart, T.C. 1985. Energy extraction and use in a nomadic pastoral ecosystem. *Science* 230(4726): 619–25.

Coulson, A. 1979. *African Socialism in Practice: The Tanzanian Experience.* Spokesman, Nottingham.

Cousins, B. 1987. *A Survey of Current Grazing Schemes in the Communal Lands of Zimbabwe.* Centre for Applied Social Sciences, University of Zimbabwe, Harare.

Cousins, B. 1992. *Managing Communal Rangeland in Zimbabwe: Experiences and Lessons.* Commonwealth Secretariat, London.

Cousins, B. 1993. Co-management of key resources in Matibi 1 communal land,

Zimbabwe. Case study paper presented at the conference on *New Directions in African Range Management and Policy*, 31 May–4 June, Woburn, UK. IIED, ODI and Commonwealth Secretariat, London.

Cullis, A. 1992. Taking the bull by the horns: NGOs and pastoralists in coalition. *Pastoral Development Network Paper* 33d. Overseas Development Institute, London.

Curtis, D. and Scoones, I. 1990. *Strengthening Natural Resource Planning Capability in Darfur*. Agricultural Planning Unit, El Fasher, Darfur.

Dahl, G. 1979. *Suffering Grass: Subsistence and Society of Waso Borana*. Stockholm Institute for Social Anthropology, University of Stockholm, Stockholm.

Dahl, G. and Hjort, A. 1976. Having herds: pastoral growth and household economy. *Stockholm Studies in Social Anthropology* 9. University of Stockholm, Stockholm.

Danckwerts, J. 1974. *A Socio-Economic Study of Veld Management in the Tribal Areas of Victoria Province*. Tribal Areas Research Foundation, Salisbury.

Dasgupta, P. 1993. *An Enquiry into Well-Being and Destitution*. Clarendon Press, Oxford.

Davies, S. 1992. Famine early warning systems and response: the missing link? Case study: Mali, 1990-91. In: Buchanan-Smith, M., Davies, S. and Petty, C. 1992. *Famine Early Warning Systems and Response: The Missing Link?* Institute of Development Studies, Brighton.

DCPU 1992. *Drought Manual, Lodwar, Turkana*. Turkana Drought Contingency Planning Unit, Turkana.

De Angelis, D.L. and Waterhouse, J.C. 1987. Equilibrium and non-equilibrium concepts in ecological models. *Ecolological Monographs* 57(1):1–21.

De Haan, C. 1990. Changing trends in the World Bank's lending program for rangeland development. In: Cincotta, R.P., Perrier, G.K., Gay, C.W. and Tiedeman, J. (eds.) *Low Input Sustainable Yield Systems: Implications for the World's Rangelands*. Proceedings of the 1990 International Rangeland Development Symposium February, Reno Nevada. Utah State University, Logan.

De Haan, C. 1991. Determinants of success in livestock development projects in developing countries: a review of World Bank experience. Paper presented at the *Occasional Symposium of the British Society of Animal Production*, Wye College, Wye.

De Haan, C. and Bekure, S. 1991. Animal health services in sub-Saharan Africa: initial experiences with new approaches. *African Livestock Policy Analysis Network (ALPAN) Paper* 29. ILCA, Addis Ababa.

De Leeuw, P., Bekure, S. and Grandin, B. 1984. Some aspects of livestock productivity in Maasai group ranches in Kenya. *ILCA Bulletin* 19:17–20.

De Leeuw, P., Diarra, L. and Hiernaux, P. 1993. An analysis of feed demand and supply for pastoral livestock: the Gourma region of Mali. In: Behnke, R.H., Scoones, I. and Kerven, C. (eds.) *Range Ecology at Disequilibrium: New Models of Natural Variability and Pastoral Adaptation in African Savannas*. Overseas Development Institute, London.

De Leeuw, P.N., and Tothill, J. 1993. The concept of rangeland carrying capacity in sub-Saharan Africa: myth or reality? In: Behnke, R.H., Scoones, I. and Kerven, C. (eds.) *Range Ecology at Disequilibrium: New Models of Natural Variability and Pastoral Adaptation in African Savannas*. Overseas Development Institute, London.

Delgado, C.L. 1979. The southern Fulani farming system in Upper Volta: a model for the integration of crop and livestock production in the West African savannah? *African Rural Economy Paper* 20. Department of Agricultural Economics, Michigan State University, East Lansing.

Demsetz, H. 1967. Toward a theory of property rights. *American Economic Review* 57:347–59.

De Ridder, N. and Wagenaar, K.T. 1984. A comparison between the productivity of traditional livestock systems and ranching in eastern Botswana. *ILCA Newsletter* 3(3):5–7. International Livestock Centre for Africa, Addis Ababa.

De Ridder, N. and Breman, H. 1993. A new approach to evaluating rangeland productivity in Sahelian countries. In: Behnke, R.H., Scoones, I. and Kerven, C. (eds.) *Range Ecology at Disequilibrium: New Models of Natural Variability and Pastoral Adaptation in African Savannas.* Overseas Development Institute, London.

De Waal, A. 1989. *Famine that Kills: Darfur, Sudan 1984–1985.* Clarendon Press, Oxford.

Diakité, C. N. 1993. *Les Peuls à la Conquête du Bourgou.* Drylands Programme, International Institute for Environment and Development, London.

Dodd, J.L. 1994. Desertification and degradation in sub-Saharan Africa: The role of livestock. *BioScience* 44:28–34.

Doornbos, M.R. and Lofchie, M.F. 1971. Ranching and scheming: a case study of the Ankole ranching scheme. In: Lofchie, M.F. (ed.) *The State of the Nations: Constraints on Development in Independent Africa.* University of California Press, Berkeley.

Doornbos, M.R., Cliffe, L., Ahmed, A.G. and Markakis, J. (eds.) 1992. *Beyond Conflict in the Horn. The Prospects for Peace, Recovery and Development in Ethiopia, Somalia, Eritrea and Sudan.* ISS, The Hague and James Currey, London.

Doppler, W. 1980. *The Economics of Pasture Improvement and Beef Production in Semi-Humid West Africa.* GTZ (German Agency for Technical Co-operation), Eschborn.

Doran, M., Low, A. and Kemp, R. 1979. Cattle as a store of wealth in Swaziland: implications for livestock development and overgrazing in eastern and southern Africa. *American Journal of Agricultural Economics* 61:41–47.

Downing, T. 1982. Climate change, variability and drought in eastern Africa. *East Africa Regional Studies Paper* 9. Program for International Development, Clark University, Worcester.

Dugué, P. 1985. L'Utilisation des résidus de récolte dans un système agro-pastoral sahelo-soudanien: cas de Yatenga (Burkina Faso). *Les Cahiers de la Recherche-Développement* 7:28–37.

Dupire, M. 1962. Peuls nomades: étude descriptive des WoDaaBe du Sahel Nigérien. *Travaux et Mémoirs* 64. Institut d'Ethnologie, Musée de l'Homme, Paris.

Dye, P. and Spear, P. 1982. The effects of bush clearing and rainfall on grass yield and composition in south west Zimbabwe. *Zimbabwe Journal of Agricultural Research* 20:103–18.

Dyson-Hudson, N. 1966. *Karamojong Politics.* Oxford University Press, Oxford.

Dyson-Hudson, R. and McCabe, R. 1983. Water resources and livestock movements in South Turkana, Kenya. *Nomadic Peoples* 14:41–46.

Eldredge, N. 1985. *Time Frames. The Evolution of Punctuated Equilibrium.* Princeton University Press, Princeton.

Ellis, J.E., Galvin, K., McCabe, J.T. and Swift, D.M. 1987. *Pastoralism and Drought in Turkana District Kenya.* Report to the Norwegian Aid Agency for International Development, Nairobi. Currently being revised for publication.

Ellis, J.E. and Swift, D.M. 1988. Stability of African pastoral ecosystems: alternative paradigms and implications for development. *Journal Range Management* 41(6):458–9.

Ellis, J.E., Coughenour, M.B. and Swift, D.M. 1993. Climatic variability, ecosystem stability and the implications for range and livestock development. In: Behnke, R.H., Scoones, I. and Kerven, C. (eds.) *Range Ecology at Disequilibrium: New Models of Natural Variability and Pastoral Adaptation in African Savannas*. Overseas Development Institute, London.

Ellis, J.E. and Galvin, K. 1994. Climate patterns and land use practices in the dry zones of Africa. *BioScience* 44(5):340–9.

Esman, M. and Uphoff, N. 1984. *Local Organizations: Intermediaries in Rural Development*. Cornell University Press, Ithaca.

FAO 1992. *Report of the International Workshop on Pastoral Associations and Livestock Cooperatives*. Egerton University, Kenya.

FAO 1993. *Report of a Workshop on Pastoral Cooperatives held at Egerton University*. FAO, Rome.

Farmer, G. 1986. Rainfall variability in tropical Africa: some implications for policy. *Land Use Policy,* October 1986:336–42.

Farrington, J. and Bebbington, A. 1994. From research to innovation: getting the most from interaction with NGOs in farming systems research and extenstion. *Sustainable Agriculture Programme Gatekeeper Series* SA43. International Institute for Environment and Development, London.

Feder, G., Onchan, T., Chalamwong, Y. and Hongladarom, C. 1988. *Land Policies and Farm Productivity in Thailand*. A World Bank Research Publication. Johns Hopkins University Press, Baltimore and London.

Ferguson, J. 1990. *The Anti-Politics Machine. Development, Depoliticization and Bureaucratic Power in Lesotho*. Cambridge University Press, Cambridge.

Finch, V.A. and King, J.M. 1979. Adaptation to undernutrition and water deprivation in the African zebu: changes in energy requirements. *Research Coordination Meeting on Water Requirements of Tropical Herbivores Based on Measurements with Tritiated Water, Nairobi*. International Atomic Energy Agency, Vienna.

Foran, B. and Stafford-Smith, M. 1991. Risk, biology and drought management strategies for cattle stations in central Australia. *Journal of Environmental Management* 33:17–33.

Fortmann, L. and Roe, E. 1981. Dam groups in Botswana. *Pastoral Network Paper* 12b. Overseas Development Institute, London.

Fowler, A. *et al.* 1992. *Institutional Development and NGOs in Africa: Policy Perspectives for European Development Agencies*. INTRAC, Oxford.

Friedel, M.H. 1991. Range condition assessment and the concept of thresholds: a viewpoint. *Journal of Range Management* 44(5):422–6.

Frisch, J.E. and Vercoe, J.E. 1977. Food intake, energy rate, weight gains, metabolic rate and efficiency of feed utilization in *Bos Taurus* and *Bos Indicus* crossbred cattle. *Animal Production* 25:343–58.

Froude, M. 1974. Veld management in the Victoria Province Tribal Areas. *Rhodesian Agriculture Journal* 71:29–37.

Fry, P. 1988. *Evaluation of Oxfam's Four Restocking Projects in Kenya*. Oxfam-Kenya, Nairobi.

Galaty, J.G. 1992. Social and economic factors in the privatization, sub-division and sale of Maasai ranches. *Nomadic Peoples* 30.

Galaty, J.G. 1993a. Individuating common resources: sub-division of group ranches in Kenya Maasailand. Case study paper for conference on *New*

Directions in African Range Management and Policy, 31 May–4 June, Woburn, UK. IIED, ODI and Commonwealth Secretariat, London.

Galaty, J.G. 1993b. Contradictions of scale and/or cooperation: why group ranches have not worked. How they might have worked. Case study paper for the conference on *New Directions in African Range Management and Policy*, 31 May–4 June, Woburn, UK. IIED, ODI and Commonwealth Secretariat, London.

Galaty, J.G., Aronson, D., Salzman, P. and Chouinard, A. (eds.) 1981. *The Future of Pastoral Peoples*. Proceedings of a conference held in Nairobi, 4–8 August 1980. IDRC, Ottawa.

Galaty, J.G. and Johnson, D. 1990. *World of Pastoralism*. Guildford Press, New York.

Gallais, J. 1967. Le delta intérieur du Niger: étude de géographie régionale. *Mémoirs de l'Institut Fondamental d'Afrique Noire* 79. IFAN, Dakar.

Gallais, J. 1975. *Pasteurs et Paysans du Gourma*. CNRS, Paris.

Gass, G. and Sumberg, J. 1993. *Intensification of Livestock Production in Africa: Experience and Issues*. Overseas Development Group, University of East Anglia, Norwich.

Gillard, P. and Fisher, M.J. 1978. The ecology of Townsville stylo-based pastures in northern Australia. In: Wilson, J.R. (ed.) *Plant Relations in Pastures*. Commonwealth Scientific and Industrial Research Organisation, Melbourne.

Gilles, J.L. 1988. Slippery grazing rights: using indigenous knowledge for pastoral development. In: Whitehead, E.E., Hutchinson, C.F., Timmerman, B.N. and Varady, R.G. (eds.) *Arid Lands Today and Tomorrow*. Westview Press, Boulder.

Gilles, J.L. 1993. New directions for African range management: observations and reflections from past experience. Case Study paper presented for the conference on *New Directions in African Range Management and Policy*, 31 May–4 June, Woburn, UK. IIED, ODI and Commonwealth Secretariat, London.

Glieck, J. 1987. *Chaos: The Making of a New Science*. Cardinal, London.

Goldschmidt, W. 1981. The failure of pastoral economic development programs in Africa. In: Galaty, J.G., Aronson, D., Salzman, P.C. and Chouinard, A. (eds.) *The Future of Pastoral Peoples*. Proceedings of a conference held in Nairobi, Kenya, 4–8 August 1980. International Development Research Centre, Ottawa.

Graham, O. 1988. Enclosure of the East African rangelands: recent trends and their impacts. *Pastoral Develpment Network Paper* 25a. Overseas Development Institute, London.

Grayzel, J.A. 1990. Markets and migration: a Fulbe pastoral system in Mali. In: Galaty, J.G. and Johnson, D.L. (eds.) *The World of Pastoralism*. Guildford Press, New York.

Grell, H. 1992. Policies promoting pastoralists. *ILEIA Newsletter* 8(3):12.

Guèye, B. 1993. Conflits et alliances entre agriculteurs et éleveurs. Case study paper for the conference on *New Directions in African Range Management and Policy*, 31 May–4 June, Woburn, UK. IIED, ODI and Commonwealth Secretariat, London. Also *Drylands Networks Programme Issues Paper* 49. International Institute for Environment and Development, London.

Gulliver, P. 1955. *The Family Herds: A Study of Two Pastoral Tribes in East Africa: The Jie and Turkana*. RKP, London.

Haaland, G. 1972. Nomadism as an economic career among sedentaries in the Sudan savanna belt. In: Cunnison, I. and James, W. (eds.) *Essays in Sudan Ethnography*. Hurst, London.

Haaland, G. 1977. Pastoral systems of production: the socio-cultural context and some economic and ecological considerations. In: O'Keefe, P. and Wisner, B. (eds.) *Land-use and Development*. International African Institute, London.

Hanan, N., Prevost, Y., Diouf, A. and Diallo, O. 1991. Assessment of desertification around deep wells in the Sahel using satellite imagery. *Journal of Applied Ecology* 28:173–186.

Hardin, G. 1968. The tragedy of the commons. *Science* 162:1243–8.

Hardin, G. 1988. Commons failing. *New Scientist* 22 October.

Heggie, I. 1991. Designing major policy reform: lessons from the transport sector. *World Bank Discussion Paper* 115. The World Bank, Washington, DC.

Hellden, U. 1988. Desertification monitoring: is the desert encroaching? *Desertification Control Bulletin* 17:8–12.

Herman, L. and Makinen, M. 1980. *Livestock and Meat Production, Marketing and Exports in Upper Volta.* Center for Research on Economic Development, University of Michigan, Ann Arbor.

Herman, L. 1983. *The Livestock and Meat Marketing System in Upper Volta: An Evaluation of Economic Efficiency.* University of Michigan, Center for Research on Economic Development, Ann Arbor.

Herskovits, M.J. 1926. The cattle complex in East Africa. *American Anthropologist* 28:230–72, 361–80, 494–528, 630–64.

Hiernaux, P.M. 1993. *The Crisis of Sahelian Pastoralism: Ecological or Economic?* International Livestock Centre for Africa, Addis Ababa.

Hiernaux, P.M, Cissé, M.I. and de Haan, C. (eds.) 1983. Recherche sur les systèmes des zones arides du Mali: résultats préliminaires. *CIPEA Rapport de Recherche* 5. ILCA, Addis Ababa.

Hjort af Ornäs, A. 1991. The logic of long term development thinking seen through the eyes of pastoralists and planners. In: Stone, J. (ed.) *Pastoralism in Africa and Long Term Responses to Drought.* African Studies Group, University of Aberdeen, Aberdeen.

Hjort af Ornäs, A. and Salih, M. (eds.) 1989. *Environmental Stress and Security in Africa.* Scandinavian Institute for African Studies, Uppsala.

Hoben, A. 1976. *Social Soundness of the Masai Livestock and Range Management Project.* US Agency for International Development Mission, Dar es Salaam.

Hogg, R. 1983. Restocking the Isiolo Boran: an approach to destitution among pastoralists. *Nomadic Peoples* 14:35–40.

Hogg, R. 1985. Restocking pastoralists in Kenya: a strategy for relief and rehabilitation. *Pastoral Development Network Paper* 19c. Overseas Development Institute, London.

Hogg, R. 1990. An institutional approach to pastoral development: an example from Ethiopia. *Pastoral Development Network Paper* 30d. Overseas Development Institute, London.

Hogg, R. 1992. NGOs, pastoralists and the myth of community: three case studies of pastoral development from East Africa. *Nomadic Peoples* 30:122–46.

Holling, C.S. 1973. Resilience and stability of ecological systems. *Annual Review of Ecology and Systematics* 4:1–23.

Holling, C.S. 1978. *Adaptive Environmental Assessment and Management.* International Institute for Applied Systems Analysis and John Wiley, London.

Holtzman, J.S. 1982a. *The Economics of Improving Animal Health and Livestock Marketing in Somalia.* Prepared for USAID/Mogadishu. Dept. of Agricultural Economics, Michigan State University, East Lansing.

Holtzman, J.S. 1982b. *The Market for Livestock and Meat in Saudi Arabia: Implications for Somalia.* Prepared for USAID/Mogadishu. Dept. of Agricultural Economics, Michigan State University, East Lansing.

Holtzman, J.S. 1984. *Review of Livestock Marketing and Livestock Marketing*

Facilities in Somalia. Small Farmer Marketing Access Project, USAID, Mogadishu.

Holtzman, J.S. 1988. Price policy induced distortions: undermining incentives to slaughter stall-fed cattle in urban areas of northern Cameroon. *African Livestock Policy Analysis Network Paper* 17. International Livestock Centre for Africa, Addis Ababa.

Holtzman, J.S., Staatz, J. and Weber, M.T. 1980. An analysis of the livestock production and marketing subsystem in the northwest Province of Cameroon. *MSU Rural Development Working Paper* 11. Department of Agricultural Economics, Michigan State University, East Lansing.

Holtzman, J.S., Ly, C. and Ndione, C.M. 1989. La commercialisation et l'organisation de la production du bétail et de la viande au Sénégal: problèmes et perspectives de recherches. In: Institut Sénégalais de Recherches Agricoles. *Actes du Séminaire: La Politique Agricole au Sénégal*. Séminaire organisé par l'Institut Sénégalais de Recherches Agricoles avec le soutien financier de l'USAID/Sénégal et du CRDI/Dakar, 7–8 juillet 1988. Institut Sénégalais de Recherches Agricoles, Dakar.

Holtzman, J.S., Kulibaba, N.P. and Stathacos, C.J.D. 1992. *Livestock Marketing and Trade in the Central Corridor of West Africa*. Agricultural Marketing Improvement Strategies Project, Sahel West Africa Office, USAID, Washington, and Abt Associates, Bethesda.

Homewood, K. 1992. Development and ecology of Maasai pastoralist food and nutrition. *Ecology of Food and Nutrition* 29:61–80.

Homewood, K. 1993. Livestock economy and ecology in El Kala, Algeria. Evaluating ecological and economic costs and benefits in pastoralist systems. Case study paper for the conference on *New Directions in African Range Management and Policy*, 31 May–4 June, Woburn, UK. IIED, ODI and Commonwealth Secretariat, London. Also published as *Pastoral Development Network Paper* 35a. Overseas Development Institute, London.

Homewood, K. and Rodgers, W. 1991. *Maasailand Ecology: Pastoralist Development and Wildlife Conservation in Ngorongoro, Tanzania*. Cambridge University Press, Cambridge.

Horowitz, M. 1979. The sociology of pastoralism and African livestock projects. *AID Program Evaluation Discussion Paper* 6. USAID, Washington, DC.

Horowitz, H. and Jowkar, F. 1992. *Pastoral Women and Change in Africa, the Middle East and Central Asia*. Institute for Development Anthropology, Binghamton.

Howell, P.P. 1954. *A Manual of Nuer Law*. Oxford University Press for the International African Institute, Oxford.

Howze, G. 1989. *Socioeconomic Profile of Pastoralists and Agropastoralists in the Central Rangelands of Somalia*. Central Rangelands Development Project, US Agency for International Development, Mogadishu.

Hubbard, M. 1982. Comparison of cattle herd performance in Botswana and their consequence for cattle production investment planning. In: Hitchcock, R. (ed.) *Proceedings of the First Livestock Development Project and its Future Implications*. National Institute for Research, Gaborone.

Hubbard, M. and Morrison, S. 1985. Current issues in cattle pricing and marketing in Botswana. *Pastoral Development Network Paper* 20e. Overseas Development Institute, London.

Hulme, M. 1992. Rainfall changes in Africa: 1931–1960 to 1961–1990. *International Journal of Climatology* 12:685–99.

Humphreys, L.R. 1991. *Tropical Pasture Utilisation*. Cambridge University Press, Cambridge.

IDA 1980. *The Workshop on Pastoralism and African Livestock Development, AID Program Evaluation Report* 4. Institute for Development Anthropology, Binghamton.

IIED 1994. *RRA Notes 20: Special Issue on Livestock*. International Institute for Environment and Development, London.

ILCA 1987–92. *Annual Reports*. International Livestock Centre for Africa, Addis Ababa.

Iles, K. and Young, J. 1991. Decentralised animal health care in pastoral areas. *Appropriate Technology* 18(1):20–22.

Ingawa, S.A. *et al*. 1989. Grazing reserves in Nigeria: problems prospects and policy implications. *ALPAN Network Paper* 22.

IUCN 1989. Rainfall in the Sahel. *IIED Drylands Programme Issues Paper* 10. International Institute for Environment and Development, London.

Jackson, J. 1989. Exploring livestock incomes in Zimbabwe's communal lands. In: Cousins, B. (ed.) *People, Land and Livestock*. Proceedings of a workshop on the socio-economic dimensions of livestock production in the communal lands of Zimbabwe. Centre for Applied Social Science, University of Zimbabwe, Harare.

Jacobs, A.H. 1975. Maasai pastoralism in historical perspective. In: Monod, T. (ed.) *Pastoralism in Tropical Africa*. International African Institute, London.

Jahnke, H. 1982. *Livestock Production Systems and Livestock Development in Tropical Africa*. Kieler Wissenschaftverlag Vauk, Germany.

Jensen, A.J. 1990. *Rural Development Project Ovamboland, Namibia: Environmental Component*. Evangelical Lutheran Church of Namibia, Lutheran World Federation, Oniipa and Geneva.

Johansson, L. 1991. Land use planning and the village titling program land policy: the case of Dirma Village in Hanang District. Paper presented at the *Land Tenure Workshop*. Arusha, Tanzania.

Johnson, D.E., Borman, M.M., Ben Ali, M.N., Laribi, N. and Tiedeman, J.A. 1988. An economic model of sheep production in the central Tunisian mixed farming systems. Paper presented at the *International Rangeland Development Symposium*. Corpus Christi.

Jones, R.J. and Sandland, R.L. 1974. The relation between animal gain and stocking rate: derivation of the relation from the results of grazing trials. *Journal of Agricultural Science* 83:335–41.

Kelly, K. 1993. *Stock Response: Oxfam's Experience of Restocking in Kenya*. Oxfam, Oxford.

Kerkhoff, P. 1990. *Agroforestry in Africa: A Survey of Project Experience*. Panos, London.

Kerven, C. 1992. Customary commerce: a historical reassessment of pastoral livestock marketing in Africa. *ODI Agricultural Occasional Paper* 15. Overseas Development Institute, London.

King, J.M. 1983. Livestock water needs in pastoral Africa in relation to climate and forage. *ILCA Research Report* 7. International Livestock Centre for Africa, Addis Ababa.

Kituyi, M. 1990. *Becoming Kenyans. Socio-economic Transformation of the Pastoral Maasai*. ACTS Press, African Centre for Technology Studies, Nairobi.

Kjaerby, F. 1979. The development of agropastoralism among the Barabaig in Hanang district. *BRALUP Research Paper* 56.

Kjaerby, F. 1980. The problem of development and villagization among the

Barabaig in Hanang District. *Research Report (New Series)* 40. University of Dar es Salaam, Dar es Salaam.

Korten, D.C. 1980. Community organization and rural development: a learning process approach. *Public Administration Review* 20:480–511.

Kulibaba, N.P. 1991. *Livestock and Meat Transport in the Niger–Nigeria Corridor.* Agricultural Marketing Improvement Strategies Project. Abt Associates, Bethesda.

Lane, C. 1991. *Alienation of Barabaig Pasture Land: Policy Implications for Pastoral Development in Tanzania.* Doctoral Thesis. Institute of Development Studies, University of Sussex, Brighton.

Lane, C. and Scoones, I. 1993. Barabaig natural resource management. In: Young, M. D. and Solbrig, O. (eds.) *The World's Savannas: Economic Driving Forces. Ecological Constraints and Policy Options for Sustainable Use.* Vol. 12 Man and Biosphere Series, UNESCO and Parthenon Publishing Group, Paris and New York.

Lane, C. and Swift, J. 1988. *Pastoral Land Tenure in East Africa.* Report of a workshop, Arusha, Tanzania. Institute of Development Studies, University of Sussex, Brighton.

Lane, C. and Swift, J. 1989. East African pastoralism: common land, common problems. *Drylands Programme Issues Paper* 8. International Institute for Environment and Development, London.

Lawry, S.W. 1987. Commmunal grazing and ranch management: the case of grazing associations in Lesotho. *ALPAN Network Paper* 13. ILCA, Addis Ababa.

Lawry, S.W. 1988. *Private Herds and Common Land: Issues in the Management of Communal Grazing Land in Lesotho, Southern Africa.* Doctoral Thesis (Land Resources), University of Wisconsin, Madison.

Laycock, W.A. 1991. Stable states and thresholds of range condition on North American rangelands: a viewpoint. *Journal of Range Management* 44:427–33.

Le Houérou, H.N. (ed.) 1980. *Browse in Africa: The Current State of Knowledge.* International Livestock Centre for Africa, Addis Ababa.

Le Houérou, H.N. 1989. *The Grazing Land Ecosystems of the African Sahel.* Springer Verlag, Berlin.

Little, P. 1985a. Social differentiation and pastoralist sedentarization in northern Kenya. *Africa* 55:242–61.

Little, P. 1985b. Absentee herd owners and part-time pastoralists: the political economy of resource use in northern Kenya. *Human Ecology* 13:131-151.

Little, P. 1987. Land use conflicts in the agricultural/pastoral borderlands: the case of Kenya. In: Little, P., Horowitz, M. and Nyerges, A. (eds.) *Lands at Risk in the Third World: Local Level Perspectives.* Westview Press, Boulder.

Little, P. and Brokensha, D. 1987. Local institutions, tenure and resource management in East Africa. In: Anderson, D. and Grove, R. (eds.) *Conservation in Africa.* Cambridge University Press, Cambridge.

Livingstone, I. 1977. Economic irrationality among pastoral peoples: myth or reality? *Development and Change* 8:209–30.

Logan, J.A. and Hain, F.P. 1990. Chaos and insect ecology. Virginia Ag. Exp. Stat. *Virginia Polytechnic Institute and State University Information Series 91–3.* Blacksburg.

Long, N. and van der Ploeg, J. 1989. Demythologizing planned intervention: an actor's perspective. *Sociologica Ruralis* XXIX (3/4): 227–49.

Long, N. and Long, A. 1992. *Battlefields of Knowledge: The Interlocking of Theory and Practice in Social Research and Development.* Routledge, London.

194

Lühl, H.P. 1992. Holistic resource management: can it beat desertification? *ILEIA Newsletter* 8 (3):10–11.

Mace, R. 1989. Gambling with goats: variability in herd growth among restocked pastoralists in Kenya. *Pastoral Development Network Paper* 28a. Overseas Development Institute, London.

Madden, P. 1993. *Brussels Beef Carve-up: EC Beef Dumping in West Africa.* Christian Aid, London.

Manger, L. 1994. Managing pastoral adaptations in the Red Sea Hills of the Sudan: challenges and dilemmas. *Drylands Issues Paper* 52. IIED, London.

Marglin, F. and Marglin, S. (eds.) 1990. *Dominating Knowledge: Development Culture and Resistance.* Clarendon Press, Oxford.

Markakis, J. 1991. Governmental support for the survival of nomadic pastoralists. In: Stone, J. (ed.) *Pastoralism in Africa and Long Term Responses to Drought.* African Studies Group, University of Aberdeen, Aberdeen.

Markakis, J. 1993. Introduction. In: Markakis, J. (ed.) *Conflict and the Decline of Pastoralism in the Horn of Africa.* Macmillan, London and ISS, The Hague.

Marsh, A. and Seely, M. 1992. *Oshanas: Sustaining People, Environment and Development in Central Ovambo, Namibia.* Typoprint, Windhoek.

Martin A., *et al.* 1992. *Evaluation of the Ishtirak Project, Oum Hadjer, Chad. A report for Oxfam.* Natural Resources Institute, Chatham.

Marty, A. 1990. *Les Organizations Coopératives en Milieu Postral: Héritage et Enjeux.* Cahiers des Sciences Humaines, ORSTOM, Paris.

MASCOTT 1986. *A Study of the Future Development of the Central Rangelands of Somalia.* MASCOTT Ltd., Mogadishu.

Maxwell, S. 1992. Food security in Africa: priorities for reducing hunger. *Africa Recovery Briefing Paper* 6.

May, R. 1973. *Stability and Complexity in Model Ecosystems.* Princeton University Press, Princeton.

May, R. 1977. Thresholds and breakpoints in ecosystems with a multiplicity of stable states. *Nature* 269:471–77.

McCabe, J.T. 1987. Drought and recovery: livestock dynamics among the Ngisonyoka Turkana of Kenya. *Human Ecology* 15(4):371–89.

McCown, R.L., Haaland, G. and de Haan, C. 1979. The interaction between cultivation and livestock production in semi-arid Africa. In: Hall, A.E., Cannell, G.H. and Lawton, H.W. (eds.) *Agriculture in Semi-Arid Environments.* Springer Verlag, Berlin.

McIntire, J., Bourzat, D. and Pingali, P. 1992. *Crop–Livestock Interactions in Sub-Saharan Africa.* World Bank, Washington, DC.

Mearns, R. 1993. Pastoral institutions, land tenure and land policy reform in post-socialist Mongolia. *Research Report* 3. Policy Alternatives for Livestock Development in Mongolia. Institute of Development Studies, Ulaanbaatar and Sussex, Institute of Development Studies.

Mentis, M.T., Grossman, D., Hardy, M.B., O'Connor, T.G. and O'Reagain, P.J. 1989. Paradigm shifts in South African range science, management and administration. *South African Journal of Science* 85:684–7.

Meyer, R.L., Graham, D.H. and Cuevas, C.E. 1992. *A Review of the Literature on Financial Markets and Agribusiness Development in Sub-Saharan Africa: Lessons Learned and Suggestions for an Analytical Agenda.* Rural Finance Program, Department of Agricultural Economics and Rural Sociology, Ohio State University, Columbus.

Mickelwait, D.R., Sweet, C.F. and Morss, E.R. 1979. *New Directions in Development: A Study of USAID.* Westview Press, Boulder.

Minson, D.J. 1990. *Forage in Ruminant Nutrition*. Academic Press, San Diego.

Monod, T. (ed.) 1975. *Pastoralism in Tropical Africa*. Oxford University Press, Oxford.

Moorehead, R. 1991. *Structural Chaos: Community and State Management of Common Property in Mali*. Doctoral Thesis, Institute of Development Studies, University of Sussex, Brighton.

Moris, J. 1988. Oxfam's Kenya restocking projects. *Pastoral Development Network Paper* 26c. Overseas Development Institute, London.

Moris, J. 1991. *Extension Alternatives in Tropical Africa*. Overseas Development Institute, London.

Mosely, P. 1991. Structural adjustment: a general overview, 1980–89. In: Balasubramaniam, V. and Lall, S. (eds.) *Current Issues in Development Economics*. Macmillan, London.

Mosely, P. and Weeks, J. 1993. Has recovery begun? Africa's adjustment in the 1980s revisited. *World Development* 21:1583–1606.

Mott, J.J., Tothill, J.C. and Weston, E.J. 1981. Animal production from the native woodlands and grasslands of northern Australia. *Journal of the Australian Institute of Agricultural Science* 47:132–41.

Müller, J.O. 1991. Die Kunst der Weidewanderung von Peul-Nomaden in Nord-Senegal. In: Scholz, F. (ed.) *Nomaden—Mobile Tierhaltung: Zur Gegenwärtigen Lage von Nomaden und den Problemen und Chancen Mobiler Tierhaltung*. Das Arabische Buch, Berlin.

Ndagala, D. 1982. Operation Imparnati: The sedentarisation of the pastoral Maasai. *Nomadic Peoples* 10.

Netting, R. 1978. Of men and meadows: strategies of alpine land use. *Anthropological Quarterly* 45:123–241.

Niamir, M. 1990. Herders' decision-making in natural resources management in arid and semi-arid Africa. *Community Forestry* 4. FAO (Food and Agriculture Organisation of the United Nations), Rome.

Niamir-Fuller, M. 1993. Range management and land use planning with displaced pastoralists: impossible or not? Case study paper for the conference on *New Directions in African Range Management and Policy*, 31 May–4 June, Woburn, UK. IIED, ODI and Commonwealth Secretariat, London.

Nicholls, N. and Wong, K.K. 1990. Dependence of rainfall variability on mean rainfall, latitude, and the southern oscillation. *Journal of Climate* 3:162–70.

Nicholson, M.J. 1987. Effects of night enclosure and extensive walking on the productivity of Zebu cattle. *Journal of Agricultural Science* 109:445–52.

Nicolis, G. and Prigogine, I. 1989. *Exploring Complexity*. W. H. Freeman and Co., New York.

Nieuwkerk, M. *et al.* 1983. *Evaluation du Mouvement Cooperatif en 6ᵉ Region du Mali*. ACORD, Mali.

NOPA 1992. *Pastoralists at a Crossroads: Survival and Development Issues in African Pastoralism*. UNICEF/UNSO Project for Nomadic Pastoralists in Africa, Nairobi, Kenya.

Noronha, R. and Lethem, F.J. 1983. Traditional land tenure and land use systems in the design of agricultural projects. *World Bank Working Paper* 561. World Bank, Washington, DC.

North, D. 1990. *Institutions, Institutional Change and Economic Performance*. Cambridge University Press, Cambridge.

Noy-Meir, I. 1975. Stability of grazing systems: an application of predator–prey graphs. *Journal of Ecology* 63:459–81.

Noy-Meir, I. 1978. Stability in simple grazing models: effects of explicit functions. *Journal of Theoretical Biology* 71:347–80.

Noy-Meir, I. 1982. Stability of plant-herbivore models and possible applications to savanna. In: Huntley, B.J. and Walker, B.H. (eds.) *Ecology of Tropical Savannas*. Springer Verlayg, Berlin.

Noy-Meir, I. and Walker, B. 1986. Stability and resilience in rangelands. In: Joss, P., Lynch, P. and Williams, O. (eds.) *Rangelands: A Resource Under Siege*. Australian Academy of Sciences, Canberra.

Oba, G. 1993. Management of patchy resources in a patchy arid ecosystem of northern Kenya. An indigenous approach to rangeland classification, assessment and management. Case study paper for the conference on *New Directions in African Range Management and Policy*, 31 May–4 June, Woburn, UK. IIED, ODI and Commonwealth Secretariat, London.

Oxby, C. 1982. Group ranches in Africa. *Pastoral Development Network Paper* 13d. Overseas Development Institute, London.

Oxby, C. 1983. Women's contribution to animal husbandry and production. *World Animal Review* 48:2–11.

Oxby, C. 1989. *African Livestock Keepers in Recurrent Crisis: Policy Issues Arising From the NGO Response*. Report prepared for ACORD. Drylands Programme, International Institute for Environment and Development, London.

Oxby, C. 1994 *Restocking. A Guide* VetAid, Roslin, Scotland.

Payne, W.J.A. 1990. *An Introduction to Animal Husbandry in the Tropics*. 4th edn. Longmans, London.

Pearson, C.J. and Ison, R.L. 1987. *Agronomy of Grassland Systems*. Cambridge University Press, Cambridge.

Penning de Vries, F.W.T. and Djitèye, M.A. (eds.) 1982. *La Productivité des Pâturages Sahéliens: Une Etude des Sols, des Végétations et de l'Exploitation de cette Ressource Naturelle*. PUDOC (Centre for Agricultural Publishing and Documentation), Wageningen.

Perrier, G.K. 1983. *The Grazing Management Strategy and Practices of Settled Fulani Livestock Producers Near Zaria, Northern Nigeria*. Report to National Animal Production Research Institute, Zaria.

Perrier, G.K. 1988. Range management practices and strategies of agropastoral Fulani near Zaria, Nigeria. In: Gay, C.W., Perrier, G.K. and Tiedeman, J. (eds.) *Proceedings of the 1988 International Rangeland Development Symposium*. February 1988, Corpus Christi. Utah State University, Logan.

Perrier, G.K. 1990. The contextual nature of range management. *Pastoral Development Network Paper* 30c. Overseas Development Institute, London.

Perrier, G.K. 1991. *The Effects of Policy Development and Organizational Structure on the Performance of Range Livestock Development Projects in Africa*. Doctoral thesis, Utah State University, Logan.

Pingali, P., Bigot, Y. and Binswanger, H. 1987. *Agricultural Mechanisation and the Evolution of Farming Systems in Sub-Saharan Africa*. Johns Hopkins University Press, Baltimore.

Place, F. and Hazell, P. 1993. Productivity effects of indigenous land tenure systems in sub-Saharan Africa. *American Journal of Agricultural Economics,* February:10–19.

Platteau, J.-P. 1991. Traditional systems of social security and hunger insurance: past achievements and modern challenges. In: Ahmad, E. *et al.* (eds.) *Social Security in Developing Countries*. Clarendon Press, Oxford.

Pointing, J. and Joekes, S. 1991. Les femmes dans les sociétés pastorales d'Afrique

Orientale et Occidentale. *Drylands Network Programme Issues Paper* 28. International Institute for Environment and Development, London.

Potkanski, T. 1994. Pastoral concepts, herding patterns and management of natural resources among the Ngorongoro and Salei Maasai of Tanzania. *Pastoral Land Tenure Series Paper* 5. International Institute for Environment and Development, London.

Potkanski, T., and Szynkiewicz, S. 1993, The Social Context of Liberalisation of the Mongolian Pastoral Economy. *Research Report* No. 4, Policy Alternatives for Livestock Development in Mongolia. Ulaanbaatar and Sussex, Institute of Development Studies.

Powell, J.M. 1986. Crop-livestock interactions in the subhumid zone of Nigeria. In: von Kaufmann, R., Chater, S. and Blench, R. (eds.) *Livestock Systems Research in Nigeria's Subhumid Zone.* International Livestock Centre for Africa, Addis Ababa.

Powell, J.M. and Waters-Bayer, A. 1985. Interactions between livestock husbandry and cropping in a West African savanna. In: Tothill, J.C. and Mott, J.J. (eds.) *Ecology and Management of the World's Savannas.* Australian Academy of Science, Canberra.

Powell, J.M. and Ikpe, F. 1992. Fertiliser factories: nutrient cycling through livestock. *ILEIA Newsletter* 8(3):13–14.

Powell, J.M. and Williams, T. 1993. Livestock, nutrient cycling and sustainable agriculture in the West African Sahel. *Sustainable Agriculture Gatekeeper Series* SA37. International Institute for Environment and Development, London.

Pratt, D.J. 1990. *Forms of Ranching and Pastoral Organizations Appropriate for Isiolo District.* ODA, London.

Pretty, J. and Chambers, R. 1993. Towards a learning paradigm: new professionalism and institutions for agriculture. *Sustainable Agriculture Programme Research Series* 1(1):48–83. International Institute for Environment and Development, London.

Prigogine, I. 1961. *Introduction to Thermodynamics of Irreversible Processes.* Wiley, New York.

Rennie, T. *et al.* 1977. Beef cattle productivity under traditional and improved management in Botswana. *Tropical Animal Health and Production* 9:1–6.

Reusse, E. 1982. Somalia's nomadic livestock economy: its response to profitable export opportunity. *World Animal Review* 43:2–11.

Richardson, F. 1992. *Challenges in Animal Production in Southern Africa.* Inaugural lecture at the Dept of Animal Sciences, University of Bophutatswana.

Rocha, A., Starkey, P. and Dionisio, A. 1991. Cattle production and utilisation in smallholder farming systems in southern Mozambique. *Agricultural Systems* 37:55–75.

Rodriguez, G. 1986. Beef supply response estimation and implications for policy analysis: the Zimbabwe case. *African Livestock Policy Analysis Network (ALPAN)* 11. ILCA, Addis Ababa.

Roe, E. 1991a. Development narratives, or making the best of blueprint development. *World Development* 19:287–300.

Roe, E. 1991b. Analyzing sub-Saharan livestock rangeland development. *Rangelands* 13(2):67–70.

Roe, E. 1993. Professionalism in sub-Saharan livestock rangeland development. *Rangelands* 15(1):16–17.

Ropelewski, C. F. and Halpert, M. S. 1987. Global and regional scale precipitation patterns associated with the El Niño/Southern Oscillation. *Monthly Weather Review* 115:1606–26.

198

Ruelle, D. 1991. *Chance and Chaos.* Princeton University Press, Princeton.

Runge, C.F. 1981. Common property externalities: isolation, assurance and resource depletion in a traditional grazing context. *American Journal of Agricultural Economics* 63:595–606.

Runge, C.F. 1984. Institutions and the free rider: the assurance problem in collective action. *Journal of Politics* 46:154–81.

Runge, C.F. 1986. Common property and collective action in economic development. *Proceedings of the Conference on Common Property Resource Management.* National Research Council, National Academy Press, Washington, DC.

Ruthenburg, H. 1980. *Farming Systems in the Tropics.* Clarendon Press, Oxford.

Said, M.S. 1994. *The Conditions for Successful Pastoral Common Property Regimes in Somalia.* Doctoral thesis, University of Sussex, Brighton.

Salih, M.A.M. 1992. Pastoralists and planners: local knowledge and resource management in Gidan Magajia grazing reserve, northern Nigeria. *Dryland Networks Programme Issues Paper* 32. International Institute for Environment and Development, London.

Sampson, A.W. 1923. *Range and Pasture Management.* Wiley, New York.

Sandford, S. 1981. *Review of World Bank Livestock Activities in Dry Tropical Areas.* World Bank Internal Report, Washington, DC.

Sandford, S. 1982. Pastoral strategies and desertification: opportunism and conservatism in dry lands. In: Spooner, B. and Mann, H.S. (eds.) *Desertification and Development: Dryland Ecology in Social Perspective.* Academic Press, London.

Sandford, S. 1983. *Management of Pastoral Development in the Third World.* Wiley, Chichester and Overseas Development Institute, London.

Sandford, S. 1988. Integrated cropping–livestock systems for dryland farming in Africa. In: Unger, P.W., Jordan, W.R., Sneed, T.V. and Jensen, R.W. (eds.) *Challenges in Dryland Agriculture—A Global Perspective.* Proceedings of the International Conference on Dryland Farming, 15–19 August, 1988, Amarillo/Bushland, Texas.

Sandford, S. 1989. Crop residue/livestock relationships. In: ICRISAT *Soil, Crop and Water Management in the Sudano-Sahelian Zone.* Proceedings of an International Workshop, 11–16 January 1987, ICRISAT, Pantcheru, India.

Sarma, J.S. and Yeung, P. 1985. Livestock products in the Third World: past trends and projections to 1990 and 2000. *IFPRI Research Report* 49. International Food Policy Research Institute (IFPRI), Washington, DC.

SCET 1976. *Essai de Réflexion sur les Stratégies Anti-sécheresse dans les Pays Saheliens de l'Afrique de l'Ouest.* SEDES/ORSTOM, Paris.

Schneider, E.D. and Kay, J.J. 1994. Life as a manifestation of the second law of thermodynamics. *Mathl. Comput. Modelling* 19(6–8):25–48.

Schön, D. 1983. *The Reflective Practitioner: How Professionals Think in Action.* Avebury, Aldershot.

Schoonmaker-Freudenberger, K. 1991. Mbegué: the disingenuous destruction of a Sahelian forest. *Dryland Networks Programme Issues Paper* 29. International Institute for Environment and Development, London.

Scoones, I. 1989a. Patch use in dryland Zimbabwe: farmer knowledge and ecological theory. *Pastoral Development Network Paper* 28b. Overseas Development Institute, London.

Scoones, I. 1989b. Economic and ecological carrying capacity: implications for livestock development in Zimbabwe's communal areas. *Pastoral Development Network Paper* 276. Overseas Development Institute, London.

Scoones, I. 1990. *Livestock Populations and the Household Economy. A Case*

199

Study from Southern Zimbabwe. Unpublished doctoral thesis, University of London.

Scoones, I. 1991. Overview: ecological, economic and social issues. In: Scoones, I. (ed.) *Wetlands in Drylands: The Agroecology of Savanna Systems in Africa.* International Institute for Environment and Development, London.

Scoones, I. 1992a. The economic value of livestock in the communal areas of southern Zimbabwe. *Agricultural Systems* 39:339–59.

Scoones, I. 1992b. Coping with drought: responses of herders and livestock in contrasting savanna environments in southern Zimbabwe. *Human Ecology* 20:293–314.

Scoones, I. 1993. Why are there so many animals? Cattle population dynamics in the communal areas of Zimbabwe. In: Behnke, R., Scoones, I. and Kerven, C. (eds.) *Range Ecology at Disequilibrium. New Models of Natural Variability and Pastoral Adaptation in African Savannas.* Overseas Development Institute, London.

Scoones, I. 1994. Exploiting heterogeneity: habitat use by cattle in the communal areas of Zimbabwe. *Journal of Arid Environments* (in press).

Scoones, I. and Thompson, J. 1993. Challenging the populist perspective: rural people's knowledge, agricultural research and extension practice. *IDS Discussion Paper* 332. Institute of Development Studies, Brighton.

Scoones, I. and Thompson, J. 1994. *Beyond Farmer First: Rural People's Knowledge, Agricultural Research and Extension Practice.* Intermediate Technology Publications Ltd., London.

Scoones, I. and Cousins, B. 1994. The struggle for control over wetland resources in Zimbabwe. *Society and Natural Resources* (in press).

Scott, J. 1985. *Weapons of the Weak. Everyday Forms of Peasant Resistance.* Yale University Press, New Haven.

Scott, J. 1990. *Domination and the Arts of Resistance: Hidden Transcripts.* Yale University Press, New Haven.

Shanmugaratnam, N., Vedeld, T., Mossige, A. and Bovin, M. 1992. Resource management and pastoral institution building in the West African Sahel. *World Bank Discussion Paper, Africa Technical Department Series* 175, Washington, DC.

Sihm, P.A. 1989. Pastoral associations in West Africa, experience and future strategies. *Professional Development Workshop on Dryland Management,* World Bank, Washington, DC.

Skerman, P.J. and Riveros, F. 1990. *Tropical Grasses.* FAO (Food and Agriculture Organisation of the United Nations), Rome.

Solbrig, O.T. and Nicolis, G. (eds.) 1991. *Perspectives on Biological Complexity.* IUBS, Paris.

Sørbo, G. 1992. *Micro–macro Issues in Rural Development: A Study of the Economic Adaptations and Environmental Problems in Eastern Sudan.* Centre for Development Studies, University of Bergen, Bergen.

Spencer, P. 1973. *Nomads in Alliance: Symbiosis and Growth Among the Rendille and Samburu of Kenya.* Oxford University Press, Oxford.

Staatz, J. 1979. *The Economics of Cattle and Meat Marketing in Ivory Coast.* Center for Research on Economic Development, University of Michigan, Ann Arbor.

Stafford-Smith, M. and Foran, B. 1990. *An approach to assessing the economic risk of different drought management tactics on a south Australian pastoral sheep station.* CSIRO, Alice Springs.

Stafford-Smith, M. and Pickup, G. 1993. Out of Africa, looking in: understanding vegetation change. In: Behnke, R.H., Scoones, I. and Kerven, C. (eds.) *Range Ecology at Disequilibrium: New Models of Natural Variability and Pastoral Adaptation in African Savannas*. Overseas Development Institute, London.

Stebbings, E. P. 1935. The encroaching Sahara. *Geographical Journal* 86:510.

Stenning, D. 1957. Transhumance, migratory drift, migration: patterns of pastoral Fulani nomadism. *Journal of the Royal Anthropological Institute of Great Britain and Ireland* 87:58–73.

Stoddart, L.A., Smith, A. and Box, T. 1975. *Range Management*. McGraw–Hill, New York.

Sutter, J.W. 1987. Cattle and inequality: herd size differences and pastoral production among the Fulani of northeastern Senegal. *Africa* 57(2):196–218.

Swallow, B.M. 1991. *Common Property Regimes for African Rangeland Resources*. Doctoral thesis, University of Wisconsin, Madison.

Swallow, B.M. 1994. The role of mobility within risk management strategies of pastoralists and agropastoralists. Gatekeeper Series SA47. International Institute for Environment and Development, London.

Swallow, B.M. and Brokken, R.F. 1987. Cattle marketing policy in Lesotho. *African Livestock Policy Analysis Network Paper* 14. International Livestock Centre for Africa, Addis Ababa.

Swift, J. 1982. The future of African hunter-gatherer and pastoral peoples. *Development and Change* 13:159–81.

Swift, J. 1984. *Pastoral Development in Central Niger*. Ministry of Rural Development and USAID, Niamey.

Swift, J. 1991. Local customary institutions as the basis for natural resource management among Boran pastoralists in Northern Kenya. *IDS Bulletin* 22 (4) Institute of Development Studies, Brighton.

Swift, J. and Bonfiglioli, A.M. 1984. Experimental development interventions: pilot herder associations. In: Swift, J. (ed.) *Pastoral Development in Central Niger*. Prepared for the US Agency for International Development, Niamey.

Swift, J. and Abdi, N.O. 1992. *Participatory Pastoral Development in Isiolo District: Socio-Economic Research in the Isiolo Livestock Development Project*. EMI ASAL Programme, Isiolo.

Sylla, D. 1985. *Evaluation des Activités Pastorales du Programme de Relance Cooperative en 7ᵉ Région du Mali*. ACORD, Mali.

Sylla, D. 1989. The experience of pastoral organizations in African countries. *Drylands Programme Issues Envelope* 3. International Institute for Environment and Development, London.

Tapscott, C.P.G. 1990. *The Social Economy of Livestock Production in Ovambo and Kavango*. Namibian Institute for Social and Economic Research, University of Namibia, Windhoek.

Tapson, D. 1991. The overstocking and offtake controversy re-examined for the case of Kwazulu. *Pastoral Development Network Paper* 31a. Overseas Development Institute, London.

Tapson, D. 1993. Biological sustainability in pastoral systems: the Kwazulu case. In: Behnke, R.H., Scoones, I. and Kerven, C. (eds.) *Range Ecology at Disequilibrium: New Models of Natural Variability and Pastoral Adaptation in African Savannas*. Overseas Development Institute, London.

Taylor-Powell, E. 1987. Fodder bank testing among agro-pastoralists in central Nigeria: feeding decisions in the use of improved forages. *Pastoral Development Network Paper* 24b. Overseas Development Institute, London.

Teklu, T., von Braun, J. and Zaki, E. 1991. Drought and famine relationships in

Sudan: policy implications. *IFPRI Research Report* 88. International Food Policy Research Institute (IFPRI), Washington, DC.

Templer, G., Swift, J. and Payne, P. 1994. The changing significance of risk in the Mongolian pastoral economy. *Nomadic Peoples* 33:105–22.

Thébaud, B. 1990. *Politiques d'Hydraulique Pastorale et Gestion de l'Espace au Sahel*. Cahiers des Sciences Humaines, ORSTOM, Paris.

Thébaud, B. 1993. Agropastoral land management in the western Sahel. The example of Sebba in the Sahelian region of Burkina Faso. Case study paper for the conference on *New Directions in African Range Management and Policy*, 31 May–4 June, Woburn, UK. IIED, ODI and Commonwealth Secretariat, London.

Thébaud, B. and Grandy, E. 1992. L'eau et les éleveurs au Sahel: L'expérience de Diffa au Niger. Le développment agricole au Sahel Tome 3. Terrains et innovations. *Collection Documents Systèmes Agraires* 17. CIRAD, Montpellier.

Thomson, J. *et al.* 1991. *Decentralisation, Governance and Management of Renewable Natural Resources: Local Options in the Republic of Mali*. OECD/Club du Sahel, Paris.

Tiffen, M. and Mortimore, M. 1992. Environment, population growth and productivity in Kenya: a case study from Machakos District. *Development Policy Review* 10:359–97. Overseas Development Institute, London.

Tignor, R. 1976. *The Colonial Transformation of Kenya: The Kamba, Kikuyu and Maasai from 1900 to 1939*. Princeton, New Jersey.

Toulmin, C. 1986. Pastoral livestock losses and post-drought rehabilitation in sub-Saharan Africa: policy options and issues. *African Livestock Policy Analysis Network Paper* 8. International Livestock Centre for Africa, Addis Ababa.

Toulmin, C. 1992a. *Cattle, Women and Wells: Managing Household Survival in the Sahel*. Clarendon Press, Oxford.

Toulmin, C. 1992b. Herding contracts: for better or worse? *ILEIA Newsletter* 8(3):8–9.

Toulmin, C. 1993. *Gestion de Terroir: Principles, First Lessons and Implications for Action*. Discussion paper for UNSO, New York. International Institute for Environment and Development, London.

Touré, O. 1990. *Applications de la Télédétection au Sahel et Utilisation de l'Information par les Communautés de Base*. Centre du Suivi Ecologique (CSE), Dakar.

Tucker, C.J., Dregne, H. and Newcomb, W. 1991. Expansion and contraction of the Sahara desert from 1980 to 1990. *Science* 253:299–301.

Umali, D., Feder, G. and de Haan, C. 1992. The balance between public and private sector activities in the delivery of livestock services. *World Bank Discussion Paper* 163. World Bank, Washington DC.

Uphoff, N. 1986. *Local Institutional Development. An Analytical Sourcebook with Cases*. Kumarian Press, Hartford.

Uphoff, N. 1992a. Local institutions and participation for sustainable development. *Sustainable Agriculture Gatekeeper Series* SA31. International Institute for Environment and Development, London.

Uphoff, N. 1992b. *Learning from Gal Oya: Possibilities for Participatory Development and Post-Newtonian Science*. Cornell University Press, Ithaca.

Upton, M. 1989. Livestock productivity assessment and herd growth models. *Agricultural Systems* 29:149–164.

URT 1992. Report of the Presidential Commission of Enquiry into land matters. *Land Policy and Land Tenure Structure*, Vol.1. Dar es Salaam.

URT 1983. *The Agriculture Policy Ministry of Agriculture and Livestock Development.* Government Printer, Dar es Salaam.

USDA 1990. World agriculture trends and indicators, 1970–89. *Statistical Bulletin* 815. US Department of Agriculture, Washington, DC.

Van Duivenboden, N. 1992. Sustainability in terms of nutrient elements with special reference to West Africa. *CABO/DLO Report* 160. CABO, Wageningen.

Van Raay, H.G.T. 1975. *Rural Planning in a Savannah Region.* Rotterdam University Press, Rotterdam.

Van Raay, H.G.T. and de Leeuw, P.N. 1974. *Fodder Resources and Grazing Management in a Savanna Environment: An Ecosystem Approach.* Institute of Social Studies, The Hague.

Van Soest, P.J. 1982. *Nutritional Ecology of the Ruminant.* O & B Books, Corvallis.

Vedeld, T. 1992. Local institution-building and resource management in the West African Sahel. *Pastoral Development Network Paper* 33c, Overseas Development Institute, London.

Vedeld, T. 1993. Rangeland management and state-sponsored pastoral institution building in Mali. Case study paper for the conference on *New Directions in African Range Management and Policy*, 31 May–4 June, Woburn, UK. IIED, ODI and Commonwealth Secretariat, London. Also *Drylands Networks Programme Issues Paper* 46. International Institute for Environment and Development, London

Von Maydell, H.J. 1986. *Trees and Shrubs of the Sahel: Their Characteristics and Uses.* GTZ (German Agency for Technical Co-operation), Eschborn.

Vrba, E. 1992. Mammals as a key to evolutionary theory. *Journal of Mammology* 73:1-28.

Walker, B., Norton, G., Barlow, N., Conway, G., Birley, M. and Comins, H. 1978. A procedure for multidisciplinary ecosystem research with reference to the South African Savanna Ecosystem Project. *Journal of Applied Ecology* 15: 481-502.

Walker, B.H., Ludwig, D., Holling, C.S. and Peterman, R.M. 1981. Stability of semi-arid savanna grazing systems. *Journal of Ecology* 69:473–98.

Walker, B.H. and Noy-Meir, I. 1982. Aspects of stability and resilience of savanna ecosystems. In: Huntley, B.J. and Walker, B.H. (eds.) *Ecology of Tropical Savannas.* Ecological Studies 42. Springer Verlag, Berlin.

Walker, P. 1989. *Famine Early Warning Systems: Victims and Destitution.* Earthscan Publications, London.

Wallich, P. and Holloway, M. 1993. More profitable to give than to receive? *Scientific American* 266:142.

Walters, C. 1986. *Adaptive Management.* University of British Columbia, Canada.

Walters, C. and Hilborn, R. 1978. Ecological optimisation and adaptive management. *Annual Review of Ecology and Systematics* 9:157–89.

Warren, A. and Khogali, M. 1992. *Assessment of Desertification and Drought in the Sudano-Sahelian Region 1985–1991.* United Nations Sahelian Office, New York.

Watson, C. and Lobuin, A. 1991. *Pastoral Institutions in Kakuma Division: A Case Study.* Intermediate Technology Development Group, Rugby.

Webb, P., von Braun, J. and Yohannes, Y. 1992. Famine in Ethiopia: policy implications for coping with failure at national and household levels. *IFPRI Research Report* 92. International Food Policy Research Institute (IFPRI), Washington, DC.

Webb, P. and Reardon, T. 1992. Drought impact and household response in East and West Africa. *Quarterly Journal of International Agriculture* 31(3):230–46.

Weins, J.A. 1977. On competition and variable environments. *Amererican Scientist* 65:590–97.

Wellard, K. and Copestake, J. (eds.) 1993. *State–NGO Interaction in the Development of New Agricultural Technology for Small Farmers: Experiences from Sub-Saharan Africa*. Routledge, London.

Western, D. 1982. The environment and ecology of pastoralism in arid savannas. *Development and Change* 13:183–211.

Western, D. and Finch, V. 1986. Cattle and pastoralism: survival and production in arid lands. *Human Ecology* 14:77–94.

Westoby, M., Walker, B. and Noy-Meir, I. 1989. Opportunistic management of rangelands not at equilibrium. *Journal of Range Management* 42:266–74.

White, C. 1990. Changing animal ownership and access to land among the Wodaabe (Fulani) of central Niger. In: Baxter, P.T.W. and Hogg, R. (eds.) *Property, Poverty and People: Changing Rights in Property and Problems of Pastoral Development*. Department of Social Anthropology/International Development Centre, Manchester.

White, J. and Meadows, S. 1980. *The Potential Supply of Immatures over the 1980s from Kenya's Northern Rangeland*. Ministry of Livestock Development, Kenya.

White, R. 1992. *Livestock Development and Pastoral Production on Communal Rangeland in Botswana*. Commonwealth Secretariat, London.

Wickens, G.E. 1980. Alternative uses of browse species. In: Le Houérou, H.E. (ed.) *Browse in Africa: The Current State of Knowledge*. International Livestock Centre for Africa, Addis Ababa.

Williamson, O.E. 1979. Transaction-cost economics: the governance of contractual relations. *Journal of Law and Economics*. 22 (October):3–61.

Williamson, O.E. 1985. *The Economic Institutions of Capitalism*. The Free Press, New York.

Wilson, R. 1982. Livestock production in Central Mali. *ILCA Bulletin* 15. ILCA, Addis Ababa.

Wilson, R. and Clarke, S. 1976. Studies on the livestock of southern Darfur, Sudan, II. Production traits in cattle. *Tropical Animal Health and Production* 8:47–51.

Wilson, R., de Leeuw, P. and de Haan, C. 1983. Recherches sur les systèmes des zones arides du Mali. Resultats préliminaires. *ILCA Research Report* 5. ILCA, Addis Ababa.

Winrock 1992. *Assessment of Animal Agriculture in Sub-Saharan Africa*. Winrock International, Morrilton.

Woodward, D. 1992. *Factors Influencing the Success of Agricultural Parastatal Divestiture in Sub-Saharan Africa*. Agricultural Marketing Improvement Strategies Project, Deloitte and Touche, Guelph.

Woodward, D. 1993. *Debt, Adjustment and Poverty in Developing Countries, Vols 1 and 2*. Pinter Publishers, London.

Workman, J.P. 1986. *Range Economics*. Macmillan Publishing Co., New York.

World Bank 1978. Annex 2: Livestock marketing performance; and Annex 3: Market prospects for Somalia livestock. In: Eberhard Reusse (ed.) *Livestock Marketing Project Identification Mission for Somalia*. World Bank, Washington, DC.

Wynne, B. 1992. Uncertainty and environmental learning: reconceiving science and policy in the preventive paradigm. *Global Environmental Change* June: 111–27.

Young, J. 1992. Do-it-yourself vet services. *ILEIA Newsletter* 3:23–4.

Zeidane, M.O. 1993. Pastoral associations: latest evolutions and perspectives. Case study paper for the conference on *New Directions in African Range Management and Policy*, 31 May–4 June, Woburn, UK. IIED, ODI and Commonwealth Secretariat, London.

Zimbabwe 1984. *Report on the Feasibility of Establishing a Fodder Bank for Drought Relief.* Department of Agricultural, Technical and Extension Services, Harare.

Zimbabwe Trust 1991. *The CAMPFIRE Programme.* Zimbabwe Trust, Harare.

Index

207

208